Published by Barricade Books Inc.
1530 Palisade Avenue
Fort Lee, NJ 07024

Distributed by Publishers Group West
4065 Hollis
Emeryville, CA 94608

Printed in the United States of America.

Library of Congress Cataloging-in-Publication Data

Allen, Steve, 1921-
    Hi-Ho, Steverino! : My adventures in the wonderful wacky
world of TV / Steve Allen
        p.   cm.
    ISBN 0-942637-55-0 : $19.95
    1. Allen, Steve, 1921-   .   2. Entertainers—United States—
Biography.   3. Television broadcasting—United States—History.   I. Title.
PN1992.4.A4A3   1992
791.45′028′092—dc20   91-40755
    [B]   CIP

Sources for Previously Published Material

How To Be Funny, 1987. New York, NY: McGraw-Hill Book Company

How To Make A Speech, 1986. New York, NY: McGraw-Hill Book Company

Meeting of Minds, Volumes 1–4, 1989. Buffalo, NY: Prometheus Books

Mark It and Strike It, 1960. New York, NY: Holt, Reinhart & Winston

The Radio Years: Orson Welles on the Air, 1988. New York, NY: The Museum of Broadcasting

TV Guide, October 20, 1984. Radnor, PA: Triangle Publications, Inc.

PROEM

"Look, the Lord is overturning the land of Judah and making it a vast wasteland of destruction.

Isaiah 24:1

When television is good, nothing is better. But when television is bad, nothing is worse. I invite you to sit down in front of your TV set and keep your eyes glued to that set until the station signs off. I can assure you that you will observe a vast wasteland.

You will see a procession of game shows, violence, audience participation shows, formula comedies about totally unbelievable families, blood and thunder, mayhem, violence, sadism, murder, Western badmen, Western good men, private eyes, gangsters, more violence, and cartoons. And endlessly, commercials, many screaming, cajoling, and offending. And most of all, boredom. True, you will see a few things you will enjoy. But they will be very, very few. And if you think I exaggerate, try it.

—Newton Minnow

ACKNOWLEDGEMENTS

I should like to thank first Cristina Gutierrez of my office staff who must now know more about me and at least some members of my family than do most of my friends in that she has had to listen to and transcribe the endless hours of dictated tapes which provided the building blocks of the first draft of this manuscript.

Also I am indebted to Karen Hicks for serving as a meticulous shepherdess of the text, typing and retyping sections of it and making frequent and wise editorial suggestions.

After the manuscript had been accepted by Barricade Books, Larry Alson and Arnold Bruce Levy of publisher Lyle Stuart's Barricade Books staff, made a number of suggestions about passages that might be profitably dispensed with so as to prevent the publication of a book too heavy to lift.

DEDICATION

To Dan, Julie, Stephanie, Christopher, Michael, Bradley, Bobby, Andrew, and Ryan, my dear grandchildren.

HI-HO, STEVERINO!

TABLE OF CONTENTS

INTRODUCTION

A public figure undertaking to write his autobiography faces at least one problem: so much is already known of him that his story can scarcely hope to surprise the reader at every turn of the narrative. The novelist is under no such handicap. Unhindered by facts, he need be guided only by his imagination, which has unlimited freedom. The autobiographer on the other hand, if he has a conscience, must conform to the details of his history, particularly those which are a matter of public record.

I choose to start, therefore, by referring to several elements of my personal history which have been reported by the media. Let me briefly set them down:

—I was born in Chicago.

—I am Jewish. My first wife was Jewish.

—I am the third richest man in the entertainment field, after Bob Hope and the late Bing Crosby, with a personal fortune of over 200 million dollars.

—I play the piano only in the key of G.

—I write every word of my own comedy material.

—I am generally pro-communist, despite which I at one time recommended bombing China's nuclear facilities.

—I am a pacifist.

—I am also a Unitarian.

—I take drugs.

—I plan to run for political office.

—I am the composer of such successful songs as "Misty," "Teach Me Tonight," and "Quando Caliente El Sol."

—I am a gifted clarinetist, as proven by my performance in the motion picture *The Benny Goodman Story.*

—I replaced comedian Jerry Lester on the *Tonight* show.

—Though generally affable, I am a man of occasionally violent temper, and in one instance broke the plate-glass door of the William Morris Agency building in Beverly Hills, after having been refused admittance late at night by a security guard.

Anyone about whom the above specifics are true must be a fascinating fellow, indeed. Unfortunately, I am not nearly so interesting. *There is no truth at all to any of the statements listed* above, though each has appeared in the public record.

CHAPTER ONE

The Beginning

I distinctly recall the first time I ever saw TV. It was in Los Angeles, in 1947. I was in my twenties. A friend had just purchased a set and a dozen of us—most of whom had no connection with entertainment—were invited to see the strange new device unveiled. For three solid hours we sat huddled together around the tiny screen—watching local game and variety shows—fascinated. But we approved of very little. We criticized, picked everything apart.

"God," our host said, "what kind of dress is that?"

"I don't know," said his wife, "but get a load of the face of that bandleader. I've seen better looking pans under iceboxes."

"That's an old joke," I pointed out.

"That's all right," said my hostess. "I picked up the habit from the so-called comedian on this program. If he can tell 'em and get paid for it, why should I have qualms?"

But even at that early point, when the general cultural level of television fare was much lower than it has ever been since, it's nevertheless significant that for three hours we did not turn off the set and do whatever human beings did with their free social time before TV intruded. Deplore it as we did, we were nevertheless hooked. And, luckily for the fortunes of the new giant in our midst, in millions of homes across the country, little groups of families and friends were sitting as we were, criticizing, enjoying, liking this, disliking that, but—above all—totally mesmerized by the talking picture box. I have never forgotten this, my initial perception of television.

In the late 1940s there was only a handful of stations scattered around the country. The black-and-white picture was fuzzy and jumpy, and so, sometimes was I, come to think of it. The general quality of those early programs is evidenced by the very first Emmy Award given to "The Most Popular Show." It went to a game series in which adults—myself occasionally included—simply sat around a living-room-like set and played Charades.

But how could it have been otherwise? The major stars of radio, films, and Broadway at first had little or no interest in the infant medium; the pay was low. Consequently, the programs were performed and created largely by beginners, semi-amateurs, and small-time professionals, many of whom would be shouldered aside within just a few years as more creative people, having carefully avoided the ground floor, jumped aboard and took advantage of the newer, better opportunities that presented themselves.

Shortly after TV opened up for business, I and many others took our places on its screens; even so it was at first the technological wonder of the new medium that was exciting, not the newly popular television personalities. East Coast celebrities like Milton Berle, Jackie Gleason, and Ed Sullivan were at first almost totally unknown in Los Angeles and most other parts of the country. Residents of large cities could identify Milton Berle, of course, but only as a nightclub and vaudeville comedian.

The first Eastern-based TV entertainer who dramatically broke through this national indifference was Arthur Godfrey. Primarily because he was already tremendously popular on radio, there was understandable curiosity to see him in action on the TV screen. No one since has achieved Godfrey's level of television renown. Oh, there've been many success stories in television's brief history. Performers like Milton Berle in the early 1950s, Lucille Ball and Jackie Gleason during their heydays, Carroll O'Connor in the early years of *All in the Family,* Bill Cosby during the first two years of his 1980s' series have been tremendously popular. But not even these superstars achieved the impact of Godfrey because they were simply one of a long list of important performers and/or programs, whereas Godfrey had not only the pinnacle but much of the mountain all to himself in the primitive 1949-51 period.

When I first began to work in television, in the season of 1947-48, I was doing my own daily network radio show from Los Angeles, and my ambitions were concentrated fully on a career in radio comedy. The mind-set was not quirky or unusual. In L.A., radio was at the time The Big Deal. Television was important mainly in New York City, where the networks' corporate headquarters were, as well as the advertising agencies that sponsored and largely controlled the TV shows. It was also where the majority of programs were produced. In most of America, in fact, there was little or no TV at all until the end of the 1940s.

I've never met anyone over the age of ten who wasn't a critic of television. What is true of television is true of life and the universe itself—part of it is magically wonderful and part of it is dreadful. The thoughtful viewer, therefore, picks his way among the assorted cathedrals and rubble, glorying in the former and avoiding the latter.

Viewers become habituated to watching certain performers or series. Lonely people may literally fall in love with a television hero, as they do with film stars and popular singers. Certainly I'm not the only TV personality to have received letters from women expressing romantic feelings, and, from men, openly and emotionally pledging respect and affection. The influence of television can be seen in fashion as well. In the early Fifties, for example, many men began wearing horn-rimmed eyeglasses or plaid sports jackets simply because I wore them.

A Jesuit priest who interviewed me not long ago on the radio, in commenting on the number of books I've written (38 including the one you're holding) said, "Apparently you've never had an unpublished thought." My bringing out one more volume, in any event, can hardly now be considered a noteworthy event, per se. This particular one, however, merits attention in that it is an account of half-a-century of experience in the two chief branches of broadcasting: radio and television.

Philosophers did not have to wait for Robert Frost to speculate about roads not taken. All of us have pondered what our fate might've been had we made decisions other than those we did make at critical moments in our lives. I've never had to indulge in such musings for the simple reason that as each professional road opened up to me I took it, while at the same time continuing to travel those paths to which I'd become accustomed.

With the advantage that hindsight gives us, it is now easy to see that my gravitating toward radio was inevitable. I'd already shown an aptitude for acting, writing, music, and comedy. Radio accommodated them all. The only more glamorous field at that point in my life—the 1930s—was motion pictures. But the figures it made famous seemed superhuman, creatures from another realm. It literally never occurred to me, even as an idle daydream, that I might profitably aspire to a film career, although in later years I would appear in a number of pictures.

Radio, on the other hand, seemed closer to reality and its ramparts not nearly as impregnable as those of Hollywood, despite the wide popularity and glamour of programs starring Bob Hope, Ed Wynn, George Burns and Gracie Allen, Rudy Vallee, Amos and Andy, Fred Allen, Fibber McGee and Molly and the medium's other major figures.

Though I didn't realize it at the time it seems, in looking

back. that at this stage of my life—the teens—fate was gently nudging me toward my later assignment as a comedian. No matter what I turned my hand to, however seriously, it always developed a comic side. In a school play a piece of scenery would fall on me as I opened my mouth to make my first speech, or if a teacher bawled me out the situation for some reason would amuse me (and consequently other members of the class). I cannot explain all this; I can only report it.

Example: one of my closest companions at this time was Richard Kiley, the actor. Dick and I have been good friends ever since eighth grade, and whenever we've spent time together we have almost invariably gotten innocently into trouble and then laughed our way out of it. I remember that one night when we were both about sixteen we went for a walk to a deserted park area on Chicago's lake front. The city had just built a playroom and shelter on the 55th Street beach that looked, to our youthful imaginations, very much like a small castle. On this particular dark and moonless night Dick and I were talking about horror movies. We both wanted very much to be actors, and so as a sort of dramatic exercise we decided to take turns portraying ghouls and zombies, each of us determined to outdo the other in giving a blood-chilling performance. Dick went first as I stood watching some distance from the stone "castle," not far from the water's edge. Stepping behind a bush to effect a change in his appearance he removed his jacket, mussed up his hair, then leaped into sight, uttered a fearful moan, and lunged toward me stiff-legged, like Frankenstein's monster. The effect was truly frightening, and I admitted as much to him—whereupon it became my turn to put on a performance.

Determined to surpass his effort I ran toward the building and retired behind the same bush to change my "wardrobe" and "make-up." On a sudden inspiration I whipped off my jacket and sweater, put the jacket on again, and then rolled the sweater up into a ball and stuck it up behind my shoulders so that I appeared to be hunchbacked. Next, like Dick, I plastered my hair down over my forehead. (Since I usually needed a haircut in those days I had a definite advantage here.) Touching my hand to the ground I picked up a bit of soil, rubbed it on my face, and then, dragging one leg and alternately snorting like a maniacal werewolf and howling like a banshee and extending my arms like some great-clawed bird, I lumbered out into sight. I had advanced perhaps twenty yards down the path toward Dick in this terrifying manner when suddenly two flashlight beams pinned me against the darkness of the night.

"Stand right where you are!" a voice rasped. Two policemen, one with revolver drawn, approached me.

For some reason, all I could think of to make myself look more like a human and less like a werewolf was to lower my arms and smile inanely.

"What the hell's going on here?" one of the policemen said. By this time they had noticed Dick.

"We're just playing, officer," I said.

"Playing?" he said, incredulously. Though young, both Dick and I were over six feet tall. After I had embarrassedly straightened my dragging leg, removed the hump from my back, and pushed my hair back the officers at last realized we were harmless. But it took quite a bit of talking. Things like that happened to me all the time.

On another evening I borrowed a voluminous Navy cape given to my mother many years before by a submarine officer, found an old black fedora, and sallied forth into the Chicago night to enact the role of Lamont Cranston, the Shadow, a popular Robin Hood-like character of the airwaves. Urged on by my less imaginative cronies I secreted myself in a dark areaway and began chuckling deeply in true Shadow fashion as people strolled by. To my surprise passersby didn't seem to get the idea at all that I was doing an imitation of The Shadow. Instead they assumed that I was a dangerous madman. This became evident to me when, after a few minutes, I peeked out from my hiding place and perceived that a small, angry, and terrified group of people had gathered a few yards down the street. A muffled chorus of guffaws and giggles from Dick and my other chums across the way convinced me that I was making quite an impression, so I ducked back into the darkness and waited for my next victim. After a moment I heard footsteps approaching. As a couple reached the areaway in which I was standing the woman gave a small yelp of fear and the man, to my utter astonishment, jammed a pistol into my gut, and pulled on my cape so hard that the snaps keeping it closed flipped off one by one in a series of small musical plinks. Again it had been my misfortune to bump into a Chicago policeman, this one in plain clothes. When I nervously pleaded that I was only a kid having some fun and meaning no harm, suggesting that he ask Dick and my other friends for confirmation, these worthies took off into the night like frightened deer, leaving me to talk my own way out of the spot. That was my last appearance as The Shadow.

CHAPTER TWO

Preparation in Radio

Many of today's talk show hosts, at least those on programs requiring some minimum knack for comedy on the part of the master of ceremonies, have a background of work in small comedy clubs. This is a sharp departure from what was common during the 1950s and '60s when Jack Paar, Johnny Carson, Merv Griffin, Mike Douglas and I emerged; our group had come out of radio.

The distinction between the two groups has to do with the fact that in clubs one need only get laughs, whereas in radio the ability to communicate coherently is the basic requirement. Our group, therefore, spoke for the most part in actual sentences. With the exception of Jay Leno, who is not only quick-minded and very funny but also a writer, today's hosts communicate in a surprisingly disjointed way, a fact which 30 years ago would have worked to their disadvantage but which, given the general cultural collapse of the past few decades, apparently at present represents no problem at all.

If the reader doubts this statement, I suggest the following simple experiment: Audio tape-record the opening monologue of the average host-comic, then have his remarks meticulously transcribed. The result will read very much like this:

Hi. What? Oh, hey, come on. Anyway, tonight we have a really—Thank you. I love you, too. Zowie! Yeah! You're beautiful!

Hey, how about Elizabeth Taylor? Isn't that something? She was— What? No, we did that last night. I think it was last night. . . .

Is this a band—or what?

And all of this, mind you, from men who have a large staff of writers and are presumably literate enough to read cue-cards.

Having established, then, the advantages of a radio background, I'll review my experiences in that medium, which—although the thought never entered my mind at the time—was ideal preparation for everything I would later do in television.

In the fall of 1942 I entered Arizona State Teachers College (today known as Arizona State University) in Tempe, a small township just outside of Phoenix, but after a few months I quit school to take a part-time job at radio station KOY. I could have continued my education at Tempe, of course, but I wanted to work in radio. So I started at KOY three years early, at a job that involved announcing, writing, playing the piano, and acting. On the side, when I thought the executives weren't listening, I even found time to sneak in a little horseplay.

One night I found out the hard way they were listening. One of my regular assignments was doing the commercials on the Alka-Seltzer news; I was the man who dropped a white tablet into a cup of hot water and said, "Listen to it fizz!" On this particular night I tipped the bottle upside down and discovered it was empty. Rushing to a drug store was out of the question; in two minutes I was scheduled to close the program. Necessity thereupon mothered a solution. Racing back to the men's room I yanked open the medicine cabinet and found a small can of Bi-so-dol that belonged to a staff newscaster who evidently hadn't been listening to my Alka-Seltzer commercials. A minute later I was back in the studio, puffing heavily but victorious, ready to go into the usual spiel. I said, "Listen to it fizz," and confidently dropped a spoonful of Bi-so-dol into the cup of water. The powder hung there on the water's surface like a white cloud—and as silent. Bi-so-dol, I learned in that instant, doesn't fizz. It just sinks slowly into the water and waits for closing time.

Two seconds passed in agonizing silence; in the control room a curious engineer turned to frown in my direction. Acting on heaven knows what inspiration I opened my mouth and did as nice a vocal impersonation of a stomach tablet's fizz as you've ever heard. So pleased was I with the sound, in fact, that all the rest of the week I disdained employing the real McCoy, choosing to continue to rely on my larynx. Then one night the boss wandered in while I was fizzing. I almost lost my job.

My years at KOY were pleasant ones and extremely educational. Although the station had hired me as an announcer I was given free rein to take on as many additional duties as I desired, as long as it was understood that I would demand no additional salary. Accordingly I wrote commercial copy, newscasts, a few episodes of a popular Arizona soap opera called *Love Story Time*, and now and then a dramatic show. Besides this I played the piano and sang, spun records, announced dance broadcasts from a local ballroom, created program ideas, and tried my hand at ad-lib, on-the-spot descriptions of such western Americana as sheriff's parades and rodeos. Being a city dude I proved something less than polished at the latter. As a result of this experience I began to have inklings that I might end up specializing in the less serious aspects of broadcast entertainment.

It might seem that describing a parade would be an easy job. It isn't. KOY admitted as much in splitting the assignment up three ways, positioning one man somewhere near the parade's starting point, another in the middle, and the third down the road a piece.

As the middleman, I took up my post on the roof of the station itself, spread my notes out on a ledge, and watched in horror as half of them blew away immediately. (Today optometrists tell me, by the way, that one of my eyes is very slightly out-of-line with the other, a condition that just might be attributable to my early attempts to keep one eye on a page of typewritten notes and another on a passing parade, calf-roping event, or trick-riding exhibition.) In any event I was nervous this particular morning as I stood in the bright, hot Arizona sunshine, leaning out and looking down the road for the approaching troops like Barbara Fritchie.

At last the sound of martial music, marching feet and the clip-clop of horses' hooves signaled the advent of the paraders. Over the radio I heard Joe Dana, the station's head announcer, say, "And now we turn you over to Steve Allen for a further description of the parade."

I took over, starting calmly enough, giving a fair description of the usual parade components: the Shriner's band, the drum majorettes from Phoenix Union high school, a sheriff's posse, a company from a nearby Army post, and so forth. Gaining confidence by the moment as the pageant flowed smoothly by, I had just started a description of a Boy Scout drum-and-bugle corps when, to my surprise, I observed that the parade was grinding to a halt.

"Well, sir," I said, "here it is, that fine Boy Scout drum-and-bugle corps, horns glistening in the sunlight as the boys march proudly by. What a fine sight they are as they—uh—pass our vantage point here. Yes, sir. What a fine sight indeed, all these—uh—Scouts. I'm sure you can hear them in the background as they—uh—play for you." On a sudden inspiration I pointed my mike down into the street below and picked up a few seconds of the Scouts' music, but that this was clearly only a stopgap measure was promptly indicated by the weary engineer who by gestures indicated that it might be wise if I resumed talking.

"Well," I said, as the boys stood slowly sinking into the boiling asphalt of Central Avenue and my dreams of one day replacing Bill Stern or Ted Husing, two famous sports announcers of the period, sank with them, "there they are, all right. They're still right here. Yes, sir. All these fine young Scouts. From Phoenix...or *of* Phoenix. They look very snappy this morning in their...in their shorts and—uh—shirts. Yes, indeed, they do, believe you me—out there—folks."

I must have gone on in this pathetic vein for another three minutes, describing the same thing over and over again before enough time had elapsed for me to throw the ball to one of the other announcers.

Even worse pitfalls were in store that same afternoon when I was dispatched to the fair grounds to do an ad-lib description of the big annual rodeo show. Fresh from Chicago, I was as un-Western as it is possible to be in Arizona without being chased off the streets as an eyesore. My knowledge of Western terminology, gleaned entirely from cowboy movies, seemed to consist solely of words like hombre, ornery sidewinder, no-good varmint, chuck wagon, and six-gun, none of which appeared appropriate to the task at hand. At this late date I naturally have no clear memory of the faux-pas-laden monologue with which I puzzled the people of Phoenix that day, but I do clearly recollect giving a lengthy description of a "steer-milking contest," a phenomenon theretofore unknown to biological science, not to mention the cattle business.

Another awkward moment that remains vivid occurred just after I had somewhat over-emotionally described the ferocity of the giant Brahma bulls that were being released directly beneath the platform on which I was positioned. "These great, powerful beasts," I intoned ominously, "are bucking and snorting down here, breathing defiance at the brave cowpokes who will shortly leap on their brawny backs and attempt to remain there when the gate is opened!" The bulls were truly snorting at that moment but as soon as I said, "I'll hold the microphone down in their direction so you can hear their fearsome grunting and snorting," they stopped and for some reason merely looked curiously up at me. Determined to deliver what I had promised, I solved the dilemma the bulls' sudden silence posed by bringing the mike back up to my lips and snorting furiously myself as I pawed the floor. The noises I made may have faintly resembled the grunt of a hog or the squeal of a horse; certainly no such sounds ever came out of the throat of a Brahma bull. Curiously enough no one ever wrote in to comment on these peculiar imitations but I did receive a sharp glance from one of the rodeo officials standing near me on the platform.

Another happy memory of the KOY days has to do with my youthful penchant for perpetrating practical jokes, a practice I am happy to say I have almost outgrown. The one of which I was proudest at the time, because it involved considerable ingenuity and cunning, regularly trapped the various announcers who worked the early-morning shift. Within a few months after starting work at the station I'd been given the job of writing a great deal of its commercial copy, and naturally I had access to all script material used at the station. This material, almost exclusively commercials, used to be put into a folder and left in the control room on a small stand in front of a microphone. As the man on duty read each announcement he simply turned it over, marked it with his initials and the exact time, and then was ready to go on to the next.

Now I'd observed from my first days at the station that the average announcer gradually developed a parrotlike approach to the drivel he was forced to read daily. This accounts for the peculiar sing-song speaking style of most announcers, and in a reverse way I think accounts for the success of the occasional announcers (Ed McMahon, Regis Philbin and Alex Trebek) who have the ability to speak like human beings and can rise to greater heights precisely because they are unlike the mass of falsely jovial, voice-conscious announcers.

At any rate, it was the purpose of my practical joke to write a commercial that was completely nonsensical and then force an announcer to read it. The pay-off would come as I lay in bed at home in the morning listening to hear if my victim realized that he was speaking drivel—and, if he did, what his reaction was. But to put this plan into effect required ingenuity. A fresh piece of copy among the dog-eared and finger-smudged sheets comprising the bulk of the average day's material would always receive careful attention by the man on duty. The very cleanness of the paper would signal that he had new words to interpret and would sharpen his attention or even suspicions. Accordingly I baited my traps by selecting and then counterfeiting a particular bit of commercial copy that had been in service for many weeks. First I would type a duplicate copy of the commercial, identical to the original except that only the first three or four lines made sense. The commercial would then read roughly as follows:

Say, men, if you're in the market for a new suit why not see the fine new worsteds and tweeds at Thew's Clothing Store on Central Avenue? Yes, Thew has a fresh delivery of good-looking new models priced to please your pocket-book. Believe me, when you try on one of these fine suits you'll find a number of small green cabbages in the pockets because Thew insists that a man working on his income tax is a man who will refuse to step on a crack for fear he'll break his mother's back home again in Indiana. And among men who know good clothing you'll find a great many chain-smokers, tobacco-chewers, and cotton-pickers. So remember, one if by land and two if by sea. There isn't a better car on the road and I'll be glad when you're dead you rascal you.

Then I would rub the paper on the floor to make it

smudged and dog-eared, rubber stamp it, forge the initials of the various announcers who had read the real commercial in the past, and then before leaving the station for the night, place my little time bomb deep in the copy book.

Since each commercial was scheduled to be read at a particular time I was able to set my alarm the following morning, wake up two minutes before the explosion, turn on the radio, and lie there happily waiting for the fireworks. You might think that you could not get very far into such a commercial without realizing that a trick had been played on you but that is because you are not a radio announcer. Announcers, as I say, often have only the foggiest notion of what they are reading, and my victims sometimes used to get almost all the way through one of these insane commercials before they realized what had happened. At home I would laugh long and loud before going back to sleep and pleasant dreams.

My most grandiose practical joke of this period was perpetrated not upon one of my fellow announcers but on the people of Arizona. It was at the time of the 1944 Democratic national convention in Chicago, a period of unutterable boredom in radio stations across the land because almost all regular daytime programming was canceled. For hours at a time the station would simply broadcast whatever fare came in over the national network line from convention headquarters. There was nothing whatever for the local announcers to do but identify their station every thirty minutes. While there are moments of high drama in any political convention, they are few and far between. Much of the time there is almost nothing going on in a literal sense because the men conducting the convention are not concerned that radio is broadcasting what transpires and are not interested in the fact that there are great chunks of dead air from time to time.

During these moments when nothing could be heard but the slow, soft mumble of the giant convention crowd I noticed that the public-address system in the auditorium in

Chicago could occasionally be heard in the background, amplifying announcements that frequently had no direct connection with the activities of the convention.

"Will delegate Charles Samuels of St. Louis, Missouri, please call his home," a distant voice would cry.

"Will the party who owns the green Cadillac parked at the south entrance please go immediately to Gate 12."

"There is an urgent message for Dr. Frank Jarecki of Detroit. Will Dr. Jarecki please report to the officer at the main entrance."

After two days of these occasional glimpses into the private lives of various conventioneers an idea formed in my mind. I knew that Ray Busey, a Phoenix paint dealer who was later to be elected mayor, was in Chicago. Suddenly I instructed a bored engineer to open a microphone in our largest studio.

"What for?" he said. "It's not time for the break yet."

"I know it," I said, "but this is pretty dull. Just open the mike and I'll take it from there."

The engineer did as instructed. I walked into the studio, stood as far from the microphone as possible and imitated, as best I could, the distant, nasal sound of the voice that came over the air through the public-address system in Chicago.

"Attention, please," I called. "Will Mr. Ray Busey of Phoenix, Arizona, please go to the parking lot back of the auditorium. Someone has just covered his car with whipped cream."

The engineer cut off the mike and we both sat down to await developments. Believe it or not, there were none! As Orson Welles had proved some years earlier people will evidently believe anything they hear over the air (except possibly a few of the more ridiculous commercials). Emboldened by this lack of censure my friend and I took another crack at the thing a few minutes later. He opened the mike again, and muffling my voice I said distantly, "Mr. Ray Busey of the Arizona delegation, will you please call home at once? They have just discovered that green paint is leaking under the door of your shop."

Evidently my imitation of the Chicago stadium announcer was exact enough to still all suspicions that might have been aroused by the content of my remarks. In any event the other announcers and I had another two days of laughs of this sort before the joke wore thin. It was at about this point in my life that I began to have something less than confidence in the interest of the masses in the political activities of their representatives.

Some years ago a staff memorandum to the House Special Subcommittee on Legislative Oversight, prepared by the Subcommittee's chief counsel, Robert Lishman, charged that some radio stations had spuriously rigged man-on-the-street interviews "in a systematic vilification of persons and companies."

Since this past decade has been a time for widespread coming clean, breast beating, and sackcloth donning it may not be amiss for me to join the parade by confessing that once in Phoenix many years ago I shamelessly rigged a man-in-the-street interview show, although not for purposes of vilification. The crime was committed in broad daylight at a supermarket not far from radio station KOY and my accomplice was Bill Lester, a fellow announcer.

Bill and I were on the air doing a fifteen-minute program the name of which was *How Do You Vote?, Who Will You Vote For?* or something of the sort. This was a public service feature that KOY put on the air from time to time during political campaigns and its format was extremely simple. A team of two announcers would go to a bus depot, busy street corner, or grocery store and take turns interviewing people selected at random. Our remarks were of a vague introductory nature and always led up to: "All right, now for whom are you going to vote in the coming election? And why?"

This was 1944 and the political contest was between

Franklin Delano Roosevelt and Thomas E. Dewey. On the afternoon in question Bill and I were soliciting endorsements for the two candidates from the assorted housewives, loafers, and breadwinners who happened to be in the supermarket. Bill conducted the first interview while I stepped away from the microphone and induced an elderly woman to submit to the next. Then while I pumped this kindly soul for her political opinions Bill quietly rounded up *his* next prospect. All went swimmingly until about halfway through the program when I looked up to notice that we were absolutely alone. There was no one left to interview. Bill was just concluding a chat with a middle-aged man; frantically looking about for prospects I signaled him to stretch out the conversation. But the man had nothing more to say and after a moment or two had to be dismissed.

With hand signals I attempted to convey the dimensions of our predicament to Bill and then was suddenly seized by an inspiration. "Bill," I said unctuously, leaning in close to the hand microphone, "I have another guest for you right here. It's Mr. Walter Kline." At this Bill's head spun around looking for Mr. Kline, but I promptly resolved his confusion by saying, "How do you do?" in what I hoped was the high, squeaky voice of a citizen of very advanced years.

Bill caught on right away. "Pleased to meet you, Mr. Kline," he said. "Tell me, where do you live?"

"Oh, out on 24th Street," I said, tiredly chewing an imaginary wad of tobacco.

"I see," Bill said. "All right, you know the name of the program. Just whom do you plan to vote for in the coming Presidential election?"

"Well," I said, "let's see." My own mind, as I recall, was not firmly made up on this point, but clearly enough I had to make up Walter Kline's mind, and fast. "Why," I said, "I'm pretty much of a Dewey man."

"Oh, really?" Bill said. "And why is that?"

"Well, I think it's time for a change."

"Is that your only reason for preferring Dewey?"

Yes," I said. "That's about the size of it."

"Well, thank you very much, Mr. Kline," Bill said. "And now, Steve, I believe you want to interview our next guest."

"Why yes, thank you, Bill," I said, speaking in my own voice. "And we have a gentleman right here. What is your name, sir?"

"My name," said Bill Lester in a strange, choked tone, "is A. K. Johnson. I'm from Tucson."

"Oh, really? How do you happen to be doing your grocery shopping here in Phoenix this afternoon?"

We went on like that for another seven or eight minutes, conscientiously splitting the votes right down the middle: half for Dewey and half for Roosevelt. We said nothing unkind about either man and so I presume that's why the House Special Subcommittee did not call us. Anyway, years later I feel much better for having made a clean breast of the whole affair.

Probably the craziest stunt ever pulled at KOY had as its victim one of the staff announcers. His assailants were his fellow spielers. The trick could never have been perpetrated in a studio that accommodated an audience, for it involved the gradual disrobing of the unfortunate man as he delivered a fifteen-minute newscast, commercials and all.

Once he'd said, "Good evening, and now KOY brings you a fifteen minute round-up of world and local news," he was of course hopelessly trapped. He couldn't protest or do a thing for the next quarter-hour but stand there at the microphone and read the news while two of his friends quietly removed his tie, unbuttoned his shirt, took it off, loosened his belt, and slipped off his trousers and underwear. There he stood, stark naked, speaking to the people of Arizona while all the other male members of the staff gathered in the neighboring booth looked at him through the glass and rolled in laughter. The sad part of this crazy stunt was this: I was not an eyewitness to it.

During my three years in Phoenix, I got married to

Dorothy Goodman, another Arizona State student, fathered a son—Steve Jr.—and began to make plans for the jump to Los Angeles and big-time radio. I worked nights as pianist and singer at a local restaurant, the Steak House, saved a thousand dollars, quit the job at KOY and took off for Hollywood.

For the next three years I worked at L.A. radio stations KFAC and KMTR, did a good deal of songwriting, and worked a few comedy dates with my fellow radio announcer from Arizona, Wendell Noble, who had preceded me to Los Angeles and been hired at station KHJ, which was affiliated with the Don Lee/Mutual network. In 1946 Wendell and I started a daily morning comedy show called *Smile Time*, which was shortly picked up by the network.

So there we were, only in our mid-twenties and already starring in our own coast-to-coast comedy show, which ran through the 1946-47-48 period before being canceled.

CHAPTER THREE

The End of the World

Films were a now-and-then treat, but radio was part of the American consciousness every day of the week, morning and night. And, one night back in 1938, I had had an experience which dramatized what should never have been in doubt: radio's power to rivet the attention of a nation.

It was in the year of our Lord 1938—the last year, I briefly thought, that the Lord was to vouchsafe to us—that my mother, my Aunt Margaret, and I (along with several million other Americans) went through an experience that few if any people will ever be privileged to share: We were on hand when the world came to an end and survived it.

The occasion was the famous Orson Welles *War of the Worlds* broadcast. I have never before told the story of my own response to that broadcast, because I have seen the reaction of those who were not taken in by Welles's radio drama to those who were. It is the standard reaction of the level-headed citizen to the crackpot. In my own defense, and in that of all the other crackpots who went squawking off into that unforgettable night like startled chickens, I offer a word of explanation. Admittedly anybody who heard the *entire* Welles broadcast from beginning to end, and believed a word of it, should be under observation. Unfortunately, millions did not. For various reasons a great many of the listeners did not hear the first few minutes of the show. If some of these were in the mood for dance music they accepted what a randomly discovered orchestra on the dial was playing, lighted cigarettes, or picked up magazines and settled back to listen.

In a suite on the eighth floor of the Hotel Raleigh, an ancient and rundown hostelry on Chicago's Near North Side that was our home that year, I was lying on the floor reading a book. Feeling in the mood for background music, I turned on our radio, fiddled with the dial until I heard dance music, and returned to my book. In the adjoining room, Aunt Margaret and my mother were sitting on the bed playing cards.

After a moment, the music was interrupted by a special "flash" from the CBS news department, the authenticity of which there was not the slightest reason to doubt, to the effect that, from his observatory, a scientist had just detected a series of mysterious explosions of a gaseous nature on the planet Mars. After this fascinating bit of intelligence, the announcer said, "And now we return you to the program in progress," and the dance music was heard once more. I ask the reader: Would you doubt anything Peter Jennings or Tom Brokaw told you on their evening newscast? Of course not.

There soon followed a series of news items, each more exciting than its predecessor, revealing that the strange explosions on Mars had caused a downpour of meteors in the general area of Princeton, New Jersey. By this time the music had been entirely forgotten, I had cast aside my book, and sitting cross-legged by the radio, listened with mounting horror while the network news department went into action to bring America's radio listeners up-to-the-minute reports on what was transpiring in New Jersey.

More meteors had landed, it seemed, and one of them, in crashing to earth, had caused a number of deaths. CBS at once dispatched a crew to the scene, and it was not long before first-hand reports began coming in. Up to now there was not the slightest reason for those who had tuned into the dance music to question the truth of a word of what had been broadcast. This granted, there was no particular reason for being suspicious of what immediately followed.

With disbelief rising in his throat, a special-events CBS man on the scene near Princeton reported that one of the Martian meteors seemed to be no meteor at all, but some sort of spaceship. It actually appeared, he said, although one could scarcely believe one's ears, that this giant blob of metal, half-buried in the New Jersey mud, was not a blind, inert fragment shrugged off by some burly planet hurtling through infinity. Rather, it appeared to have been manufactured somehow. Bolts and hinges were in evidence. The National Guard had roped off the area, allowing no one near the gargantuan hulk. This, as far as one could determine, was simply a formal precaution, for it seemed clear that even if some strange form of life had made the flight from Mars inside the meteor, it could certainly not have survived the crushing impact when the weird craft plunged into the earth.

By this time my mother and Aunt Mag were huddled around the speaker, wide-eyed. The contents of the news broadcast were inherently unbelievable, and yet we had it on the authority of the Columbia Broadcasting System that such things were actually happening.

But if our credulity had been strained up to now, it had yet to face the acid test. The network next presented an army officer who made a dignified plea for calm, stating that the National Guard and the New Jersey police had the situation completely in hand. He requested that motorists give the area a wide berth, and concluded with a few words conveying his complete assurance that it would be only a matter of hours until order had been restored.

But it at once developed that his confidence had been badly misplaced.

The network interrupted his sermon with another report

from the scene, frankly emotional in nature, which confirmed the suspicions that there might be life of some kind inside the rocket. Fearful listeners were now treated to the benumbing description, by a patently frightened newsman, of the emergence of strange, leathery creatures from the spaceship.

I suppose if one has been convinced that there is life on Mars it matters little whether Martians be leathery, rubbery, or made of Philadelphia Cream Cheese. The description of grotesque monsters by this time seemed in no detail too fantastic; what was fantastic was that there were any creatures in the rocket at all. Their slavering mouths, jelly-like eyes, and the devastating fire they directed toward the soldiers who dared stand and face them, were all minor, almost unimportant, details, and even now they are not clear in my mind.

To our horror, the National Guard troops dispatched to the scene were massacred almost at once by the huge interplanetary invaders (there were several of them now, for other ships were landing). In the confusion of the battle, the network's facilities were impaired and its "man-on-the-spot" was cut off in mid-sentence.

CBS, however, was equal to the occasion. Civic and government spokesmen were rushed to microphones; dutifully—and ineffectively, as it turned out—they instructed the populace not to panic. An airplane was sent up over the trouble area and the network continued its blow-by-blow description from the clouds. My mother, my aunt and I didn't wait to hear more. We looked at each, hardly knowing what to say.

"Good God," Aunt Mag gasped, her face pale, "what's going on?"

"I don't know," I said. "What do you think we ought to do?"

"There's only one thing to do," my mother responded. "We can all go over to church and wait there to see what happens." She referred to the Holy Name Cathedral, not many blocks from our hotel.

"I don't know if that's such a good idea," I cautioned. "There might be crowds."

Just then we heard the word *Chicago* on the radio. "More spaceships have been reported," a voice intoned. "Observers have seen them over Cleveland, Detroit and Chicago!"

"Jesus, Mary and Joseph!" Aunt Mag shouted. "We'll be killed right here in this hotel!" She ran back into the other room and grabbed her coat.

"What are you doing, Maggie?" my mother asked.

"What do you think?" Mag replied. "We can't stay here and be killed. Let's get out of here."

"You're right," Mother said. "We'll go over to the church. Who has the key to the room?"

"Who the hell cares about locking the door?" Mag said. "It doesn't matter now."

I was putting on my coat, still too shocked to say much. Oddly enough, and this I recall quite clearly, my predominant emotion was not fear, but blank stupefaction. I remember saying "Gosh," idiotically, over and over again, and frowning and shaking my head from side-to-side. I couldn't believe it, and yet I had to, on the basis of years of conditioning. CBS news had never lied to me before.

Aunt Mag was still fluttering around the room. The door was now ajar, but she was like a bird that, with its cage opened, doesn't know just where to fly.

"What are you looking for?" Mother asked.

"My glasses," Mag said, in a mixture of anger and panic.

"You're not going to have time to read anything, Maggie," Mother told her. "Just get your hat and let's get the hell out of here!"

"If I don't need my glasses, what good is my hat?" asked my aunt.

"Never mind," said my mother. "Let's go!"

They both stopped to look at me. Perhaps I was a bit pale.

"Are you all right?" my mother asked.

"Gosh," I said, resourcefully, and we headed for the door. By this time people all over the nation were reacting similarly. Many stayed glued to their radios and heard the reassuring conclusion to the program, but millions, like us, rushed off wildly. They had not heard the introduction to the broadcast, and they did not stay to be calmed by its finale.

Police stations, newspapers, and churches were badly shaken by the first wave of frightened, fleeing citizens. In one New Jersey town, a terrified man rushed into the First Baptist Church during evening services and announced that the end of the world was at hand. The pastor made a futile attempt to quiet his flock by leading them in a prayer for deliverance.

Switchboards at radio stations from coast-to-coast were clogged for hours by callers, some angry, some panicky.

In New York's Harlem more than one police station was besieged by terror-stricken men and women seeking refuge.

Conscience-plagued sinners all over the country began making efforts to return stolen money, confess undisclosed sins and right old wrongs. People in houses rushed into the streets, and people on the streets rushed into houses.

About this time Welles and the members of his cast, glancing toward the control room of their mid-Manhattan studio, perceived that it was crowded with policemen. They must have finished the program in a state almost as disturbed as that of many of their listeners. Needless to say, none of this was known to us at the time.

"Button your overcoat, Stevie," my mother said. "You'll catch cold when we go out."

This remark did not at the moment strike any of us as amusing. I buttoned my overcoat, and we hurried out. My mother and aunt ran down the hall. I followed at a slower pace, not because I was trying to maintain a shred of discretion, but because I was too stunned to move with speed. Rounding a corner, we burst suddenly upon a dignified-looking young woman holding a little girl by the hand.

"Run for your life!" my mother cried at the woman, at the same time jabbing a shaky but determined finger at the elevator button. In response, the woman looked at her with no expression whatsoever.

"Pick up your child and come with us!" Aunt Mag shouted, wide-eyed. The woman paused a moment and then laughed right in my aunt's face.

Mag was outraged. "Oh, yes," she sputtered with withering sarcasm. "Go ahead and laugh! But for the sake of that dear baby in your arms, don't you laugh!"

At this the young woman drew back in alarm, evidently concluding that she was confronted by three violently deranged people who might do her physical harm. She looked at me questioningly.

"We just heard on the radio," I said, "that there's, er, 'something' up in the sky."

The merest flicker of bemusement crossed her face, but the woman did not speak. It was clear that she was hovering between two alternatives, Alan Funt and his Candid Camera not having yet been let loose upon the world: Either we were a trio of incredibly inventive and determined practical jokesters, or we were insane. The third possibility—that there might actually be "something" up in the sky—apparently was never given serious consideration. Instead, she shifted her child in her arms to a more secure position and retreated a few steps down the hall, walking backwards so as to keep an eye on us. But my aunt was not to accord this gesture the honor of understanding. She moved angrily toward the woman, and her right hand pointed up toward the heavens. She must have looked like a witch calling down a curse.

"You ought to get down on your *knees,*" she shouted like a complete nut, "instead of laughing at people! We're going to church to pray, and that's what you ought to be doing right this minute—praying!"

Before the woman could interpret this admonition, a soft whir and click announced that the elevator had reached our floor. A moment later the door slid back and the smiling face of the Negro operator greeted us. Never have I seen a smile fade so fast. If this scene were to be enacted in a motion picture, the man's role would be to open his eyes wide with fear and say, "Feet, get movin'!" In any event, the violence with which we dashed into the elevator at once convinced the operator that all was not well. My mother's first words confirmed his suspicions.

"Hurry up and take us down," she gasped. "They're up in the sky!"

"Who is?" asked the man, aghast.

"How do we know who is?" my aunt shouted. "But you'd better get out of this hotel right now while you've still got the chance!"

"Yes, ma'am!" he whispered, withdrawing completely to his corner of the elevator. For perhaps ten seconds he regarded us warily, holding the car-control handle at full speed. Then, torn between fear and curiosity, he succumbed to the latter. "What did you say the matter was?" he said, timidly.

Aunt Mag's patience was exhausted. How many times did you have to explain things to people? "They're up in the sky!" she repeated. "Haven't you been listening to the radio?"

"No, ma'am."

"Well, you'd better do something, let me tell you. The radio just said they're up over Chicago, so you'd better run for your life!"

I am sure that if the elevator operator had been convinced that an interplanetary invasion was underway, he would have faced the challenge as bravely as the next man. But instead, he apparently concentrated on the idea that he was cooped up in an elevator with three dangerous lunatics. As a result, he became positively petrified. Fortunately for his nervous system, the elevator arrived at the main floor at this point. He yanked the door release and shrank back against the wall, as we thundered past him into the lobby.

Though we had met with icy disbelief twice in quick succession, we were still ill-prepared for the sight that now greeted us. The lobby, which we had expected to find in turmoil, was a scene of traditional lobby-like calm. Nowhere was there evidence of the panic we had come to accept as the norm in the last few short minutes. Aggravatingly, people were lounging about, smoking cigars, reading newspapers, speaking in subdued tones, or dozing peacefully in thick leather chairs.

It had been our intention to sweep through the lobby and proceed right across Dearborn Street, pausing only in the event that a sudden spaceship attack should force us to take cover, but something about the tranquillity around the registration desk presented a challenge we did not feel strong enough to resist. Indeed, we felt it our duty to warn the unfortunate souls who thought all was well to prepare for ultimate disaster.

The elevator man peered after us from what was now the safety of his cage as we raced up to confront the blasé desk clerk. "Is something wrong?" this worthy asked quietly, evidently hoping that if something were amiss he could contain the area of alarm within his immediate vicinity.

"Well," replied my aunt with a contemptuous sneer, "it's the end of the *world*, that's all that's wrong!"

The clerk's face was an impenetrable mask, although after a moment he permitted a suggestion of disdain to appear on it. I started to explain that on the radio—and then, in some clear, calm corner of my mind I heard soft sounds in the corner of the lobby. It was a radio, and the sounds were not the sort a radio should be making at a time of worldwide crisis. The sounds, as a matter of fact, were of a commercial nature. Some other announcer on some other station was extolling the virtues of a brand of tomato soup.

A wave of shock passed through me as, in the instant, I saw things as they really were. Turning to my mother, I began speaking very fast, explaining what I presumed had happened: It was all make-believe on the radio. For a split second she wavered, hoping, yet fearing, and then for her, too, the ice broke.

Light, followed by painful embarrassment, also dawned on Aunt Mag. Like bewildered sheep we retreated back towards the elevator, excruciatingly aware that all heads were turned toward us, that the clerk was smiling at us in a frightfully patronizing way, and that never again as long as we lived would we be able to walk through that lobby without casting our eyes to the floor.

"We'll have to move out of this place," my mother said.

Our next reaction, upon us before we could even stagger back into the elevator, was one of wild hilarity bordering on hysteria. We laughed until our sides ached and tears poured down our cheeks. We fell into heavy chairs and laughed some more, and at long last, we pulled ourselves together, still shrieking with laughter, and started back toward the elevator. We laughed so hard going up that I don't recall the elevator operator's reactions. I'm sure he must have assumed we were now in the hilarious stage, still nutty as three fruitcakes, probably no longer dangerous.

We spent a restless night, alternately laughing and repeating, "We'll *never* be able to face all those people again!"

The next day on the way to school, I glanced at the blazing newspaper headlines and knew that we had not been alone.

CHAPTER FOUR

The Wild World of Wrestling

My earliest foray into television was in a rather odd role for a comedian: I was an ABC-TV wrestling announcer.

Ron Powers, in his book *Super Tube: The Rise of Television Sports,* asserts that back in the late 1940s I frequently "sat in" as announcer of the televised wrestling matches at the old Olympic Auditorium in Los Angeles. Actually, I did considerably more than sit in. Over a period of several weeks, I made my living describing the contortions of assorted habitues of big and tall men's shops—though as humorist rather than in deadly earnest. There were some potentially deadly elements to the experience, I suppose, but perhaps we should start at the beginning.

In the fall of 1949, while doing a nightly ad-lib comedy show for the CBS radio station in Los Angeles, I got a call from an ABC television executive. "We're thinking of trying something with our wrestling matches," he said. "We believe it might be interesting to hire somebody to do funny commentary on what's happening in the ring. We think you could do that. What do you think?"

"It sounds like fun. I'm willing to try." I didn't tell the gentleman that I knew nothing whatever about wrestling.

There have always been a good many Americans dubiously qualified for their jobs, so I figured I would perhaps go unnoticed in the general incompetence.

In the 1940s, wrestling, even more popular than it is today, was a television staple. Consequently, I suppose it was assumed that almost anyone who owned a television set would know something about the manly art of attempting to maim a colleague without the aid of a concealed weapon.

In any event, I prepared for the assignment during the following two weeks by paying careful attention to a popular wrestling announcer of the time, a former film actor named Dick Lane. After concentrating on Lane's hold-by-hold descriptions for three nights, I realized I was party to a secret that could have rocked the republic—Lane didn't know a hell of a lot more about either wrestling or the human body than I did. He did have a knowledge of the more common holds—the full Nelson, the half-Nelson, the flying mare and so forth—but the terms he applied to other more obscure or random positions seemed to be solely his own. Nor was he always consistent. A position he'd clearly called a stepover toehold on one night might be called a Boston land-crab the next.

There were no rehearsals scheduled, so as the night of my first broadcast approached, my only preparation was to write a few wrestling jokes and hope that somehow I'd find an opportunity to throw them in. A witty friend named Bill Larkin gave me a few more, but I realized I would have to ad-lib exactly as if the proceedings were absolutely legitimate.

At the appointed hour on the appointed night, I arrived at the old Ocean Park—not Olympic—Arena and took my place beside Bill Stern, Graham MacNamee, Ted Husing, and other great sportscasters of that era. Five minutes into the first match I'd used up my meager supply of prepared material. All I had left was a combination of creativity and panic.

After a few more minutes, I was able to recognize one or another standard positions the burly professionals assumed, but for the most part, as the evening wore on, the bulky bodies rocked and rolled before me in positions rarely seen this side of the *Kama Sutra*. These were positions for which I had no terminology. Had I been hired for my sports expertise, I would have been in serious trouble, but inasmuch as my task was to get laughs, my ignorance actually turned out to be a plus.

One of the stars of the show was a gentleman named Baron Leone, whom I have reason to suspect was not actually a member of the Italian nobility. Since, in my opinion, he was very funny himself, I had no qualms about describing him in suitable terms: "Leone gives Smith a full-Nelson, slipping it up from either a half-Nelson or an Ozzie Nelson. And now the boys go into a double pretzel-bend, with variations on a theme by Veloz and Yolanda (a ballroom dance team of the day). Whoops, Leone takes his man down to the mat! He has him pinned. Now they roll—it's sort of a rolling-pin."

During the filmed commercials and after every broadcast, I would quickly jot ad-libs like this into a notebook, since I knew that during the weeks ahead the opportunity to use some of the lines, with slight switches, would present itself again.

The Ocean Park Arena in those days was a bizarre, noisy, animalistic sort of place with an atmosphere I imagine was similar to that of the Coliseum in ancient Rome. The air-conditioning system in the arena was unable to cope with the smoke of thousands of cigars and cigarettes that hung in the air, adding a sort of Ingmar Bergman-touch to the general ambiance.

"There's sure a lot of smoke in this auditorium," I ad-libbed one night. "In fact, this may be the only arena in the country where they cure hams from the ceiling."

In most sports, even the most rabid of fans shout only

every few minutes. Not so in wrestling. During every moment of every match, the air at the Ocean Park Arena was
filled with a constant roar. Raucous cries, bloodthirsty lynch-
mob imprecations, and general incitement to riot led me to
conclude, perhaps unfairly, that true-blue wrestling fans are
not our most civilized citizenry.

Perhaps the aspect of audience misbehavior that I found
most depressing was that a good many of the loudest, most
maniacal ringsiders were women. If this seems a sexist
statement, then so be it. If there have to be loudmouthed
nuts in this world, I honestly prefer that they all be male.

In any event, some of the faces in the front rows looked as
if they'd been borrowed from the Missing Persons telecast
and, since none of them could hear me, I would frequently
comment on the more colorful characters as they became
visible on camera, a shtick that would later evolve into one of
my standard comedy show routines. "There's a man down in
the third row yelling boos and catcalls—and if I'd had that
much booze, I'd call a few cats myself. By the way, it's Ladies'
Night here at Ocean Park, folks. There's still time to come on
down—and you don't even have to prove that you're a lady."

Oddly enough, my comments about the audience never
received any criticism, although my lines about the wrestlers
did. "If you think wrestling is so funny," one correspondent
wrote, "try getting into that ring yourself, wise guy." After a
few weeks, however, no more death threats or other complaints were received, apparently because listeners got used
to my unorthodox approach.

Actually I was, from time-to-time, in the general prox-
imity of physical danger, not in my announcer's perch high
atop the arena, but later, after the matches, when I would
venture into the locker room for some post-bout interviews
with the winners and losers. I was never absolutely certain if
the animosity the wrestlers displayed toward each other was
real or faked, so heated were their exchanges. Sometimes I
found myself nervously separating two hulking athletes who

seemed fiercely determined to continue their battle in the dressing room. And on at least two occasions I received painful electrical shocks because I was holding a microphone as about two inches of water splashed out of the nearby showers and eddied around my feet.

Fortunately, the pre-game locker room interviews never lasted very long because the mayhem-lovers gathered upstairs could wait no longer for the punishment to start, and hundreds of them would pound their heels on the floor. The effect in the first floor dressing area was rather like being inside a tom-tom during Gene Krupa's solo on "Sing, Sing, Sing."

Those were the golden days of wrestling and some of the new representatives of the artform became not only popular within the narrow context of sports but celebrities in the larger world, rather like certain rock-music performers of the present day. The best known, of course, was a man named Gorgeous George, a hulk with wavy blond hair. George would enter the ring followed by an adoring entourage of managers, servants, agents, butlers, etc., some of whom would spray him with perfume from a large can of the sort customarily used to discourage the growth of aphids. I once called George the Human Air-Wick, but he didn't seem to mind since his approach to wrestling was rather like that of Liberace's to nightclub entertainment.

Another of my favorites was the aforementioned Baron Leone who, long before the Beatles introduced feminine hairdos to American males, wore the long, flowing tresses of a medieval philosopher. The Baron would've made a great actor in silent films because he could convey so much by the art of pure pantomime. One of his stock routines was to inquire of the referee before the match, by gestures, whether it would be permissible to pick his opponent up and fling him not just outside the ropes but to the topmost reaches of the auditorium. The referees would patiently explain to Leone that such conduct was *not* to be countenanced, after

which the Baron would turn to the audience with a Mediter-
ranean shrug as if to say, "How can a man be expected to
perform his appointed task under such restrictions?"

Also among the artists of the grappling game at the time
were Chief Little Wolf, the Navajo Indian Deathlock Artist,
Gino and Leo Garibaldi (a clean-cut father and son team
popular in tag-team matches), Brother Frank Jares who'd
been trained by Brother Jonathan, the Mormon Crusher (I
once asked how many Mormons Jonathan had crushed,
which perhaps did not endear me to his co-religionists), and
Argentina Rocca, who I alleged was the brother of Almond
Rocca and one of the sweetest guys in town. Rocca's crowd-
pleasing move was a prodigious high-jump, at the apex of
which he would wrap his thighs around his opponent's head
with intent to do bodily harm.

I've always suspected that at least some percentage of
those watching at home did not really attend clearly to what
Dick Lane, I, or any other wrestling announcer said. One
night I tested this theory by waiting until a particularly
dramatic moment of the match and then shouting excitedly,
"Leone now has his krelman frammised over the arm of
Hayes' kronkheit, but the referee doesn't seem to zelman the
croyden. Ladies and gentlemen, the zime is going absolutely
mactavish!" Not entirely to my surprise, not a single fan ever
wrote in to say, "What was that again?"

In New York a while back I saw a televised Madison
Square Garden match between "Cowboy Bob" Orton and
Tito Santana. Little seemed to have changed over the years.
There were still power slams, back-breakers, chokeholds,
kicks in the gut, forearm smashes to the face. The reactions
to these assorted blows and holds, as ever, were incredibly
exaggerated, not at all what they'd be in reality.

I detected only one difference, which I took to be significant. The screaming, booing, shouting, frothing-at-the-
mouth crowd reaction appeared to be chiefly a sound effect
since members of the audience who appeared on camera, in

reaction shots, were usually taking the proceedings relatively calmly.

After the Orton/Santana bout, Greg "The Hammer" Valentine opposed a man named Hulk Hogan. Both Hogan and Valentine, I noted, had long hair, of the sort boasted in the earlier generation only by Gorgeous George, Baron Leone, and a few others. Hogan seemed determined to make short work of his opponent, who was seconded by what appeared to be the oldest, fattest Hell's Angel in the world.

The action, needless to say, was by no means one-sided. After taking what appeared to be a terrible beating, Valentine suddenly turned the tables, placed his locked hands under Hogan's chin while sitting on the Irishman's back, and seemed determined to tear the man's head from his body.

After another beating, Hogan threw Valentine mightily against the ropes and, when he bounced off, kicked him in the face. Valentine staggered, half-crazed, fell out of the ring and down on the floor, where he was pursued and pummeled again.

Hogan then climbed back into the ring. When Valentine didn't immediately follow, Hogan came back to the floor, beat Valentine soundly and then threw him back into the ring. Valentine retaliated by kicking Hogan in the face and beating him to the mat. When Hogan finally pinned his opponent, he burst into a paroxysm of conceited delight.

Legitimate wrestling—that engaged in by amateurs in schools and in the Olympics—is one of the least interesting sports in the world, which explains why it is so rarely seen on television. The more theatrical sort engaged in by professionals is vastly more entertaining and at least served the purpose of introducing me to the Southern California television audience.

CHAPTER FIVE

Out of Radio and Into Television

My first network TV assignment was for CBS—a low-key daily 11:00 a.m. mix of comedy, music and ad-lib starting December 25, 1950, shortly to be converted to a nightly 30-minute TV comedy series in the 7-7:30 p.m. time-slot. There was a serious complication, the program had to be done from New York rather than my home city of Los Angeles. This was not just a whim on the part of CBS; at the time it was not possible to use Los Angeles as a live network origination point since the West Coast was not yet hooked up to the telephone coaxial cable that carried the TV signals which linked the East and Midwest.

I was quite confused emotionally at the time because my first marriage was in a state of collapse. As the father of three dearly-loved sons I was seized by strong feelings of guilt and depression, hardly a propitious background against which to launch a career as a network television comedian.

Another problem emerged in my first meeting with my new employers, the New York-based network programmers. They were a likable and talented bunch although I now can recall the names of only two: Hubbell Robinson and Marlo Lewis. Because they were accustomed to dealing with established personalities of the Bob Hope, Burns & Allen, Red Skelton, Fred Allen-type, or else with rigidly formatted game shows, they had some trouble getting me into focus, given that I worked in a loose and largely extemporaneous way. I had not given much thought as to what the title of my new program would be but had assumed, on the basis of the long history of radio, that it would bear my own name, just as Jack Benny or Eddie Cantor's programs had borne theirs.

"But we'd like to come up with some sort of cute, fresh name for the show," one of the executives said. "Not just *The Steve Allen Show*. You know, something like *Strike It Rich* or *You Bet Your Life*."

"Those are perfectly good names," I admitted, "but they suggest formats or games. I have no format nor do I play games. I just plan to do thirty minutes of this and that."

"But we're not *creating* anything that way," Marlo Lewis said.

"Godfrey does all right," I pointed out.

"Godfrey's different," they said.

"We're not trying to be difficult," Robinson said. "But you know how buyers are. They want a peg."

"How about Peggy Lee?" (Oddly enough, Ms. Lee would later become part of the show.)

"No, no. You know...something to hang your hat on. A place to start."

"A gimmick," a third executive chimed in.

"Yes," said a fourth. "A springboard."

"Something definite," said Robinson. "A hook."

"A peg," I said.

"That's it," they said. "Now you've got the idea."

"Wait a minute," said one, snapping his fingers. "Of course I'm just talking off the top of my head but how about *The Fun House?*"

"Why not call it *The Top of My Head?*" I asked.

They smiled thinly.

"I'm just throwing this on the table for what it's worth," one said, "but how about *Time to Smile?*"

"Well," I said to the others, "what's it worth?"

Robinson stood up.

"Maybe we ought to kick this thing around by ourselves for awhile and get together again in a day or two," he said. He turned toward me and continued, "Why don't you kick it around and see what you come up with?"

"All right," I said.

I kicked it around all afternoon. My foot got sore. Then I sent them the following list of names for my program:

The Jack Benny Show
Strike It Poor
Arthur Godfrey and A Friend of His

(On Arthur's programs he is frequently replaced by substitutes. On this one he would not have to bother to show up at all.)

Words and Music
Music and Words
Words and Words
Music and Music
Finn and Haddie

(I am willing to change my name and get a partner.)

Burns and Allen

(Only if George were willing, of course.)

Allen and Burns

(If George was careless.)

What Else Is On?
Clara, Lu and Em (a radio sitcom of the 1930s)
The Stork Club

(I would appear in a small enclosure and spend the entire thirty minutes attempting to club a stork.)

What's My Lion?

(A panel show I'd like to do with animal trainer Clyde Beatty.)

The Format Hour

(With Joe Gimmick and his orchestra. Would also feature Sally Framework and George Peg, who recently

appeared at the Hook Room and who have also been seen in the show *Something to Hang Your Hat On*, which was adapted from the novel *The Boys Need Something Definite*.)
Springboard

(Which would open with me doing a half-gainer through a pane of glass and coming right into their homes—get it?)

The program was called *The Steve Allen Show*.

Since the success of this late night radio show led to my being signed to network TV, it's ironic that one of the first instructions I was given upon being hired made my jaw drop.

"We'd like you to stop doing those audience interviews," Hubbel Robinson said.

"Really?" I asked. "Why?"

"Well, the routine has sort of, you know, a daytime feeling to it."

"I've been getting big laughs with it on the *late-night* show," I said.

Thank God I did not permit myself to be talked out of a routine that was not only working well for me at the time but would, when I moved to NBC in 1953, prove to be a staple of the original *Tonight* show.

People often profess to marvel that I was able to ad-lib for as much as an-hour-and-forty-five minutes each night, five-nights-a-week, with little help from script or TelePrompTer and often with no panel of guests. I appreciate their praise but do not deserve it. Philosophers tell us that we only use a small part of our potential brain power. A proof of this is our ability to speak extemporaneously. We express surprise that a man can get up in front of an audience and speak without a piece of paper in his hand; yet we all do precisely the same thing every waking day.

When you walk into a meat market you don't spend anxious moments at the door wondering what you will say to the butcher. When you meet friends you don't waste time planning in advance how you're going to address them. Obviously the ability to communicate is something most of us share. The trick, of course, is in being relaxed enough to speak on the air as easily as you do in the living room.

People seem to think that I make the studio audience my straightman. I see it the other way around; much of the real humor in audience interviews comes from the people themselves. When I say to a guest, "What is your name, sir?" and he answers with calm assurance, "Boston, Massachusetts," he is the funny one, however unintentionally, and I his willing straightman.

All that settled, the series went on the air—and encountered a third major problem almost immediately: a call from an official of the New York local of the American Federation of Musicians. "Who are those guys doing the music on your show?" he asked.

"They're the Four Freshmen," I said. "Aren't they terrific?"

Not long before leaving for the East, a friend, music publisher Mike Gould, had taken me to a small Hollywood jazz club on Sunset Boulevard to hear a new vocal and instrumental group. I was so impressed by their performance that when Mike introduced me to them after the show, I told them, "CBS has just asked me to go to New York and start a new nightly TV show. It strikes me that you guys would be terrific as the musical group on the program. Are you interested?"

Needless to say they were. Within the next few days the fellows checked out of their separate living quarters, disposed of excess baggage, and took off for New York. They were, to be sure, well received on the show, but then came the fateful phone call.

"You've got to get rid of those people," the man from the musicians' union said.

"Why?"

"Because you're doing the show from New York. That means you have to hire New York musicians."

And, believe it or not, the hand had to be played out in that way. The embarrassed network official who had forgotten to check on such technicalities agreed to pay the Freshmen for the full-term of their contract, thirteen weeks, and they went home, naturally crestfallen. Fortunately their great talent later led to a long and successful recording and concert career.

In any event, right off the bat we began doing creative, experimental stunts on the nightly show. Al Span, our producer, who'd earlier worked for me as a soundman in Hollywood, booked a nightclub-vaudeville novelty act on the first show, the chief gimmick of which involved an acrobat setting four champagne bottles on a table and putting the legs of a kitchen chair on top of the bottles. The acrobat then climbed up on the chair and balanced himself in a variety of poses, after which he called, "Steve, why don't you come up here and join me?"

I was honestly surprised.

"It's easy," the acrobat said. "Just come on over here and sit on the edge of the table."

I had very little interest in following his instructions, but since we were on the air live and in front of a studio audience, I didn't want to appear chicken; I did as he requested.

"Now what?" I asked, my obvious nervousness eliciting laughter from the audience.

"Just stand up," he said.

Once I was erect, he said, "Now listen carefully. I'm going to get out of the chair and help you up here so you can sit in it."

"Where will you be at the time?" I asked, to the accompaniment of more laughter from a now doubled-up studio audience.

"Never mind that," he said. "Just ease yourself up here. That's it, hang onto my arm."

Somehow I got into the chair, at which the fellow held himself out in space so as to counterbalance my own weight, and then tipped two of the chair legs up in the air so that I was sitting much too high in the air on an angled chair that rested only on two champagne bottles.

At this the audience clapped wildly.

"Stop that lousy applause," I said, "or this guy will have me up here all night." I was actually quite ill-at-ease and consequently was resorting to the kind of sarcastic Irish humor I'd heard all during my childhood from the many wits in my mother's family. The approach seemed to play well with the studio audience.

Our stage manager on the series, by the way, was Joseph Papp, called by *Time* magazine when he died in November of 1991 "the most influential figure in the American theater for the past quarter-century."

And our gofer and cue-card holder was a young fellow named Dan Melnick, who would go on to considerable fame as a television network programmer, studio executive and motion picture producer.

As another example of the show's creativity, we one day originated the program not from our regular network studio but from the swimming pool of the Hotel St. George in Brooklyn. This led to one of the most remarkable program-openings I've ever been involved with. Those who tuned in that morning would've noticed nothing unusual because I was wearing a conventional two-piece suit and standing in front of what appeared to be our customary backdrop curtain.

In reality, the curtain was miles away back in our regular theater; we had instead taken a portion of the small sparkly blue material and placed it over a large, lightweight wooden frame. When the announcer, Bern Bennett, introduced me at the top of the show, I quickly walked into the picture and bowed, acknowledging the applause by looking to the left and the right as if nodding to people in different parts of our theater.

For the first couple of minutes, I did a purposely par-for-the-course opening monologue and then said, "Well, I guess it's time to get over to the piano," at which point I began walking to my left. Since I was actually standing on the diving board of the hotel's pool I naturally did not continue on the same plane but suddenly, upon reaching the end of the board, plunged into the chilly blue water below me. At that point the camera director, Gene Kelly's brother Fred, pulled out to a very wide shot so the audience at home could see me falling into the pool. Home viewers later told me it came as a total surprise.

It was almost a more sobering surprise, actually, because since I was fully clothed and am not a terribly good swimmer, I immediately sank beneath the surface. Unable to clear the water from my eyes when I came up, I began to thrash off-course instead of heading directly to the side of the pool. The weight of my shoes and other clothing continued to drag me down. Fortunately, former swimming champ Buster Crabbe, star of the old *Flash Gordon* films, was a guest on the show; he reached out from the side of the pool and rescued me.

A more spontaneous stunt occurred to me one day when the studio audience was fairly listless. They weren't laughing heartily and nothing we were doing in the way of comedy, conversation, or music seemed to impress them. I suddenly heard myself say, "I'll tell you what, ladies and gentlemen, why don't we do something else? Would you like to play a game?"

A few apathetic voices said "Yeah, sure."

"All right," I said. "Then why don't we play Follow the Leader? I'll start down here in the aisle and you can follow me, row-by-row. There's only one rule to the game—whatever I do, you have to do."

For whatever reasons, the audience responded favorably, the band played crazy marching music, and we shortly had on camera about 300 people in a big conga-line, snaking

their way up the aisle, across the back of the theater, down
another aisle, across the stage, backstage, out the other side,
and finally through the lobby and out into the open air. I
made an arbitrary left turn in front of the theater and led
our little band to the corner at the end of the block. Acting
on a sudden inspiration, I shouted, "Wait here!" and turned
and ran, as fast as I could, back into the theater. Once inside
the lobby, I shouted to the ushers, "Lock the doors!" then
walked back up on the now quiet stage. The musicians
looked at me in wonderment since we had about ten minutes
of airtime still to fill.

"Guys," I said, "anybody got a deck of cards?"

The floor manager produced a deck from backstage, and
the musicians and I gathered around the piano-top and
began a quiet game of poker. There was very little conversation, just some card playing, pictures of which our
camera-director took, revealing the cards in our hands.

All through the game, the at-home audience could hear
people knocking on the front doors, trying to get back in.

When the time came for the show to go off the air, I
looked up at the nearest camera and said, "Oh, thanks for
watching, folks. See you tomorrow."

In later years, two of my favorite young comedians, Steve
Martin and Andy Kaufman, would do precisely the same
routine, minus the poker-game finish.

The CBS program was well-received by the critics. I can't
recall whether there was much interest in our ratings in
those days; but for whatever reasons, during the next three
years the network kept moving the program about in its
schedule. From our 11 a.m. schedule we were moved to the
7 p.m. to 7:30 p.m. slot. After several months in the early-
evening spot we were moved back to 2 p.m. In 1953 the
network advised me that they had decided to remove the
show from their television schedule altogether and make it
available only on the radio.

Taking the creative approach to the very end, I decided that on the last day of the TV version it would be interesting for the at-home audience to see the actual physical dismantling of our little circus. Accordingly, about thirty minutes before the finish I told the audience that the program they were watching was our last—at least until further notice—and that I wanted to take the opportunity to thank those who for the previous three years had been such loyal viewers.

As I made these and similar remarks, the stagehands quietly began to take the set apart. I played one final piano solo and then, during the last few minutes, put on my trench coat, fedora, and scarf, waved good-bye to the studio audience, and stepped out the open scene-dock door to the street. At that point my departing figure was picked up by an already in-position camera, and, to the accompaniment of the slow playing of our theme song, I simply sauntered off into the distance, mingling with a number of passersby who had no idea they were being seen all over the nation on television.

Although I considered the closing as simply a clever way of winding up the series, we later got several poignant letters from the mothers of young children who happened to be watching. "Please, please," one woman wrote, "write to my daughter and tell her you're still alive and on earth. That you didn't just disappear into outer space. She thinks she's never going to see you again, and she cried and cried when she saw you disappearing into the crowd."

Speaking of the tears of children reminds me of a mild paradox which has never occurred to me before. Although trade commentators have often used adjectives such as *sophisticated, egghead, satirical,* and *modern* to describe the various programs I have done, all of them, with the exception of those that were broadcast at very late hours, have invariably had a powerful appeal to children, perhaps because we were nothing more than big kids playing on stage.

Undoubtedly one of the reasons this particular CBS program had been popular among children was the frequent presence of an adorable animal I named Llemuel the Llama. Another was Floyd the Fly. We had to pay Llemuel a salary larger than that earned by over 99 percent of the breadwinners in the world, but Floyd, I'm happy to say, worked for nothing—or to be more precise, for coffee and cakes. The reason was that Llemuel had an agent and a manager, whereas Floyd represented himself. Even his first guest appearance on the program was an offhand matter.

Since I have always been a late sleeper and since after several months the program had become a midday affair, I worked at a common kitchen table covered with a blue-checked tablecloth. I would usually arrive at the theater about half-an-hour before the program went on the air, sit down at the table, and go over the jokes, letters and newspaper clippings that Bill Larkin, Larry Markes, Gene Levitt, Bob Mitchell, and our other writers had prepared. At airtime I would dig into the ice-cold orange juice, sweet rolls, and hot coffee that were my real breakfast and make-believe lunch. One day as I was about to pick up one of the pastries I noticed that a fly was circling just above it.

"An unexpected guest has just dropped in, ladies and gentlemen," I said. "Camera two, let's see if you can get a close-up of him." Fred Kelly obliged, and the home audience was treated to a tight close-up of the fly as he came in for a neat landing on the plate of pastries. The fly rubbed his forelegs together, craned his "neck," strolled about a bit, and made all the customary gestures, which I narrated as if giving a play-by-play description of President Bush about to set off around the world. Our drummer, Ed Shaughnessy, who years later would join Doc Severinson's *Tonight Show* orchestra, caught Floyd's movements with appropriate rolls and rimshots.

"Folks, we're very honored today to have that world-famed show business personality, Floyd the Fly, with us. As you can see, Floyd has just landed on a saucer near a Danish here in our CBS theater and now he's bowing to the audience and waving his arms in that famous hands-locked gesture so familiar to boxing fans. Now he's up in the air again, circling the table and looking over my jokes. He's landed on the one about Macy's basement—seems to be giving it the once-over. And it seems that he didn't care too much for it because now he's back on the Danish."

The bit ran for five minutes or so, and almost every day thereafter Floyd (or possibly other flies who bore a marked resemblance to him) dropped in for a breakfast visit. Within a few days Floyd, like Llemuel, was receiving fan mail from small fry all over the country. It must have been such free-wheeling goings on that made the show popular with children as well as adults.

As I've already mentioned, during those same early-1950 years with CBS, I did a number of other network series. One of these involved serving as host—I think for about a-year-and-a-half—on an entertaining production called *Songs for Sale*. Thousands of amateur songwriters from all over the country contributed numbers. The finest of these were skimmed off each week, and four or five famous singers would perform the tunes, after which a panel of judges decided which was the best of the lot.

The one sad aspect of the *Songs for Sale* program is that although some of the songs introduced on it were at least as good as much of what one heard on the radio, there were no real success stories that came out of the series. Quite a few of the songs were recorded, in some instances by popular and talented vocalists, but none made a splash in the record industry.

Meanwhile, something odd happened that gave my career a major boost. One January afternoon in 1952, a year after I had arrived in New York, I received a panicky phone call from CBS programming. Arthur Godfrey was snowbound in Miami and couldn't get back to New York that evening to host his top-rated *Talent Scouts* show. Could I fill in for him?

I'd seen the program only a few times but agreed to replace Godfrey and ran right over to the studio.

Not long ago, at an intimate birthday party for 96-year-old George Burns, my friend and fellow-comedian Jan Murray was reminiscing about Arthur's popularity during the early-1950s. "You couldn't turn on a radio or a TV without seeing the guy," he said. "He was on during the morning. He was on at night. No matter what you turned on in the house—radio, TV, Waring Blender, Mixmaster, no matter *what*—there was Godfrey."

Talent Scouts had a contest format in which new entertainers performed their acts, with the winner determined by audience applause read by an electronic meter. When I arrived at the theater that Monday evening I knew I was in trouble: As I've mentioned I'd rarely seen the show, certainly had never studied its procedures, and we would be on live!

As it turned out, the very fact that I was unacquainted with the production details amused the audience. I got the message at once and proceeded to purposely goof up even more than my ignorance justified.

Godfrey always did his own commercials on the show—which was sponsored by the Thomas J. Lipton Company—making a cup of the company's tea or a bowl of their chicken soup on-camera. He also often played his trademark ukulele on the program. That night when the time came for the first commercial, I—partly out of klutziness and partly deliberately—made a total mess of things—combining chicken soup and tea in a pot, then pouring the whole concoction into the ukulele's hole, sloshing it around and playing a few mushy chords. The audience went wild. In his charming report of his own experiences in television, *Prime Time,* written in collaboration with his wife Mina Bess, Marlo Lewis is kind enough to write, "Steve was so hilarious on the show that five minutes after it was over Arthur Godfrey called to say that he had laughed so hard he still had tears in his eyes."

On Wednesday, *Variety*, the show-business Bible, said:

Chalk up the first five minutes of Monday's *Talent Scouts* display as one of the most hilarious one-man comedy sequences projected over the TV cameras in many a day. One could have wished that, for the occasion, the Talent Scouts format of bringing on semi-pro performers could have been tossed out of the window to permit Allen greater latitude as a stand-up comedian in his own right....The guy's a natural for the big time. He rates kid-glove attention.

It's embarrassing to quote one's favorable reviews—almost as embarrassing as quoting the unfavorable—but the point is that, again a challenge, a problem, even what might have been a disaster, had led to good results.

Later, when I replaced Arthur on subsequent broadcasts during the early '50s, I sometimes met with the comment, "You ought to be doing that show instead of Godfrey; you're funnier than he is." Those who expressed the opinion, flattering as it was, entirely missed the point of Arthur's popularity.

It was not difficult to be funnier than Godfrey since he was not essentially a comedian. Almost any established comic sitting in Arthur's chair on his *Talent Scouts* or *Arthur Godfrey and His Friends* (a variety-type show with regulars that included Julius LaRosa, The McGuire Sisters, tenor Frank Parker, and a Hawaiian woman named Haleloke) would have made him look bad by comparison if the only important aspect of his work were humor.

Such, of course, was not the case. People laughed at what Godfrey said because they liked him, not because what he said was especially amusing. His material was often, as a matter of fact, weak, if not in poor taste; but it is an indication of the tremendous power of his personality that he triumphed over it. Godfrey was more important than anything he said. This lent a great deal of authority to his comments.

He had such a vital personal magnetism that it was difficult not to be pleased by almost anything he presented. Somehow when Arthur said, "Well, the weather is certainly nice today," one felt that the weather was unusually pleasant. When he told an ancient joke one was inclined to be vastly amused, and when he extolled the virtues of a brand of cake flour the viewer received such a strong psychological impression that it was difficult to avoid acting on it when out shopping the following day.

Although Arthur Godfrey is not ordinarily thought of as a TV talk-show host, his style of television entertaining in the 1950s helped set the stage for the talk-show formula that would shortly emerge. In addition to the singers, musicians, and announcers who worked with him, he would from time-to-time interview guest stars, always on an ad-lib basis. He was actually doing a talk show of sorts. His original daytime radio and television programs set the easy, natural tone for all subsequent TV ad-libbers.

My replacing Godfrey, that winter night in 1952, was a big help to me professionally because it brought my abilities to the attention of many of the "right" people.

That, in turn, led to other favorable developments: a Broadway play, *The Pink Elephant,* a light comedy in which I played the role of a crusading Washington journalist; a few months spent hosting an ABC-TV series called *Talent Patrol,* an amateur hour in which all the contestants were drawn from the military service; and a year-long stint as a regular panelist on the top-rated *What's My Line?,* concerning which I'll have more to say in a later chapter.

CHAPTER SIX

Inventing the Talk Show

To explain how I happened to develop the talk-show formula—and *happened* is the proper word since the evolution of the form was not purely a matter of calculation—we'll have to briefly go back to the years 1946-47, in Los Angeles, when I did a daily fifteen-minute comedy-and-music program, *Smile Time,* for the Mutual Radio Network. I'm sure I did not appreciate at the time how unusual it was to be given one's own coast-to-coast comedy program at the age of twenty-four. The daily struggle to come up with scripts (there was no money for writers in the budget) occupied practically all of my creative attention.

In 1948, after a two year run, the *Smile Time* show was dropped by the Mutual Network and my partner, announcer/vocalist Wendell Noble, and I were out of work and undecided about our next course of action. After a few weeks it became apparent that since we could find no radio work together we would have to fend for ourselves individually. Wendell accepted an assignment as a record spinner for Los Angeles station KHJ and did other radio work as a singer while I gratefully acknowledged an offer from the local CBS outlet, station KNX, to do a nightly 30-minute records-and-talk program. I called the show *Breaking All Records* because I used to literally break old records rather than play them.

At the time I looked upon the move from network back down to local radio as embarrassing, decidedly in the wrong direction, and dictated only by financial considerations. The moral is that we often do not recognize our greatest opportunities. Far from being the end of my career as a comedian the move to KNX opened entirely new vistas. Accident and necessity called forth abilities I might never have realized I possessed had I stuck to the traditional radio format of scripted comedy.

When I went to work for KNX the instructions I received were simple; but I made it my business to disobey them at the earliest opportunity. "Just play the records," my new employer told me, "and in between do a little light chatter. We don't want either a straight announcer or a disc jockey for this assignment. We'd like somebody who'll handle the show with a humorous approach."

Perceiving at once that by playing a great many records I would be performing an estimable service for Bing Crosby, Frank Sinatra, Dinah Shore, and the like but doing very little for myself, I determined to make the music on the new late-night program secondary in importance. I therefore wrote out a seven- or eight-page comedy script each evening, read it in an offhand, conversational manner to create the impression that I was speaking extemporaneously, and played a little less recorded music than instructed, though I did a bit of piano work.

The reaction from listeners was immediate and encouraging. Within a very few nights the program—to my great surprise—had a group of avid fans. Cheered by their reaction, I took to talking more and playing even fewer records. This continued for about two months—until one day I received a memo from Hal Hudson of the KNX programming department. His directive said, in substance, "We hired you to play records, not to do a comedy program."

Here was a formidable obstacle to my plans, vague as they

were. Although a number of my announcer friends had made reading aloud a satisfying and lucrative profession, to me spending a lifetime as a disc jockey or announcer was a fate worse than death. I solved the dilemma by reading the executive memo on the air. As I had anticipated, listeners came to the rescue at once. In the following two days over four hundred letters flowed in, all of which stated the case precisely as I perceived it myself. "If we want to hear music," was the general idea, "there are a dozen other stations in Los Angeles playing it night and day. The reason we listen to this particular program is that it gives us something different."

The following day I walked into Hudson's office carrying a large box of mail. "I think you'll be interested in these letters," I told him.

It was gratifying that after Hal had sampled the contents of the box he immediately reversed his position. "Well," he conceded, "you win. Go ahead and talk. But play a *little* music, okay?"

I assured him that I would, but by the time another eighteen months had passed there were no records played on the program at all. The metamorphosis had begun promptly. Within a few days after I had been given free rein, people in the business—song-pluggers, musicians, writers, actors, friends—began dropping into the tiny studio where I worked. If anything happened to strike them funny, they laughed. Listeners at home heard the laughter and began writing for permission to visit the show.

"Since ours is not the sort of program that has an actual audience," I wrote in reply, "there are no tickets we can send you. If you care to drop in on a catch-as-catch-can basis, however, we can probably put you up."

Within a few days we had an audience of ten or twelve at each show, although I could not understand why they would travel across town late at night to see a man in his shirt-sleeves sitting at a table reading from a script and introducing an occasional record. Feeling that I ought to give our visitors a little more for their money, I replaced the table with a piano. At first I did no solos but used the instrument only as a means of gracefully dissolving from a recording into speech and then back into another record. Although I'd played piano and sung on the air at KOY in Phoenix, my playing was hardly of the quality that would entitle me to work on a Hollywood radio station. But oddly enough, listeners began to request certain piano selections rather than recordings, and after a few weeks I had summoned enough nerve to play one or two solo numbers each evening.

Twelve people laughing in a small room sounds like a much larger number; the studio audience now began to snowball. The station soon offered a larger studio, one that could accommodate over a hundred people. Within a few months our studio audience had swelled to fill the new space. Considering that our broadcast time was 11 p.m. in an early-to-bed town, this was regarded as phenomenal. At this point something marvelous happened, although at first I regarded it as an annoyance: Because the show in its 30-minute form had become successful, the station decided to lengthen it to an hour.

Unfortunately, though the show's time and responsibilities increased, the salary didn't. A little embittered at this, I decided not to spend additional hours writing comedy material but to fill the extra time by the easy and time-honored expedient of interviewing guest singers and musicians. It was this casual decision that led, by a fluke, to my doing ad-lib comedy and consequently to the opening of an entirely new line of work.

One night our scheduled guest was Doris Day, then a popular singer, later a film actress. Fortunately she never showed up. I say fortunately because if she had I might never have gotten into network TV. The press agent who had promised that Miss Day would appear had evidently neglected to communicate this information to her and at 11:30 I was suddenly faced with twenty-five minutes of dead air. I had used up all the prepared script, had played both sides of Doris' record, and was, frankly, at a complete loss.

Luckily in such situations something within me seems to take charge, almost without my conscious volition. It is as if some inner power says to my outer, bumbling self, "If you'll just step aside, old boy, I'll get you out of this scrape. But you must put yourself in my hands."

I suddenly heard myself saying, "Well, Doris Day evidently isn't going to join us tonight. But no matter; I'll just take this microphone and interview some of the ladies and gentlemen who *did* arrive this evening." So saying, I picked up the heavy floor microphone and, carrying it around like a large, unwieldy pipe, began chatting with people in the audience. I don't recollect the jokes during the next twenty-five minutes, but I had never gotten such laughs before. Whatever was said was greeted with almost hysterical laughter.

When the evening was over I was in a state of intellectual elation usually associated with an important scientific discovery. For two years I'd been slaving away at the typewriter and reading scripts, with only moderate success. Now I was astounded to learn that audiences would laugh more readily at an ad-libbed quip even though it might not be as funny as a prepared and polished joke. And I had not just hit it lucky one evening as I initially thought. I had not merely run into a red-hot audience. From that night on I made audience interviews an important part of the program. Never once, to this very day, has the routine failed.

Because of the change in format the program now became more than popular; it became a late-night institution in Southern California. For four nights of the week I worked in the Sunset Boulevard CBS studio usually reserved for the use of Jack Benny and other major stars. It seated 350. On Friday nights such a large crowd would show up, waiting in line for hours to get in, that we broadcast from Studio A, which seated 1000. On that evening we taped two shows—an early show, to be aired the following Monday, and a second one which was live.

Lucille Ball's mother was an occasional visitor; she told us that Lucy was a nightly listener. So, I learned, were such giants as Ethel Barrymore, Fanny Brice and Al Jolson, the last of whom was at the time riding the crest of a new wave of popularity because of the release of the motion picture version of his life (in which actor Larry Parks played Jolson). He was kind enough to say for the public record that ours was "the best radio program on the air." Jolson appeared one night, in fact, as a guest, and his incredible performance is fortunately preserved in the form of a record album titled "Al Jolson and Steve Allen."

Oddly enough, although the show was carried only on the network's Los Angeles station, KNX, it was heard in many parts of the country. Late at night radio waves from 50,000-watt stations can be picked up thousands of miles away, with the result that we used to get fan mail from Florida, the New England states and some parts of the Pacific Northwest.

In the 1990s, when programs with even quite simple formats are staffed with dozens of people, I suppose it's worth pointing out that the late night show had no producer, no director, no writers, no band leader or musical group— no help at all, really, except on certain nights from Tom Hanlon, a genial, heavy-set staff announcer who'd occasionally try to read a live commercial while I did assorted pantomime nonsense behind him, over which he would break up.

One night, for example, while he was doing a commercial for a brand of hair oil, I happened to be leaning against a grand piano. As he mentioned the tonic, I ran my right hand through my hair as if to say "I use the stuff myself." A moment later I looked down at my hand and pretended to be shocked by the fact that the palm was covered with grease. I then pantomimed rubbing it off on my tie and, after a moment, pretended to be annoyed by the fact that the *tie* was now supposedly grease-soaked.

The next step in this somewhat Chaplinesque routine— which was totally spontaneous—involved my wringing the tie out, which of course led to the grease supposedly being transferred to the lower part of my suit jacket. I then grabbed that part of the jacket and wrung it out, too, after which I made a sort of "Well, that's that" face, only to pretend a moment later to discover that the carpet to my right was now soaked with the hair oil.

Since poor Hanlon was trying to read with a straight face—although partly breaking up—I continued the pantomime by kneeling down, grabbing a handful of the velvet curtain that hung from the ceiling and rubbing it vigorously into the carpeting, as if to remove the offensive grease-spot. God knows what I would have done next had not Tom finally completed his reading of the commercial.

The KNX program lasted for almost three years: 1948, 1949, and 1950. During that time I also did other things, of course. In 1949, for example, the West Coast CBS network affiliate gave me a more traditional, scripted, early-evening radio comedy program. The first few shows of this series I wrote myself but after several weeks two talented writers, Bob Carroll, Jr. and Madelyn Pugh, were assigned to me. (A few years later these two would write the delightful *I Love Lucy* scripts during the heyday of Lucille Ball's television career.)

Madelyn, sensibly, used to go home at night when her day's work was done. But Bob and I would sometimes hang around either the CBS building on Sunset Boulevard or at one of the nearby coffee shops trying to outdo each other in thinking up offbeat jokes, some of which were too zany to use on the air. One night I asked Bob if he'd ever heard of Walter F. Doontan, the inventor of Doontanite.

When he replied, "What's Doontanite?" and I said, "Oh, nothing much; what's doin' at *your* place tonight?"—we saw at once that we had a new formula which might promptly be run into the ground. Thereafter we created such characters as Joseph K. Upton, inventor of Uptonite, and Samuel W. Gononton, inventor of Gonontanite.

Besides this prime-time CBS radio series, which for want of a better name was called *The Steve Allen Show*, I did a comedy-quiz program that ran for about a year called *Earn Your Vacation*. It didn't give winners money but sent them winging across the nation or around the world to various vacation spots, presumably whether they wanted to go or not.

In 1950 I also did a summer replacement full-network series for Eve Arden's *Our Miss Brooks*. It was on this program that I gave national exposure to a routine that had earlier worked successfully on the local Los Angeles production. At a certain point in one show I said, "You know, the latest ratings have just come in and, frankly, I admit to being surprised that this program's ratings aren't higher. I'm constantly seeing very kind reviews, lovely mail, and hearing good word-of-mouth, but the ratings arithmetic doesn't seem to reflect this sentiment. Well, I've finally solved the puzzle. Because of the time at which our program is aired millions of our listeners are picking us up while driving, and of course there's no way that ratings measurement companies can ask drivers what they're listening to.

"To resolve that difficulty engineers at CBS stations all over the country have set up audiometers to measure the volume of sound produced by car horns in your local communities. So in just a moment I'm going to count to ten. When I do, I want every one of you who's listening in an automobile—all over the country—to give a good long blast on the horn."

I counted to ten. Horns blared all over the U.S.

All the talk about audiometers and measurement ratings was, of course, nonsense; the whole thing was a practical joke. But I later heard it had some peculiar results. I got letters from three people, in different parts of the country, telling me that they were listening to a central radio hookup at a drive-in theater while waiting for the film to begin. When I reached the number 10 every single car—of the hundreds gathered—set off a blast that must have been heard in neighboring counties.

Another letter came from a man who told me he had been physically attacked for blowing his horn. He was stopped at a red light at the moment I said ten, and a large, burly pedestrian, startled by the sound, attack the driver's side of his car, swore at my correspondent, and even threw a couple of punches.

The late-night KNX program seemed to roll along almost on its own power. Once the pattern was established, I stopped writing comedy material altogether and usually showed up at the studio only ten or fifteen minutes before airtime. I'd select a few letters and newspaper articles for the ten-minute monologue that opened the program. Then there were only three things to do: interview the guest for the evening, play the piano—perhaps sing a number—and, with whatever time remained, talk to members of the studio audience.

Naturally the totally unexpected success of a low-budget and largely unpromoted local program didn't escape the attention of radio and television programming departments. After the radio network gave me a weekly, prime-time radio show, the TV people suddenly became interested.

In the fall of 1950 CBS said they'd like me to move into the new field of television, where I'd already done a bit of local work: the comedy-narrating of wrestling matches described in Chapter Three, and another show—with Wendell Noble—called *Comedy Store,* which was really little more than a thirty-minute commercial for the sponsor, a food company whose wares were displayed on the shelves of the set and who insisted on an inordinate number of plugs as well as out-and-out commercials. The program lasted, as I recall, five weeks. We were fired on the spot one evening because of something funny that happened.

I was doing a pitch for the sponsor's packaged dried beans, a pound of which was wrapped in cellophane. The copy on the cue-card led me to say, "Note how securely the beans are packaged," at which point I was to tap the bag twice on the counter top. Well, you can guess what happened. At the first tap beans flew all over the stage—and I just stood there and laughed. I was still laughing backstage a few minutes later when a stern-faced advertising executive

told us that the sponsor was very upset and that he personally doubted that the series would continue.

He turned out to be right.

The few weeks' experience on the program, however, had
been invaluable because it helped us make the transition
from radio to a medium in which we were not only heard but
seen. No longer could we hold scripts in our hands. Anything written was now either memorized or—more often—
read from cue-cards. Since the industry was new, there were,
of course, no experienced cue-card holders. Consequently,
there was many a clumsy moment when a card was dropped
or card number three was in the position of card number
two. Also, we'd moved from the physical comfort of radio
studios to the discomfort of television facilities. These were
invariably too warm because of the massive amount of light
necessary in those days to transmit an acceptable picture.
Heavy makeup was also called for; at least in this area we
were serviced by experienced personnel who'd formerly
worked in films.

The history of talk shows in television has been, like the
history of other TV forms, cyclic. Some years ago the TV
talk show became something of a glamour stock. In addition
to those hosts who'd already been on the air for a good many
years—Mike Douglas, Merv Griffin, Johnny Carson—newer
faces had entered the field—Chicago columnist Irv Kup-
cinet, TV producer David Susskind, David Frost, Dick
Cavett, Joey Bishop. Suddenly it seemed that *everybody*
wanted to do a talk show. Because of the success that Dinah
Shore had enjoyed with the form, two other singers—Toni
Tennille and John Davidson—were assigned to do similar
programs. At that point I started on a book manuscript titled
simply *The Talk Shows*. After an introductory chapter I then
did separate commentaries on a dozen or so of the leading
practitioners of the conversation-show form. I never submitted it to publishers, however, because by the time I'd
completed the project, some four years later, talk shows had

fallen on hard times. NBC was concerned with *Tonight* show ratings, Toni Tennille had gone off the air; so had John Davidson and Dinah Shore. Even the Merv Griffin and Mike Douglas ratings were reported to be slipping. I changed the title of my manuscript to *The Life and Death of the Talk Shows,* set it aside, and concentrated on other writing projects.

By the late 1980s the situation had again changed and the talk formula was once more considered of major importance. By this time Douglas and Griffin had finally concluded their long and successful careers, but Joan Rivers took advantage of popularity derived from *Tonight Show* appearances to start a similar venture of her own. Comedian David Brenner started a daytime version, as did Regis Philbin. Phil Donahue, coming from modest beginnings in Dayton, Ohio, had become a dominant figure in daytime TV syndication, and Geraldo Rivera and Oprah Winfrey would shortly borrow his theme-show formula, to be followed by Sally Jesse Raphael. Tom Snyder followed *The Tonight Show* on NBC's 1:00 a.m. program *Tomorrow.*

Though the Joan Rivers challenge to *Tonight* was not successful, CBS elected to start another program of the traditional late-night sort featuring game-show host Pat Sajak, and after a number of incredibly embarrassing experiments with its late-night hour, the Fox network finally settled on a mature but youthful-looking comic, Arsenio Hall, who would soon be followed by Jay Leno, Chuck Woolery, Rick Dees, Maury Povich, Jenny Jones, Ron Reagan, Jr., and, by late 1991, apparently everybody in the business who wasn't otherwise occupied at the time.

I'm often asked what I think explains the remarkable longevity and popularity of television talk shows. There is no one answer; a number of factors are involved. The basic ingredients of a typical talk show are, obviously, (1) the host and (2) his or her guests. There's nothing particularly mysterious about the popularity of the latter factor—mankind has long been fascinated by the various military leaders, film stars, singers, Broadway actors, nightclub performers, comedians, authors, musicians, sports heroes, political figures, and others who have gained national or worldwide prominence. This is particularly true in the United States where we've developed an apparently insatiable appetite for celebrities—whether old, new, short-term, long-lasting, legitimate, manufactured, or scandalous. Indeed, were it not for this popular if bizarre appetite, massive publishing empires would go out of business overnight.

The reasons for the popularity of talk-show hosts, however, are more elusive. What is the magic factor that separates successful hosts from the rest of their entertainment world colleagues? First, it has apparently nothing whatever to do with talent. Talent, as the word has traditionally been understood in the arts, refers to the ability to perform a creative task with excellence. There's no such thing as talent in the abstract. When we employ the term we're referring to such specific activities as acting, doing comedy, singing, dancing, playing a musical instrument, or—to move outside the performing context—painting a picture, sculpting a statue, or writing a poem, novel, or play. But for hosting talk shows such abilities have no necessary connection at all.

This is not to say that talk-show hosts have no talent. Some do; most do not. What's fascinating is that there have been success stories and failures in both categories. There've been cases where highly talented entertainers proved to be poorly suited for the role of conducting a talk show. Jerry Lewis, as funny a comedian as our culture has produced, was totally miscast introducing other entertainers and interviewing them. The great Jackie Gleason, too, briefly attempted a talk-show formula, with no success. You can't be much more talented than was Sammy Davis, Jr., but he, too, proved inept at the talk-show assignment, as did another of my personal favorites, the gifted and lovable entertainer Donald O'Connor.

But if it's not talent, as that term is generally perceived, that accounts for success in the talk-show field, what is it? Well, until recently anyway, it seems to involve having an easy-to-take personality, being generally soft-spoken rather than pushy, not noticeably eccentric, and not so socially dominating that one will overshadow one's guests.

Dinah Shore, for example, succeeded as talk hostess partly because her personality is so relaxed that she may someday be arrested for loitering while on the air. As Dinah would readily concede, she is not particularly polished at interviewing. But because she is truly nice, viewers were willing to watch her five days a week.

A slightly naive quality seems to help a talk-show host succeed. It's not that a literal boyishness or immaturity is required, or the eternally boyish Regis Philbin would have been more successful than Johnny Carson, but a certain freshness of outlook must be retained. A jaded, bored talk-show host would not last long. The host, in a sense, represents the audience, and like the audience, he must actually be—or pretend to be—entranced with his guests and their doings, ideas, and comments. One of the reasons for Phil Donahue's success is his intense concentration and interest in the subjects discussed on his program. Merv was also excellent at retaining the "Gosh, really?" freshness of his responses, even after more than twenty years at the game.

Talk-show hosts, of course, have to be at least moderately articulate, though not much more so than the average disc jockey or afternoon game-show emcee. Having myself served early in my career as announcer and disc jockey, it's not my intention to cast aspersions on those two worthy professions. Some of the nicest people I have ever met have been radio announcers. In fact, if we apply the old would-you-want-your-daughter-to-marry-one? test it could easily be argued that a good, sensible announcer is preferable to the average stand-up comedian. The point is that neither of the two professions made sense, for me, as a lifelong commitment, in the same sense, remaining in his original job—that of joke-writer for other comedians—would have made no sense for Woody Allen.

Another characteristic seemingly required for success as a chatter-program leader is a degree of blandness. The TV medium is so intimate that hyperintense people—even if gifted—are perceived as vaguely annoying if seen often. This was Joan Rivers' problem with some viewers although with the success of shows like *Geraldo* and *Arsenio Hall* the more flamboyant approach may finally have found its audience.

Those talk-show hosts who have been most successful over the years—Jack Paar, Mike Douglas, Johnny Carson, Merv Griffin, your obedient servant, et al—were not only trained in radio but also had the advantage of prior experience as entertainers, which is to say we were accustomed to working with *audiences* as well as with guests. And they had the ability to engage in easy, relaxed banter with those who came to view their shows in the studio.

Another factor in the success of talk-show people is simply their appearance night-after-night rubbing shoulders, seemingly as equals, with famous actors, singers, politicians, and other celebrities. TV talk-show hosts are like radio disc jockeys in this connection. While a few artistically talented individuals have briefly spent time introducing recordings early in their careers, no one would otherwise dream of relating talent to the work of disc jockeys. A disc jockey, after all, is simply a radio announcer; and a radio announcer is just someone with a pleasing voice, which may be interpreted as a winning personality by the radio audience. The major comedians of 1930s and '40s radio—Jack Benny, Fred Allen, George Burns, Edgar Bergen, Eddie Cantor, Bob Hope, Red Skelton—all had as announcers genial gentlemen who themselves became famous simply because they appeared, week after week, with the gifted stars featured on their programs. As mentioned earlier, neither occupation—radio DJ or TV talk-show host—calls for artistic talent as it is generally defined.

When I created *Tonight,* the original example of the genre, it was not a creative act of the traditional sort as was, for example, the later development of my PBS-TV series *Meeting of Minds.* The *Tonight* show formula emerged out of something as casual as a personal "workshop" process, discovering which entertainment forms were most effective for me and gradually constructing a new type of program based on those strengths. The low-key opening monologue, the jokes about the orchestra leader, the home-base chatter with the announcer sidekick, the kidding with the studio audience, the celebrity interviews—all of these were selected for personal convenience but in time came to seem the "natural" talk-show formula.

Inventing the talk program was, frankly, rather like inventing—oh, the paper towel. The result is useful, a source of enormous profits, and the world is somewhat better off for it. But it's hardly to be compared with doing a successful weekly prime-time comedy series, painting an unforgettable picture, composing a beautiful musical score, or discovering a cure for a crippling disease.

I assume that a million years ago there was a man sitting on a tree stump in some jungle or forest idly exchanging pleasantries with two men to his right, seated on a fallen log.

"You guys catch any fish this morning?" he probably said.

"Well," one of his companions might have responded, "I caught a pretty big one, but it got away."

And that, ladies and germs, is really all there is to a talk show. I mean that quite literally. You can make minor adjustments such as exchanging the tree stump for a desk and chair, replacing the log with a couch, adding a bit of background scenery or an orchestra, but such additions are clearly not of the essence.

But why, then, do talk shows seem so important despite their almost nonexistent format and the simplicity of the host's task? The answer is simple, and a bit scary. What makes the programs seem so significant is simply that *they're shown on television*. Ask yourself, in all seriousness—would you pay the price of a Broadway theater ticket to go inside and see, oh, Maury Povich idly chatting with Miss Wyoming, an aging actress promoting a book she did not actually write in which the main attraction was the revelation of the identities of a number of fellow performers with whom she had had sexual relations, a doctor promoting a new diet, and a transvestite demanding to know why the church refuses to let him study for the priesthood?

Of course you would not.

But add the factor of television exposure to these same dreary proceedings and now your former and quite sensible disinterest will be transmuted to an almost morbid fascination.

Nevertheless, despite its inherently lightweight quality, it would seem that no other television form has so consistently affected, for better or worse, the national consciousness. That conversation-programs can make books best-sellers, rush entertainers from obscurity to popularity overnight, hype box office for motion pictures, concerts, and plays is clear. Foreigners can learn a great deal about our culture by doing nothing more than watching our talk shows. American dramas and comedies give a distilled and distorted impression of our social reality. Our newscasts, too, though they deal with reality directly, have time to show only thin slices of it. But the talk program—except for the fact that it presents mostly the prominent among us—at least shows us as we are, without scripts, being ourselves. We are heard discussing events of the day, currently controversial issues, the latest jokes and humorous references, politics, religion, sex, war, peace, revolution, sports—whatever is going on or in the wind.

While I am frequently introduced on television as "the Father of the talk show," or "as a talk show host, the granddaddy of them all," and so on, it was actually Jack Paar who set such programs more narrowly in their present mold. I indeed did a talk show, but it's not correct to describe *Tonight* during my three-and-a-half years as host (1953-56) as *essentially* a talk show. It was something much more creative—an experimental TV laboratory. One night we'd book, say, the Count Basie band and let them do twenty-five minutes of music. The next evening our show might be structured in the form of a debate between teams of political opponents; on other occasions we might present a full-fledged, thirty-minute drama, ad-lib comedy routines in the street, or do exciting remote telecasts from Hollywood, Miami, Chicago, or Niagara Falls.

Sometimes a guest would be so special—comedian Fred Allen, composer Richard Rodgers—that I'd do an entire program with him alone, the kind of show Dick Cavett years later did so well with people like Orson Welles, Laurence Olivier, and Katherine Hepburn. One such instance on *Tonight* occurred the night we were told we could have poet and Lincoln biographer Carl Sandburg for a brief five-minute chat. When at the end of the short exchange I thanked Mr. Sandburg for having joined us, he said, "You've made me feel at home here. I feel I have friends out there in the dark." Declining to leave, Sandburg almost displaced actor Charles Coburn, throwing the control room into a panic. But when Sandburg, Coburn and I finally closed the show with a three-part harmony rendition of "Home on the Range," it was one of the most thrilling experiences in my entire professional history.

The tragedy of this otherwise wonderful event was that the program is not retained on kinescope film because NBC intentionally destroyed thousands of its early films and tapes on the grounds that—if you can believe the rationale—they were running short of shelf-space at their New Jersey storage facility.

In any event, on certain evenings on *Tonight,* we'd invite three or four people in to "chew the fat," as my mother's family used to say, and those were our pure talk-show nights. But it was Jack Paar who "invented the couch." Evidently perceiving that this particular approach was far simpler to execute than coming up with fresh and creative ideas every night, Jack simply decided to book amusing or interesting guests nightly, and leave it at that. He did it very well.

Our production people during those first few years, in contrast, were so experimental, so creative, so innovative, that literally nothing has been done on subsequent talk shows—network or syndicated—that was not originally introduced, in some form, during the first three years of *Tonight* and the first year of the New York-based late-night *Steve Allen Show* which preceded it.

Some of today's hosts, for example, like to take a hand mike, wander out into the studio audience, and interview visitors as we did. On the Carson *Tonight Show,* members of the audience were sometimes invited to "Stump the Band" by thinking up obscure songs the orchestra might not know. That comes from our original NBC series. Answering questions visitors have written on cards was also part of the original show; I still do the routine in my personal appearances. *The Late Show Pitchman,* a standard comedy bit from our 1950s' program, was presented on the Carson *Tonight Show* as *The Tea-Time Movie with Art Fern,* right down to the showing of old film clips and Art Fern's wearing of a dark wig and mustache. In fact, the word *fern* itself was one of the original *Tonight* staff's standard double-talkisms, with Louis Nye as the originator.

The strange, off-camera cry "Whoa-oh," which mysteriously greets talk-show hosts at the beginning of a telecast was originated by trombonist Frank Rosolino on my show a good many years ago. And, of course, *The Great Carnac*—as scores of journalists have observed—is a precise copy of *The Question Man* with a funny hat.

There are times, if one comedian "borrows" another's material, when there's at least an attempt to disguise the act. A prop may be added, an accent, a bit of business that at least puts a new frame around the original picture, but in the case of one more sketch from the original *Tonight* show the recent version simply took it lock-stock-and-barrel. In 1954 writers Stan Burns, Herb Sargent and I introduced an idea so fresh and funny that to this day it would still be hip. For some time I'd been getting laughs—on an ad-lib basis—by taking tight close-up shots of people in the first two or three rows of our audience, giving them names other than their own, and doing some sort of spontaneous nonsense with them. Building on this base, Stan and Herb wrote a number of wonderfully funny routines sometimes constructed as the summation of an ongoing soap opera story, in other cases identified as a "Missing Persons" report, and sometimes identifying the faces in the audience as those of the FBI's "10 Most Wanted" criminals. Before the show started, during the warm-up, we would size up the audience and make notes as to which faces seemed the funniest. Anyone wearing an odd hat, or having a front tooth missing or a strange-looking hair-do would be marked by Dwight Hemion, our director, as the object of a close-up once the sketch got underway. Stan and Herb's first draft would then be placed on my desk, and I would read from it as the separate shots of our visitors were taken. But ad-libbing was always required, based on whatever I noticed about the individuals we had selected. For example, one fellow—upon seeing himself on one of the studio's television sets—might suddenly burst out laughing, at which I would ad-lib something like, ". . . and of course you will recognize Burt by the notoriously goofy laugh by which he has so often been identified by his victims." Or if a woman, spying herself on the screen, suddenly clapped her hand over her mouth in embarrassment I would say, "Freda can, of course, be recognized by her tendency to clutch at her upper plate in moments of emotional stress."

We performed the sketch every so often and it was always warmly received. I would do it again, during a 1962-64 talk-comedy series and then, in a third instance, during the daily series that ran from 1968 to 1972.

A few years later I began to get calls from people who reported having seen the exact sketch on the *Tonight* show. Since the then-incumbent and/or his writers had already occasionally borrowed from our repertoire I at first thought that the new instance was not especially noteworthy. But eventually I realized that the latest theft represented not a one-time offense but had become something of a fixture. One day I got a letter from Mel Chase, who'd written several versions of the sketch for me during the '69-72 series. Quite incensed, he implored me to at least write a letter of protest to the *Tonight Show* producers, perhaps on the grounds that if they could not be made to desist at least they might be induced to feel a twinge of guilt. The response to my letter—alas—was a blank-faced denial of plagiarism and a claim that their own writers had thought of the idea independently. Even in the unlikely event that they had, the simple fact that our show had repeatedly done the sketches starting more than 20 years earlier would have settled the issue had the matter been taken to court, or even to Writer's Guild arbitration.

Since the news media thrive on controversy it is probably inevitable that these observations, though entirely factual, will somehow be taken as justification for some sort of Allen-puts-down-Carson stories. If only to forestall that possibility, I will set down here, once and for all for the record, my opinion that Johnny Carson has done an absolutely superb job of hosting the *Tonight Show* during his years at the helm. I enjoyed his work long before he had had experience at talk show hosting and used to occasionally book him to do his own always clever routines on my prime-time NBC comedy series. Unlike some popular comedians, Johnny has always written a certain amount of his material and has deservedly become a national institution due to his over quarter-century of experience as America's king of late-night TV.

Indeed the obvious fact of his success has provided him a remarkable degree of Teflon-like protection against the

constant charges of plagiarism to which he has been subjected, by both other comedians and professional critics,
during his long tenure on the show. Concerning this Dick
Cavett wrote in his autobiography titled *Cavett:*

> I'm sure that Johnny is as riddled with doubts about his
> identity as any of us who have gravitated toward comedy
> for a living, and I think it shows in his work. His style is an
> accretion of Bennyisms, Grouchoisms, Hopeisms, and, to
> drop the ism-ism, later additions of Don Rickles, Don
> Adams, Dean Martin, and a large dose of Jonathan Win-
> ters. Here and there are touches of both Allens, Fred and
> Steve. Fred Allen had a department called The Mighty
> Allen Art Players, a witty adaptation of Stanislavsky's name
> for his company, and Steve Allen's Question Man went into
> swami drag and became Johnny's Carnac. Also, Johnny's
> appropriation of Oliver Hardy's look of dismay into the
> lens was a shrewd choice for television.

Dick's reference to "a large dose of Jonathan Winters" of
course refers to the fact that Johnny—like the rest of us—
was so amused by Jonathan's Maude Frickert old-woman
character that he somehow managed to guiltlessly appropriate it, in its every detail, except that his character was called
Aunt Blabby.

This relates to the fact that two forms of entertainment at
which Johnny has always been quite gifted have, oddly,
scarcely been mentioned by the reviewing media. For example, reader, were you personally aware that Johnny is a gifted
card-manipulator? Well, he is. I've often wondered why he
did not more often publicly display his remarkable prowess
with a deck of cards.

The second ability for which, at least to my knowledge, he
has never before been praised, is that he has always been
quite a good impressionist. Indeed one of the excellent
monologue routines he did on my old Sunday night show
involved his credible imitations of Ed Sullivan, James Garner

as Bret Maverick, and myself. In another of his routines he did very good impressions of Edward R. Murrow and Jack Benny.

It's probably here that we find an explanation of what has always been Johnny's tendency to use other people's material. No one complains, he may reason, when an impressionist does a precise imitation of Jimmy Cagney, Cary Grant, Jimmy Stewart, George Burns, or any other established entertainer, even when those impressions include lines and jokes created by the originator. Perhaps it does not seem like a very large step, in Johnny's mind, from one form of appropriation to another.

The moral distinction between the two, obviously, is crucial but it is characteristic of our time that moral distinctions are now commonly obliterated.

The foregoing list of appropriated materials is actually rather short, not for the reason that the original *Tonight* show did not create a great number of production ideas—we came up with them almost every night—but rather because Jack Paar's formula of doing nothing more than booking a group of guests has come to dominate the field. Consequently, there's no longer any particular demand for creativity on the part of either producers, writers, or hosts of most programs of this sort. This is not a criticism. The programs are enormously successful in their present form. It would therefore be difficult to think of any reason they should be changed.

There *was* one eventual sharp departure from the stock formula, however: that now associated with Phil Donahue. We had occasionally done "theme shows"—programs on which only one issue is discussed—on both the original *Tonight* and a program I would later do in the early Sixties which was syndicated by Westinghouse. But by concentrating on this format exclusively and dealing with the more controversial issues Phil did develop a fresh formula. By the 1990s, of course, there were so many versions of the Donahue formula on the air that the freshness had worn off.

While it's no exaggeration to say that many Americans have been significantly educated on various important social questions as a result of watching Phil over the years, the recent much-publicized competition among Donahue, Winfrey, Rivera, Rivers, Jenny Jones, Maury Povich, and Sally Jesse Raphael has led to a frantic search for ever more sensational and controversial subject-matter, which in turn has attracted the attention of the nation's comedians. But those of us who write jokes on that subject have trouble devising satirical lines that are wilder than the issues these programs now typically present. A few years ago, when the matter first attracted public attention, I did a line in which I pretended to be doing a promotional announcement for one of these shows: "Lesbian nuns: should they be permitted to have abortions? Today on *Geraldo*." But, as I say, the exaggeration is not now all that far removed from the reality.

Young viewers sometimes assume that David Letterman's late-night program represents a creative departure from the norm; but as David himself has often graciously conceded it is nothing of the sort. He used to watch my 1962-64 show almost nightly and has subsequently often been generous enough to report that it formed his own comic con-sciousness. David used to get a kick out of my spontaneously taking cameras backstage or down the hall, showing people on the street outside our studios, making funny phone calls to various parts of the country, reading viewer mail, and doing wild physical stunts. As a result, when he and his production people were assigned by NBC to do his present late-night show they made a conscious decision to simply revive as many of my old routines as they could recall. Billy Crystal, Steve Martin, Dennis Miller, and Andy Kaufman, among others, have also been kind enough to state for the public record how much of their own approach to comedy was influenced by our early comedy-and-talk shows.

CHAPTER SEVEN

Early Days in TV

I'll never forget the first time I actually performed comedy in a television studio. Accustomed to the tomb-like silence of radio studios, the "Quiet, please!" or "On the Air" signs, and the rapt attention of the visitors in the seats, I was horrified to learn that instead of being separated from the audience only by one thin microphone, I was now required to reach them through a jungle of cameras, lights, props, microphone dollies, and scenery inhabited by three camera operators, two men working movable microphones, numerous stagehands creeping around in the darkness—upon rare occasions even visible on-camera—assorted stage managers who strode around with headphones on muttering audibly while receiving communications from the control booth, and a general collection of producers, announcers, musicians, actors, dancers, and hangers-on.

Trying to make an audience laugh under these distracting circumstances was, in those hectic early days, a little like playing the Palace while between you and the footlights the Harlem Globetrotters mapped out a few fast-moving plays.

One of the first comedy routines I ever performed on television concerned a particular technical problem—an annoying glitch called *rollover,* in which the picture would suddenly start sliding up—or down—the screen. Sometimes you could fix it by making an adjustment on your set but in most cases the attempt was to no avail since the problem originated at the point of transmission.

In 1950 I wrote a routine incorporating this glitch, which I performed on my show the following year. I had noticed, as a television viewer, that when rollover started, a thick black horizontal line—approximately an inch in width—would precede the picture as it rolled up or down the screen. I therefore instructed my prop people to take a 2-by-4 piece of wood, wrap it in black velvet, and then have it held aloft by two men standing on either side of me just outside camera range. I then assumed my usual center-stage position. At a prearranged cue they lowered the black bar slowly into the picture, at which time I bent my knees so as to make the upper half of my body slide down the picture at the same rate at which the bar was moving. On the home screen it looked almost exactly like rollover, although whenever I did this bit our engineers were never able to figure out a way to make me appear on top of the picture a moment later, as would've been the case with an actual rollover.

The studio audience, who could see both the routine on the in-house monitors and the seemingly magical means by which the illusion was produced, always laughed heartily. Those watching at home, now that I think of it, must've been more puzzled than amused.

In general, though, there was never any sharp line of demarcation between my radio comedy and what I later did on TV, probably because what I do as an entertainer is behave the way I do all day long, at home or anywhere else. Certain sensible adaptations were required by the full-time move to TV, but my style didn't change. It depended on spontaneous reaction to the reality of the moment.

For example, on our 1948 daytime CBS radio comedy-and-talk show, I once heard an annoying clatter coming from just outside the upstage doors of our studio. There was no sense going on with the business of the moment; the noise was too loud to ignore. So I asked a couple of our ushers to open the back door, took a hand mike, and went outside to find out what was going on. It turned out that an elderly Italian fellow was running a cement mixer. I hand-signaled him to turn the thing off, then interviewed him for several minutes, to the accompaniment of screaming laughter from inside the studio. To this day I don't think the man had any idea that people were hearing him all over the country. He said he was sorry if the noise was disturbing us, but he had a job to do and had to knock off work at a certain time. It didn't matter much what either of us said—it was the situation itself that was funny.

It was from that radio incident that I got the idea of interviewing fewer celebrities and more Just Plain Folks. On my television talk shows of the early Fifties, in fact, I not only interviewed working people but had them actually perform their professional function while we chatted. One time, for instance, a tailor fitted me for a suit while we talked. He was an old fellow from Europe, and to this day I remember the volume of laughter when he suddenly knelt before me, quite unself-consciously, and measured my inseam. To kick the laugh along a bit, I turned my head to the right and coughed, which naturally got a great reaction from the men in the audience and blank stares from the women.

We also had a barber on the show who gave me a shave and a haircut; someone else gave me a shoeshine. There was a good deal of that sort of thing, which David Letterman would revive some thirty years later (having watched my Sixties Westinghouse Show, although most of the routines originated years before that on my radio series and the original *Tonight* show).

Only because of my radio background could I have taken that approach to entertaining on television. None of the great comedians of vaudeville or nightclubs would have thought to do that kind of comedy. They did their acts, for the most part, or shows based on their acts, but for those of us who came out of radio and into TV in the early '50s—

Godfrey, Dave Garroway, Jack Paar, Garry Moore, Johnny Carson, and others—that radio background was invaluable.

All in all it was an exciting and stimulating time. In 1948 both CBS and ABC had begun regular network TV service. NBC and DuMont (the innovative but fleeting fourth network in business between 1946 and 1955) had already started sending programs over their stations two years before, NBC being first when its WNBT-New York outlet began feeding shows to Philadelphia and Schenectady.

At the same time that CBS was signing me to a TV contract, a fellow who was spoken of as the other hot young comic in Hollywood was being wooed by NBC. Don "Creesh" Hornsby was the network's first choice to host its planned late-night program, to be called *Broadway Open House*. Had Hornsby undertaken the assignment, Jerry Lester, Jack Paar, Johnny Carson and I might not have succeeded, at least in the way we did.

The energetic Hornsby might well have become one of the leading lights of the Golden Age of television comedy. I'd been hearing about him for some time, although I had neither heard nor seen him because he didn't perform on radio or television. A number of friends in the music business had told me that Don, also in his late twenties, and I worked in somewhat similar fashion, in that we both ad-libbed, did one-man shows, and got laughs in what was then a new way. Curious, I went to see Hornsby one night in 1950 when he was working at old vaudevillian Charlie Foy's Supper Club on Ventura Boulevard, not far from Hollywood.

Watching him, I perceived the few similarities in our styles that had been pointed out but noticed mostly the differences. Hornsby, husky and with light-brown hair, worked in a much louder, more physical, extroverted fashion. Like myself he entertained partly from a piano bench and was also the composer of a number of novelty songs. But he did some of his performance from a crazy trapeze-bar swing—from which he would loft himself out high above the first few tables while carrying on a nonstop patter. I can't recall a single one of his jokes, unfortunately, merely that he performed in a very free-form fashion.

One gimmick I do remember, because it worked so well, involved his holding one of those enormous five-battery railroad-yard flashlights that casts a powerful beam. He would point it now at one table and now at another, which had the effect of suddenly spotlighting some embarrassed customers. He would ask them questions to get them talking, somewhat in the manner of my own studio-audience interviews, and then do a combination of prepared jokes and ad-libbing, which went over wonderfully.

Hornsby may also be the originator of a type of act that many later comedians have done, the sort where the entertainer uses one crazy prop after another and makes a joke about it. Rip Taylor, Gary Muledeer and Gallagher come to mind in this connection. And he was not above such *aren't-we-devils?* gimmicks as walking through the audience with a large and all-too-realistic rubber gila monster. He would also from time-to-time pick up a giant cheerleader's megaphone and, instead of speaking into it, place it over his head, dunce-cap style. Pretending to be displeased with one segment or another of his audience he would spray ringside tables with pressurized dry ice from a fire extinguisher and then tell those on whom the chilly dust had settled that in a few minutes holes would begin to appear in their flesh.

Another certain laugh-getter in those pre-feminist days was the clothed, life-size, blonde, window-dummy model which sat behind Don onstage. Whenever the mood struck him, he would whirl about and slap the "woman" in the mouth.

Hornsby had the gift of being funny with whatever was going on at the moment: a bartender serving a drink, a waiter carrying a tray of dirty dishes, a customer heading for the men's room. In his teens he'd worked as a pianist in small jazz clubs around the country, but before long he'd evolved from a funny piano player into a full-fledged comedian.

Don was, because of the physicality of his style, a natural for television, which was just then summoning up a small army of entertainers from radio, nightclubs, theater, and films. Early in May, 1950, he flew to New York to sign a network TV contract with NBC. A *New York Times* clipping refers to his arrival in the city:

> The network thinks so highly of its new acquisition that it has sold him to Anchor-Hocking as master of ceremonies for its nightly series of hour-long variety shows scheduled to start May 16 in the 11 p.m. to midnight time. The Milton DeLugg Trio has been assigned to supply the music for the programs....

Though it sounds like a twist in the plot of a bad movie, Hornsby was stricken with polio on the very day he was to have auditioned for his new late-night show. He was placed in an iron-lung at the Grassland Hospital in White Plains, New York and seemed at once to be aware that he would not survive. "When I go to sleep," he said to his wife, Dorothy, "I'm not going to wake up." Two days later he was dead.

Don would have been the first late-night spontaneous comic. It is tragic that he was deprived of life and that millions of the rest of us were deprived of his ability to entertain.

But when, instead of Hornsby, two veteran comics, Jerry Lester and Morey Amsterdam, were signed to host the Anchor-Hocking show (Jerry three nights a week, Morey the other two), the show became popular almost at once. Amsterdam left not long after the program premiered, but the delightful *Broadway Open House* for a little over a year turned out to be a potpourri of comedy skits, music and dance, though in no sense a talk show. Its biggest hit was the deadpan buxom blonde called Dagmar (Virginia Ruth Egnor) who, wearing black dresses with plunging necklines, sat on a stool and read bad poetry while Jerry Lester did burlesque-style double-takes.

Another clever performer on the Los Angeles scene in the late '40s was Jim Hawthorne, who I've sometimes referred to as the West Coast Ernie Kovacs since both men specialized in fresh, inventive sight gags and camera tricks rather than simply doing radio comedy on TV as other comedians of that time did. Hawthorne looked like a cross between Garrison Keillor and me. After CBS brought me to New York, I understandably lost track of the local Los Angeles scene and therefore was no longer able to enjoy Jim's creative work. It was not, in fact, until July of 1989 that I learned Hawthorne had been considered, in 1953, as a replacement for Jerry Lester on the *Broadway Open House* show. I was a guest on Larry King's radio program one night when a listener from Toronto called in to ask if Hawthorne had ever been considered as Lester's replacement. I said that although I'd always enjoyed Jim's work, I had never heard that particular report. Hawthorne, fortunately, happened to be listening and, in a letter to me a few days later, said:

> Jerry Lester was leaving the program and my manager/ agent called me one night asking if I was interested in going to New York as *Broadway Open House* emcee. Obviously I said yes and thought my big break had arrived. Unbeknownst to me, the agent said the money was not enough...$1600 a week. I said I wanted the show anyway and would do it for nothing. The next thing I knew I was no longer in the running. My "rep" had blown the deal, and I was in tears. By the way, later I was told that Bob Hope had recommended me.

Show business history is full of such sad stories.

Those of us fortunate enough to have performed on television in both the 1940s and the 1990s are inevitably referred to as pioneers. Oddly enough, none of us ever thought of ourselves in such terms in those early days. I suppose it was simply my ability to create humor spontaneously—which, as mentioned, was perhaps a character defect conditioned by having grown up in a witty, quick-minded Irish family—that largely accounted for my being given so many opportunities in the new medium. It also helped that I was an easy-going type, with a face not likely to alarm small children, that made television programming executives—for the most part themselves young and inexperienced—so frequently offer me employment.

In the life stories of some men and women of achievement one can detect a running thread of goal-setting, determination, sometimes fierce ambition. All three would appear to be lacking in my own case. While what I assume are accidents of genetic nature provided me with several marketable talents, I might nevertheless have lived out my life in obscurity had I not had the blind luck to enter adulthood just as the newly conceived medium of television was entering its infancy.

So far as conscious ambitions are concerned, I had intended to become a journalist, poet, and writer of fiction. As a freshman at Drake University in 1941, the year of the Japanese attack on Pearl Harbor, I had quite casually taken a snap-course in radio production and immediately perceived that, while the newspaper business was likely to be a demanding profession, almost anyone not cursed with an annoying speaking voice could find work in radio. And several years' experience in that medium accidentally placed me in that enormous job-pool from which the first wave of television personalities were drawn. Thus, far from having to make any willed attempt to get into TV, I was pulled into it, along with hundreds of others, as if we all were in the grip of an enormous vortex. It was simply a matter of being in the right place at the right time.

I am often asked—did I—or anyone I knew—have any grand vision for our new professional home at the time? I think not; I certainly didn't. As noted previously, TV wasn't nearly as good then as it is now. Those of us who appeared on it saw the same things that everyone else saw when we turned on our home sets. In Los Angeles we found game shows, amateur hours, reruns of old low-budget cowboy movies, bottom-of-the-barrel films from studio vaults suddenly marketable on *The Late Show,* newscasts presented by rather stiff journalists or radio announcers just learning their new trade, little musical shows featuring mostly unknown singers, with rare examples of excellence. Programs were better in the New York area since many of America's comedians and jazz musicians were residents there, but in the rest of the country local TV was the slimmest of pickin's as of 1950.

Network programs were, of course, of a generally higher quality level, but in those early days many of them left a great deal to be desired. We newcomers—whether as professionals or viewers—had no idea that television would turn into the world's most powerful medium and its biggest, most influential advertising vehicle.

In time, however, the quality began improving. The shakedown was concluding and out of the general mass of largely talentless on-screen personalities there gradually emerged such attractive and interesting entertainers as Dave Garroway, Arthur Godfrey, Jerry Lester, Milton Berle, Jackie Gleason, Ernie Kovacs, Sid Caesar, Imogene Coca, Jack Carter, Jan Murray, Red Buttons, and Wally Cox.

Gifted young dramatists, too, began to perceive that they might have better luck on television than on hard-to-crack Broadway. Reginald Rose, Paddy Chayefsky and Rod Serling were among others who began to provide powerful scripts, which fortunately fell into the hands of such talented directors and producers as Delbert Mann, Martin Manulis, Sidney Lumet, Franklin Schaffner, and Fred Coe.

But all that came later.

It is difficult for us to recall now, the glow of nostalgia being so beguiling, just how terrible much of television really was in the early-1950s, particularly on local programs. I recall being a guest, along with famed songwriter Arthur Schwartz and other dignitaries, on one New York program, whose host was designer Oleg Cassini's brother Igor.

I don't believe I'd ever seen the program before I appeared on it, nor do I remember seeing it thereafter. The only reason I recall the experience at all is that the entire 30-minutes—done from a swank midtown restaurant—was one endless disaster for poor Mr. Cassini. Microphones that were supposed to be turned on weren't, so only lip-readers could follow parts of the conversation. Lights came on and went off at odd moments. If two people were speaking, the camera director seemed to prefer a shot of the listener rather than the speaker. A full cup of coffee was noisily spilled on the tablecloth. Mr. Cassini mispronounced one guest's name and momentarily forgot another's. There were mysterious—sometimes hilarious—off-stage sounds and voices. At the end of this brain-numbing experience, poor Igor, charming as ever though obviously shaken, said, "Steve, I can't thank you enough for being with me today."

"That's right," I replied, relieved that the ordeal was finally over. "You can't."

Network programs, too, had their share of snafus. On our *Tonight* show hang-ups were, as some writers like to put it, not infrequent. Sometimes right in the middle of a comedy monologue—either the opening remarks or some more involved routine I was doing within the show—a stagehand or technician, not realizing which camera was on, would actually walk right across the stage between the audience and me. On the old kinescopes you can sometimes clearly see the man's shadow as he crosses in front of a light. Anybody who had done that on, say, an old Bob Hope or Jack Benny radio show would have been shot at sunrise, if permitted to live that long; but on television in the early days such goofolas were common, and terribly distracting. Literally every head in the house would turn away from the performer and watch the moving body as it walked across the stage carrying a chair, a prop, or whatever. The next joke could have been better than anything Mark Twain or Voltaire ever wrote, but it wouldn't get a peep from the audience for the simple reason that nobody had heard it.

Viewers at home would know nothing about the background factors. All they perceived is that the comedian suddenly didn't seem so funny.

Often I would have to fill up a minute or two of unplanned time just because it was taking the stagehands and other technicians that long to move scenery, cameras, props and microphones into place for an upcoming number. Obviously I never saw the *Tonight* show in those days because I was doing it live five nights a week; but now, as I look at the few old films available, I can easily see the precise moments at which I realized that instead of being able to say, "And now, here's Eydie Gorme," I suddenly became aware that I was just going to have to talk—about something—until further notice. And in some cases I can detect the trace of annoyance I was feeling at the time.

Another reason we early-birds had not the slightest sense that we were making television history is that most of us were much too busy to indulge in such introspection. One summer I not only did *Tonight* but played the title role in a motion picture called *The Benny Goodman Story*—a murderous schedule both physically and psychologically. Later I not only produced ninety minutes of material for the nightly live *Tonight* show but was also doing a prime-time Sunday night comedy show for which I helped Stan Burns and Herb Sargent write original sketches each week.

Additionally, my co-workers and I just didn't consider our shows a big deal. We knew people like Bob Hope and Bing Crosby were important stars, but we were just a bunch of young guys having a hell of a time.

Oh, I saw my picture on magazine covers, read the lovely reviews and heard about the high ratings we were getting, but somehow all that never seemed to relate to me. It was almost as if I were reading about someone else named Steve Allen. All we were concerned about was: God, what will we do tomorrow night? We knew we were a hit tonight, but each day was a brand new slate and the audience's attitude was then, as ever, "What have you done for me lately?" So we did no looking ahead whatever and very little appreciating of what critics said we were accomplishing.

Incidentally, working on television in the early days was wonderful therapy for me personally. For one thing it helped me get over my tendency to shyness. I'm somewhat withdrawn by nature, and when I was first in television I was painfully insecure. It's odd that at a time when observers in the other media were kind enough to refer to my competence as an interviewer, I myself was a generally disappointing subject for others to probe. There were occasional exceptions—if the journalist putting questions to me was extremely bright or had a hip sense of humor—but often newspaper and magazine people would later report: "Allen is surprisingly introverted and not nearly as communicative as he is on the air." They were right and it took me about five years to work my way out of that phase. But once I did I was so relaxed on the air I could have a cup of coffee, eat dinner, sing, dance, play the piano, give blood to a Red Cross nurse or, almost literally, fall asleep.

There are many strands of humor running through the history of television, of course, in addition to sketch and situation shows that were intentionally comic. In the days when most programs were done present-tense live, there were occasional disasters on serious dramatic programs which, though funny in retrospect, made nervous wrecks out of those involved.

In a tense moment on one show, for example, on which my wife Jayne was featured, actor Wendell Corey was shot, dutifully clutched his chest, staggered back, fell to the floor, and "died." Naturally such players do not lie motionless forever; they are cued by the floor manager as to when they may get up and walk away. Mr. Corey thought he heard such a cue, opened his eyes, sat up, dusted himself off, and marched off the set. Which would not have been so unusual were it not for the fact that he was still on camera.

Then there was the time when Burr Tillstrom and his delightful Kuklapolitan Players—puppets Kukla, Ollie and

Beulah Witch—together with their charming straightwoman Fran Allison, were guests on my show. *Kukla, Fran and Ollie* was a marvelous, largely ad-libbed children's show that was also popular with hip grownups. When they appeared on our program, Burr as usual provided the behind-the-scene voices of the puppet characters, naturally having his own microphone for doing so. Ollie, the snaggle-toothed dragon, was at one point having a chat with Fran when I suddenly noticed that the off-screen operator of the boom mike was doing exactly what he would have to do if two humans were having a conversation—he was constantly pointing the microphone back and forth to whichever puppet was supposedly speaking at the moment, as if they were actually doing the talking.

How could I not have great fun working in a field where such things happened?

Undoubtedly the wildest, most infamous goof-up is that related by director John Frankenheimer, a young member of the *Armstrong Circle Theatre* production staff at the time. He clearly recalls the incident, he says, which took place in a relatively small studio space at Leiderkranz Hall on New York's 58th Street. The unlucky actor who was the center of both the scripted and real-life dramas was Francis L. Sullivan, who played a missionary working with an assistant Frankenheimer maintains was portrayed by Eva Marie Saint. (Eva says she was not the actress on this particular program, although she has her own similar incident to relate.)

In John's account, the script called for the couple to fly over the Himalayas in a small two-seater plane piloted by Sullivan. Suffering engine trouble, they would then be forced to land in mountainous country where they would be rescued by a team of Chinese ski troops.

The resulting debacle grew out of the fact that Sullivan was apparently not quite familiar with his lines when it was time for the live telecast to begin. Recalls Frankenheimer:

> Sullivan was pretty shaky. And I must explain that there wasn't a great deal of room in Leiderkranz Hall and right

beside the airplane set was the area where the commercials, also live, were to be done. Another factor was that we had had to find eight Chinese actors to play the parts of the ski-troopers. Unfortunately none of us knew where to find that many Chinese actors so one of the production people, with an interpreter, went down to Pell Street in Chinatown and walked up to people on the street until he found eight who were willing to cooperate.

Another problem was that in the scene the Chinese guys had to be seen moving on skis. Naturally none of them knew anything about skiing, and there could be no snow in the studio anyway. Somebody got the brilliant idea to put rollerskate wheels on the bottom of the skis so that the troops could at least be seen moving through the picture; if their feet were below camera range it would look real enough. While the scene in the airplane was going on, the eight Chinese fellows were over near the commercial area, on their skis, waiting for the interpreter to tell them to move through the other shot.

Now we return to the scene in the small plane, which was presumably flying at about ten thousand feet and losing altitude fast. Sullivan, by now glassy-eyed from insecurity and the knowledge that he was the object of at-home scrutiny by millions around the country, suddenly sank into a mental air-pocket and hadn't a clue as to what he was supposed to say next. He simply looked at Eva Marie Saint and said, 'Well, my dear, what have you got to say for yourself?'

She looked at him and said, 'I think I'll just go to sleep,' and put her head on his shoulder, at which point Sullivan looked desperately at the camera and said, 'My stop. I think I'll get off.'

At that moment, apparently, director Don Medford understandably panicked and decided that the only thing he could do was cut away from the now pilotless airplane and go to commercial. The temporary solution would no doubt have been helpful, had it not been for the fact that the live commercial was not scheduled to start until several minutes later. Consequently the announcer, who was not listening to the on-camera dialogue, had no idea that his services were suddenly and unexpectedly called upon. He happened at the moment to be casually chatting with a representative of the Armstrong Cork Company, the sponsor, and that is precisely what viewers around the nation saw—two unidentified gentlemen engaged in relatively idle banter.

But out of the corner of his eye the announcer suddenly perceived both the red light on the camera aimed at him and the frenzied waving of a floor manager. Realizing that he was on the air he simply walked away from his companion, approached the camera, and began to read his prepared commercial copy. Unfortunately, the audio engineer in the booth had neglected to turn the announcer's mike on, so all that was viewable at home was a man moving his lips, gesticulating, but making no discernible sound. Even worse, the engineer had forgotten to turn *off* the mike back at the airplane set, so what was heard was the by now half-mad Sullivan bemoaning his fate in highly colorful language.

Hearing this, Medford shouted for the addled audio specialist to cut the mike, which he did. He also opened the announcer's mike so at last he could be heard. But in the general confusion, someone waved, which the eight Chinese gentlemen on the skis equipped with wheels took as their cue. They slowly trudged through the live picture of the announcer extolling the virtues of Armstrong's products. Since at that point there had been no reference in the script to Chinese ski troops there was no possible way the program's viewers could make any sense whatever of the intrusion of the confused and wobbly-footed Orientals.

Obviously there was literally no way that all the pieces of the dreadful puzzle could be corrected. It was not even physically possible to continue the program. The pale, shaking Medford called master control. "For God's sake," he shouted, "get us off the air any way you can!"

The next thing viewers saw was some unidentified and of course irrelevant film feature.

When I wrote to Eva Marie Saint concerning the above account she wrote back that she had broken up laughing while reading it, but that she wasn't the actress involved. The foul-up to which she was connected happened—she believes—on *One Man's Family,* a '50s prime-time soap opera-type drama, transferred from radio, in which she starred as Claudia Barbour Roberts.

CHAPTER EIGHT

The Birth of the
Tonight Show

In the fall of 1953, both my professional and personal life began looking up. The ABC television station in New York had a five-nights-a-week variety program on the air from 11:00 p.m. to midnight. Its format was reminiscent of Jerry Lester's *Broadway Open House,* though not nearly so entertaining. But I used to watch it frequently because one of its comics, Louis Nye, amused me greatly.

In those days, Ted Cott was head of NBC's New York outlet. Cott coveted the brewery account, Ruppert Knickerbocker Beer, that ABC had landed with its night-owl variety hour. As I later heard the story, he approached the Ruppert people and said, "Why don't you come over to our station? I can give you the same sort of program, only better, and to head the show I can give you a fellow who specializes in this sort of work." The deed took several months, but when it was set Cott had the Ruppert account in his pocket and had hired me to emcee the program on his station. Although it was to be broadcast only in the New York-New Jersey-Connecticut area, I accepted the assignment.

WNBT provided us with trombonist Bobby Byrne and his orchestra and announcer Gene Rayburn. We auditioned several singers, and hired a young blond seventeen-year-old named Steve Lawrence whom I'd earlier booked for an appearance on my CBS radio show. Several weeks later we added a dark-haired vocalist by the name of Eydie Gorme.

The program appealed to TV viewers tired of a diet of old Charlie Chan movies and the frenetic tempo of *Broadway Open House,* which it replaced, and it enjoyed popularity from the start. For the first time since coming to New York I felt completely in my element in television, partly because the new program was much like my old Hollywood radio show, only instead of a table I now sat at a desk. There was very little script, mostly ad-lib chatter, questions from the audience, guest and audience interviews, piano music, and songs from Steve and Eydie, the band, and myself.

When we first started doing the show, I had no writers at all; none were needed. Occasionally I would write a comic monologue or a simple sketch for a guest and myself, but all I actually required on a typical night was a piano, a couple of amusing letters from viewers, a newspaper article that had caught my fancy, an unusual toy that a member of my staff had picked up, a guest or two to chat with, and an audience to interview.

After several weeks the program's mushrooming popularity made it a more profitable venture for the station, as a result our budget was somewhat enlarged. It became possible to raise the question of getting some help in creating that small part of the show which could be prepared in advance.

At about that time I met an affable young writer named Stan Burns. He said he'd like to work for me if the opportunity ever presented itself. Stan amused me, so I spoke to our production people and he was hired. Not long thereafter he mentioned that if there was enough production money to afford another writer, a friend of his named Herb Sargent might profitably be considered.

For the next year or so, Stan, Herb and I handled all writing duties, not feeling the least bit put-upon in doing so. Other writers were eventually added, but this was because the program had become so profitable that extra production dollars were available.

This reminds me of an Emmy Award program I was watching a few years ago on which the *David Letterman Show* won an award for comedy writing. I had the impression that half the audience got up to accept it. I think David actually had something like seventeen writers at the time. To this day I do not understand why it takes that many people to do what little writing such programs require.

There were happily no critically negative reviews of our new show at all. Something about the freshness, energy, and relaxed spirit of the program—which had the general atmosphere of a fraternity house—seemed to please viewers with all sorts of tastes. One of the reasons for the show's kind reception, I suppose, is that all of us on it were having a perfectly marvelous time. In recent years I've read about cliques, back-biting, and rivalries on *Saturday Night Live,* which is sad if the reports are true. In our case doing the program was remarkably like going to a party every night. There were good jazz players in the band, the singers were terrific, and the studio audiences warmly responsive. It therefore came as no surprise when after several months Pat Weaver, NBC's programming chief, called me in and said he hoped to put the program on the network at some point in the not-too-distant future.

From a failed marriage and a worn-out welcome at CBS, things were finally improving. My ex-wife Dorothy was happily remarried, I was working for NBC, and I'd met film and Broadway actress Jayne Meadows, whom I would marry in the summer of 1954. I missed the children terribly, flew out every few weeks to see them and brought them East whenever I could, but otherwise life was once again getting back on an even keel.

Around the time of its one-year anniversary, the program was renamed *Tonight* and put on the full NBC network. On September 27, 1954, the night we went national, I told the audience:

In case you're just joining us...I want to give you the bad
news first: This program is going to go on—forever....It's
a *long* show. Goes on from 11:30 until one in the morning.
We especially selected the Hudson Theatre for this show
because I think it sleeps about eight hundred or so.

This is a mild little show. Just look at it for about a week
and then decide what you think of it. It's not a 'spectacular.'
It's going to be more a 'monotonous,' I think.

Because I've had few preconceptions about radio, television, films, or Broadway over the last quarter century,
nothing has come as a particular surprise to me. The one
glaring exception, however, concerns the extent to which the
public record of my doings has been distorted. I do not refer
to those inconsequential errors which are a daily part of
normal human discourse and communication. Or perhaps
in another sense I do. If your Aunt Mabel says that your eyes
are blue, when in fact they happen to be brown, that is
hardly a matter of great consequence. When the *New York
Times,* however, says precisely the same thing, obviously
readership by a wide audience profoundly alters the significance of the error.

I detected the phenomenon as soon as my own activities
began to be written about. Shortly I had noticed enough
errors of fact that I began keeping a separate collection of
them. Now enormous, it continues to grow to the present
day. To dramatize the point I will state only that *Current
Biography,* a primary research resource, had, the last time I
looked at its entry on me, a longer list of errors than any
other article I have read, 37 in all.

Another interesting thing about published mistakes is that
they never stop. And they often emanate from sources that
ought to know better. In a recently published book about the
Tonight show, written by a charming gentleman who's had
long personal connection with the program, it's stated, and
will unfortunately now be accepted as fact by the thousands
who read it, that the *Tonight* show was created by an NBC

programming executive—oddly unnamed—and that its first host was Jerry Lester! Since such errors are not trivial and bear on the history of one of television's most important programs, they naturally require correction.

Incidentally, it's interesting that during the 1950s and '60s I never had to mention the matter because everyone knew the facts. But new generations have now been born that never saw the original *Tonight,* millions who did see it have died, and a few of those who remain would appear to be suffering from what I call old-timer's disease; so before the record is hopelessly obscured, it needs to be reaffirmed.

The unidentified NBC executive alluded to in the book is the gentleman I mentioned earlier, Sylvester "Pat" Weaver, father of actress Sigourney Weaver and brother of comedian "Doodles" Weaver. Pat and I have long constituted a mutual admiration society. He was kind enough not only to put me on his network for ninety-minutes-a-night five-nights-a-week but later asked me to do a far more important NBC prime-time weekly comedy series. For my own part, I've always thought that Pat was one of the best programming executives in television history. But it needs to be settled now, once and for all, that he had nothing whatever to do with "creating" *Tonight.* The program, as I've described it here, had already been created—with no input from NBC programming people—over a year before Pat and his assistant Mort Werner had the wisdom to add it to the network's late-night schedule. The only change was that it was no longer called *The Steve Allen Show* but became known as *Tonight* because the network already had initiated its still-successful morning experiment called *Today.*

At this point, a sharp-eyed researcher should ask, "But isn't it possible that in converting the program from local to network either Weaver or his programming associates made certain changes, subtle or otherwise, that would have at least entitled them to claim that they had participated in the show's creation?"

No, it is not.

Pat and his associates did indeed attempt to make some
minor revisions in the program, each of which left those of
us who were actually creating it night-by-night open-
mouthed with astonishment. Weaver, it bears repeating, was
a gifted network programmer but that profession has no
necessary connection at all with the actual creating and
production of programs. A programming executive simply
decides which programs he will carry, and secondly where
they will be placed in his schedule.

To deal with specifics, the first change the NBC people
recommended was a nightly report on skiing conditions
around the country. As Jack Paar used to say, I kid you not.
When our producer Bill Harbach first told me about this, I
laughed heartily, as if he'd just said, "The fellas think we
should have a segment every night where we tell people how
to cast voodoo spells," or "They think it would be a very good
idea to have a nightly segment on Buddhist theology." The
really funny thing is that the NBC people were absolutely
serious. I sent a memo to them in which I said, "I wonder if
you gentlemen have conducted any formal research as to
what percentage of the American viewing public is involved
with skiing at all, and secondly which subsection of that
minuscule group might actually be planning to ski as of a
given date."

Needless to say, no such thought had been given the
matter and, to the credit of the programmers, they came to
realize that it was pointless to force us to inform our millions
of listeners all over the country that there was light snow at
Stowe or poor conditions in Aspen. The segment was, after a
very brief period, dropped and forgotten.

A second suggestion was also completely wrong for
Tonight, which emphasized comedy. The network fellows
thought we should add a serious drama critic—a friend of
Jayne's and mine named Robert Joseph. The suggestion was
that he become a regular member of our on-camera team for
the purpose of reviewing all the new plays that opened on
Broadway. In explaining why the proposal was absurd for

the show, I pointed out that (a) a tiny fraction of one percent of our audience would be interested, (b) most of them would live and die without ever having seen a Broadway production, and (c) most plays with unknown actors in leading roles were failures.

I added that, on those all-too-rare magical Broadway nights when a truly distinguished drama or a great musical opened, almost none of our listeners would know—on the show's opening night—that it was eventually to be recognized as important. If they did want to hear anything about the event, their interests could easily be satisfied by our having the stars appear as guests, doing a number from the musical or something of that sort. Furthermore, Mr. Joseph, although a dear fellow and a perfectly competent critic, was not exactly a walking bundle of charisma, so that even if some such regular segment could have been justified, he was far from ideal casting for the assignment.

This idea, too,—after a short time—was fortunately tossed overboard.

Among the people who came into my life as a result of the show were Dwight Hemion, still the best camera director in television, and Bill Harbach, our producer. These two men have rarely received the media credit they deserve for the success of both the late-night show and our award-winning prime-time comedy program that followed it. Dwight, who looks like George Peppard, went on to do brilliant specials for Barbra Streisand, Burt Bacharach, Shirley MacLaine, and others; Bill, to produce *The Hollywood Palace* with another friend and member of our staff, Nick Vanoff.

Harbach, who looks like an actor (he once played a small part in one of Jayne's pictures, *Song of the Thin Man*) is a cheerful enthusiast with a warm and wacky manner of handling people and getting their finest work out of them. Best of all, considering that he produces comedy shows, he loves to laugh. But Bill is funny himself without knowing it. He does not mean to be; he is not a jokester or a cut-up. But the combination of his ferret-like nervous system and a certain difficulty in expressing himself when he is excited makes him say some of the most outlandish things this side of Sam Goldwyn. A few examples:

One day while in a heated debate with Jules Green, our executive producer, Bill hit the ceiling at one of Jules's suggestions. "There you go, Jules," he shouted. "For the first time you're wrong again!"

Once, wanting to conclude our program with a religious number that was not too slow in tempo, he came running into my office and said, "What's a good *up* hymn?"

Bill says things of this sort with a perfectly straight face and in all seriousness. One time, when we did our show in Havana, he was asked when the various members of our group were dispersing to return home. Bill replied, "I'm dispersing Wednesday."

Then there was the day he came into my office to discuss something and I noticed he was wearing a heavy overcoat. "Do you have a chill?" I asked.

"No," he said. "Why?"

"Well, you're walking around indoors with your coat on."

"Oh." He looked surprised. "I forgot to take it off. No! I forgot to go *home*!" And with that he dashed out of the room and ran for the elevator.

Another peculiarity of Bill's is that he has the world's worst memory for names. He doesn't just forget them; some tantalizing shred remains in his mind causing him to cry out weird variations. Trying to instruct his secretary to call Charlton Heston for rehearsal one afternoon he shouted, "Get me—uh—Charleston Huston; er, uh—Charleton Hudson. You know: Chester Moses."

But the funniest thing Bill ever said came out one day when he was trying to call to mind the title of the world-famous poem by Joyce Kilmer. "You know," he snapped. "Only whatsisname can make a tree!"

Many of the production innovations that Dwight Hemion introduced on the original *Tonight* show are now commonplace in the trade. One of the reasons Hemion is such a polished comedy-variety show director is that he has a sharply defined sense of his expertise. He is master in the use of cameras, lights, studio or remote facilities. He has sensitive taste and impeccable judgment. And he is a good photographer who happens to use a TV camera rather than a still camera as his instrument.

Quite importantly, he's aware that his professional competence does not extend to the area of comedy. During all the years of the *Tonight* show and our prime-time Sunday evening series I cannot recall his once making a suggestion to any of our comedy players as to how they might improve the reading of a line or the performing of a bit of physical business. Nor did he ever offer suggestions to our writers about jokes or sketches. There have been many comedy and comedy-variety shows during the last forty years on which the directors were not nearly so wise. Apparently what was involved was a simple error in thinking: They assumed that since they were (a) directors and (b) worked on a comedy show, it was therefore logical that they should (c) direct the comedy. But that does not necessarily follow.

Jules Green, our financial chief, had also been my agent since the Hollywood radio days. Like Bill, he's something of a character and frequently amusing without intending to be. He, too, sometimes lets his emotions run away with his tongue. Once, in talking about a right-wing political figure who had died and for whom someone in the room was expressing sympathy, Jules snapped, "To hell with him. There are dead men walking the streets tonight because of him!"

Stan Burns and Herb Sargent, too, seem like a couple of characters out of fiction. Stan is a big, husky ex-Marine with the most pleasant personality in the world. In forty years I have never known him to have a glum moment, and his wife and children seem as jovial as he. Oddly enough, his specialty in comedy is what has come to be known as the Sick Joke. His subject matter is apt to include death, Hitler, accidents, and national catastrophes. Needless to say, some of his best lines could never be used on the air. He was the originator, for example, of that much-quoted sick classic, "Remember, folks, _____ Airlines is the airline of the stars: Carole Lombard, Grace Moore, Will Rogers. . ." And I was not surprised one afternoon during a plane flight to see Stan wandering up and down the aisle with a small box of sweets borrowed from a stewardess, saying, "After-crash mints, anyone?"

Sargent, tall, good-looking, and quiet, is also a brilliant jokesmith. Given to wearing tweed sports jackets, he has the Connecticut haircut and the grizzled Ivy-league look of men in cigarette ads. While lost in thought he may stand in the middle of a room, arms held out from his sides, shrugging his shoulders and quietly flapping his fingers. When I would go into his office to talk to him I would often make this gesture; he would laugh and then we'd go on with the conversation. (I say go on rather than start because in our office conversations were never really begun or concluded. They all seemed to begin in the middle, taking off from some point of earlier reference, and were invariably broken off in midsentence or interrupted by another party.)

An indication of Stan-and-Herb's sense of humor—I connect their names with hyphens because around the studio they were usually spoken of as if they were two lobes of the same brain—is the Christmas present incident. Every year at Christmas I inform those working for me that my name is not to appear on any gift list. One year I sent a memo to all hands pointing out that I was the proverbial man who had everything and thus didn't want anyone to give me anything for Christmas. I was surprised, therefore, when on December 24th I found a beautifully wrapped gift from Stan and Herb on my desk. Opening it I could see that it was a framed object of some sort, perhaps a special portrait or a historic document. It was a document all right; the fellows had given me a tastefully framed copy of my memo.

Another time they gave me a handsomely trimmed photograph of themselves for which my then-rival Ed Sullivan had been kind enough to pose.

These five—Green, Harbach, Hemion, Burns and Sargent—formed the original team of our late-night TV show. They were some of the many men and women behind the scenes who over the years have made my on-camera work so much easier than it would have been without them.

Another was Sam Homsey, dark, thin, nervous, who was in charge of booking eccentrics (he called them left-fielders) for our show. We called Sam "The Prince of Darkness" because he always wore black. Today half the people in our country, and probably 90 percent of those in the music business, seem to prefer weird attire, but in those days, at least in the New York scene, Sam had the field pretty much to himself. Every day he'd parade his finds into our office: health nuts, Oriental seers, ancient Native Americans in warbonnets, circus freaks, people who wanted to teach me to breathe, to do exotic exercises, read my kneecaps, or whatever.

Then there were the "regulars" of the studio audience, those hardy souls who seemed to have no purpose in life but to spend every waking moment—and some sleeping ones— at radio and TV shows. Some MCs avoid them and issue instructions that they are to be penned off like cattle to the rear seats when possible. Personally I like the regulars. They entertain and amuse me, and I think they do the same for audiences watching at home. Given a choice between a regular and an unknown quantity I'll head for the regular eight times out of ten. It isn't only that I get more comedy mileage out of the steady customers; I'm constantly on the lookout for the eccentric and extroverted people who are willing to talk, and this is a good description of a regular.

One of our most dependable steadies was an oddly clad elderly woman of obviously small financial means known simply as Mrs. Sterling. We never did know her first name or where she lived. Perhaps she resided in the fourth row of some New York TV studio and only went home occasionally to change clothes. Like most of the regulars, she was present nightly, partly because she liked the *Tonight* show and partly—perhaps mainly—because she liked to carry home prizes.

Mrs. Sterling had a simple act, but it seemed to amuse audiences. First she complimented me lavishly, then she demanded a gift, usually a "Pomeroy" camera. The camera's name was actually *Polaroid,* but Mrs. Sterling wasn't particular. Our conversations, which rarely varied, went something like this:

STEVE: Good evening, Mrs. Sterling. How are you tonight?

MRS. STERLING: Mr. Allen, you're wonderful.

STEVE: That may well be, Mrs. Sterling, but I didn't come over here to listen to your compliments again, flattering as they are.

MRS. STERLING: But I just want everybody to know what an angel you are, Mr. Allen. I hope you're feeling well.

STEVE: But Mrs. Sterling, I—

MRS. STERLING: You're not working too hard, are you?

STEVE: Up until now I wasn't, no.

MRS. STERLING: That's fine. Say, I'd like to have one of them Pomeroy cameras.

I don't recall how many cameras we gave Mrs. Sterling, but we did shower her with a wide assortment of stockings, record albums, enormous salamis, wristwatches, perfumes, furniture, and electrical appliances. Whether she used these articles, hocked them, sold them, or stored them away on the Collier Brothers' Hoarding Plan remains a mystery.

What our millions of viewers never knew was that from time-to-time after the show Mrs. Sterling would lurk in the darkness outside the theater, waiting for me to come out. When I did, she would rush up and hand me a wrinkled paper bag or package. It always contained a little present, usually a handkerchief or candy.

Another regular who visited us two or three nights a week for almost a year was a tall, thin fellow named John Schafer. To say that John talked a lot doesn't begin to give you the idea. He was a man with a long-playing tongue. I stumbled over him one night in the audience and started a conversation with the usual, "And what's your name, sir?"

"Well," he said, speaking extremely rapidly, "my-name-is -Schafer-John Schafer-I-work-as-a-farmer-upstate-That-is -it's-not-*my*-farm-you-understand-but-my-uncle's-farm-but-I -figure -*eventually* -it'll -be -my -farm -I -mean -if -everything -turns-out-all-right-We-raise-quite-a-few-nice-things-on-the -farm-It's-about-a-hundred-acres-and-we've-been-up-in-that -section -for -the -last -two -three -generations -I -just -come -down-to-town-once-in-awhile-to-see-the-sights-and-have-a -little-fun-Watch-your-show-once-in-awhile-and-thought-I'd -drop-in-and-see-it-What-was-it-you-wanted-to-ask-me?"

"To tell you the truth, Mr. Schafer," I said, "I had five or six questions in mind but you've already answered all of them."

One night I happened to ask John where he'd been the night before.

"Well-I-seen-this-movie-*Mogambo*-with-Clark-Gable-and -this-Ava-Gardner-woman-and-it-was-a-pretty-good-picture -but-to-tell-you-the-truth-I-couldn't-figure-out-what-old -Clark-was-so-interested-in-this-Gardner-woman-for-when-I -figgered-he-would've-been-better-off-with-this-blonde-girl -whatsername -this -Kelly -girl -Her -father's -from -Philadelphia-'Course-it-sure-was-something-when-all-those-old -gorillas-came-running-around-and-Old-Clark-had-to-step -lively-to-keep-things-on-an-even-keel."

Schafer went on in that vein for a full five minutes, during which time I did not say a single word, blank-faced takes into a close-up camera being sufficient reaction.

When he finished I said, "So that's what you did last night, eh?"

But we realized there was value to John's monologues. Not only were they the longest straight lines in the history of comedy, but his synopses of motion pictures had a childlike sort of charm. We actually signed him up for a series of movie reviews, which were well received by our audiences, if not by the motion picture studios. ·

Another regular visitor was the ever-popular, short, be-spectacled "Mrs. Miller"—actually Miss Dorothy Miller—who got her "start" in my audiences at KNX in Hollywood and then followed me to New York. Incredibly, she came to our show almost every night by train from Philadelphia, where she worked as a clerk-typist for the U.S. Army Quartermaster Corps. She later spent years in the audiences of Jack Paar, Merv Griffin, Joey Bishop, Mike Douglas, and Johnny Carson, as did another regular, a sweet, elderly woman known only as "Lillian Lillian." The oddest thing about Lillian was that wherever we went, she showed up. When we did the *Tonight* show once at Niagara Falls, there she was, smiling up from the front row. And she followed our circus to Havana, to Hollywood, and to Fort Worth, Texas. I never knew how she got her tickets, how she managed to get a front-row seat, or where she stayed in the various cities to which she followed us. But she was always there, and until recent years was often on hand when I made guest-appearances on New York shows. We, in fact, ex-changed letters from time-to-time.

Perhaps our most unusual regular was a gentleman we discovered one summer when we originated the program in Hollywood for a period of several weeks while I was filming the life story of bandleader Benny Goodman. He brushed aside the customary query about his name with the sugges-tion that he sing a song for us. He was a short, stocky man with a heavy, and to me still unidentifiable accent, though it may have been Italian. I later learned that his name was Carmen Mastren. "What song would you like to sing?" I asked.

"Allaganzanada's Ragatima Band."

"What key do you sing it in?" I said, hoping to pick up a cue for Skitch Henderson, our conductor.

"A," said Carmen. It developed he sang every song in the key of A, or at least said he did. As a matter of fact, we never could figure out what key he sang in because he did every song *on one note*, like a Gregorian chant. His appearances were a popular feature of the show for several weeks, and one record company even signed him to a contract and cut a few sides. Evidently the experiment didn't pan out, but for a time Carmen was one of the most popular singers on television.

Another fascinating visitor to our studios was a little old man named Ben Belefonte. He called himself a *rhyming inventor*. This did not mean that he invented rhymes but that he was an inventor who incidentally happened to write rhymes. I shall never forget his weird inventions. One of them was a Hanger Bank. This was not a device for hanging banks or for banking hangers; it was just a common transparent plastic hanger in which Mr. Belefonte had cut slots large enough to permit the passage of small coins. You simply dropped pennies, nickels, and dimes into the hanger until it was full. Then you had a hanger full of coins. Don't ask me who needed such a thing.

Another of Ben's brain-children was an enormous device for eliminating pedestrian congestion at busy intersections. In his sketches it looked like the four sets of steps that lead up to elevated train stations. Instead of a waiting platform at the top, there was a big sort of lazy Susan turntable which shuffled the pedestrians around, and then—by centrifugal force—shot them off, hopefully in the right direction. Ben spoke in rhymed but not rhythmic verse. His most fantastic invention was a rhyme that had never fallen from the lips of man before and never will again. Somehow he managed to make the word *the* rhyme with the word *inventor* by saying, in a heavy New York accent:

I'm Ben Belefonte, the
   Rhyming inventuh!

A particularly wild character, also a regular, was a man known as Professor Voss. The Professor was a well-preserved chap in his late sixties who spoke with a slight German accent, liked to walk around with a bare chest in the coldest of weather, and had unusual ideas about diet and exercise. One night a dreadful thing he said made the audience laugh for such a long time that I regret nobody timed it with a stopwatch.

"Tell me, Professor," I said, as he sat half-naked in a large tub filled with freezing water and large blocks of floating ice, "to what do you attribute your remarkable physical condition?"

"Well, it's water that does it. You've got to start off each day by drinking plenty of water."

"Do you do that?"

"Oh, yes, indeed," he said. "The first thing you must do when you get up in the morning is drink four quarts of warm water."

"Wow! Four quarts! That's a lot of water. And what do you do then?"

"Well," he said, as matter-of-factly as if he were discussing the weather, "you stand about three feet from the toilet. . . "

Naturally I cut him off immediately, but there was no stopping the audience. This, of course, was in the days when the chatter on talk shows was devoid of the leering vulgarity that now seems almost a requirement.

One night we'd booked as a guest a woman who was an expert on the care and feeding of cats. She had brought about a dozen of them to the studio and on my desk had placed a doll's house about which five or six of the cats were crawling, sleeping, and playing. As soon as I walked into the theater and saw this, the phrase *cat house* (brothel) flashed across my mind, so I gathered Steve and Eydie, Gene Rayburn, Skitch, and other members of our crew around me. "Be sure," I instructed, "that when we start talking to this lady about her cats and the little house that they're playing in...be sure that no one uses the phrase *cat house*." They chuckled and of course agreed to avoid the term.

A few minutes later we went on the air and shortly thereafter I began to interview the woman with the cats. "What is this thing?" I said, pointing to the little structure.

"Oh, that," she said amiably, "that's a cat house."

The regulars who appeared on our show became so much a part of the family they were often the recipients of fan mail. Audiences came to look forward to seeing them almost as much as they enjoyed our guest stars.

One *Tonight* regular that people still ask about was a cheerful young Italian immigrant by the name of Joe Interleggi, whom I dubbed the Human Termite because he ate wood. He didn't actually swallow and digest it, I suppose, but his claim to fame was that he had jaws and teeth of such prodigious strength that he could bite holes in any piece of wood in the house. He could also open beer bottles with his teeth and grind the bottle caps into small twisted wads by rolling them around in his mouth. Joe became tremendously popular with our viewers.

He prefaced almost every sentence by addressing me as MistaSteveAllen, as if that combination of syllables was a single entity.

"MistaSteveAllen, I wanta thank you for havin' me here. MistaSteveAllen, you a good guy. MistaSteveAllen, we all love you. MistaSteveAllen, I will now lift a kitchen table witha my teeth."

On one occasion, after Joe had ground several bottles into small bits, leaving a pile of broken glass on the stage, he brought an overweight young woman up out of the audience, introduced her as his girlfriend, sat her in a chair, and quickly put a length of simple clothesline rope around both her waist and the chair. Then, grasping the knot of the rope behind the chair in his teeth, he stood up full-length. The unfortunate woman was suddenly suspended in mid-air, supported only by a thin piece of rope across her spacious abdomen. Understandably enough, she squawked like a pig hoisted in a slaughterhouse, which apparently unnerved Interleggi so much that he let the rope slip from his usually mighty jaws. The young woman immediately fell about three feet into a pile of broken glass, giving her lacerations on both kneecaps—not to mention ruining her hose. She bled slightly but fortunately was not seriously hurt. It did not require sadism on the part of the audience to be driven to hysterics by this unplanned demonstration.

Besides our parade of eccentric amateurs, we also booked talented professionals. One of these was Genevieve, a young French singer who got laughs by mangling English. She would later work with Jack Paar. Then there was Rosaria, a cute little brunette from South America who spoke Portuguese better than she spoke English; comedian Don Knotts who performed brilliant monologues he had written; and the always funny Louis Nye.

Then there was one of the modern giants of comedy— Jonathan Winters—who made a good many appearances. He was so unfailingly funny that we invariably called him when we were booked to originate the program from some other part of the country. Not content with being funny on the air, Jonathan would keep us in stitches almost every hour of our travel days, starting early in the morning at some central hotel-lobby gathering point, then on the bus to the airport, through the terminal, on the plane, in another bus at our destination, in the hotel lobby when we arrived, in the dining room that night, the rehearsal hall the next day— Jonathan's spontaneous creativity never stopped.

Stan, Herb, and I would sit with him and throw him challenges. First we'd say something like, "Be a German," at which Winters would begin speaking in dialect. Then one of us would say, "Make the German a little effeminate." A few seconds later, "Make him an effeminate German nightclub singer." It didn't matter how many elements we added to the characterization, Jonathan never balked. Readers who admire Robin Williams—don't we all?—should know his greatest inspiration was Winters.

One problem with Jonathan was that he was a little hard to work with; all you had to do was stand next to him and in a moment you'd be laughing. The only two TV performers who ever were able to play straight for him were, I think, Jack Paar and myself. We, too, did our share of laughing; but at least we were able to feed him lines and suggestions that would spontaneously fuel his remarkable comic creativity.

Once, when I was doing a guest-appearance on Jonathan's own show, I appeared as a "bush pilot." When he asked me what kind of plane I flew, I said, "No, no. I don't fly planes. I fly bushes," and pointed to a large hedge which happened to be part of the set. Some comics would've just chuckled and taken another tack. But not Jonathan. Nothing could ever throw him.

CHAPTER NINE

The *Tonight* Show: Wild Ad-Lib Routines

W hat wild nights there were on the old *Tonight* show, what crazy ad-lib routines. One of my favorites—because it was true, extemporaneous and unpredictable comedy—was when we used to open the back door of the theater and point a TV camera out into the night. With no idea that they could be seen on television from coast-to-coast, passersby would saunter by, do a double-take, and then casually drift back to look into the theater—which meant that they were looking right into the camera. After a few minutes drunks would pile out of the TV-equipped neighborhood saloons to wave at the nation and then it would be time to end the routine, but those first few minutes were always priceless. I would keep a microphone open and make off-the-cuff comments about the faces that loomed on the screen like strange fish floating before a submerged camera. Audiences loved this spot. It was as if we were all in on a gigantic practical joke. The bit became so popular that one night Sid Caesar did a take-off of it on his own marvelous show, playing the part of one of the passersby.

Another of my favorite routines was to open the back door, point a camera outside, walk quickly out into the night dressed in some peculiar costume, and engage strangers in extemporaneous conversation. The wildest thing that ever happened on the show, I suppose, occurred the night I donned a realistic New York policeman's uniform, charged into the street, and began stopping automobiles. I had no idea what I was going to say to the drivers but figured that just the sheer, insane idea of stopping actual cars on live TV and saying *anything* would be unusual enough.

Because I'd lived in the West and been stopped by the State Guard on the Arizona-California border on several occasions, I was not surprised to hear myself saying to the first motorist who slowed down, "Sorry, sir, but this is the Arizona border patrol, and we're making a spot-check for contraband."

"What band?" the man asked. Since the bright lights from the theater prevented his seeing the TV cameras or from even recognizing that the building to his left was a theater, he had no reason to doubt that I was a real policeman.

"I just want to know," I said, "if you're smuggling any fruits or nuts."

"No. Absolutely not!" From inside the theater came a great roar of laughter.

"Drive on," I said, "and remember, the life you save...may not be worth it."

When I raised my hand to stop the next car, its driver suddenly stepped on the gas and sped by, almost knocking me down, which the audience found vastly amusing.

"Border patrol," I shouted to the driver of the third car as he skidded to a stop. "Are you smuggling anything?"

"No, *sir*," the occupant, a middle-aged black man said, blinking at the lights.

"Well, then," I said, signaling to an associate who brought me a huge, three-foot Hebrew National salami, "take this to the river."

"To the what?" he said, accepting the salami.

"Never mind. Just get going. And don't stop till you hear from me!" He sped off as instructed.

The next car was a taxi. I grabbed another salami and flagged the driver down. "Where to, chief?" he asked amiably.

"Just take this to Grand Central, and hurry!" I said, opening his back door and flinging the giant salami in. He roared off at once into the night while the audience laughed so loudly it sounded like a crowd at a football game. No, we never heard from the driver again. I have often wondered why he sped away down the street following such an insane order.

Another popular—and ultimately much-copied—routine that evolved on the *Tonight* show was called *Crazy Shots,* which had the odd distinction that it was originally created right on the air in full view of our audience. I was playing a moody piano solo one night when it occurred to me—as I glanced at a stage-side TV set—that Dwight Hemion was taking the same TV pictures that he took on almost every other similar occasion.

Suddenly I stopped playing and said, "Dwight, I've just noticed that although you take beautiful pictures, there really isn't much variety you can get photographing a piano solo. Since night after night my fingers on the keyboard look the same, eventually a certain monotony could creep in. I'll tell you what. I'll start the number again, and this time I don't care what you photograph, just don't take the standard pictures, okay?"

He got the idea immediately and a loud "Sure" was heard over the intercom. When I started the number again, Dwight took pictures so incongruous that they were automatically funny. One was a very tight close-up of my left eye, another a shot of my right ear. Another camera concentrated for several seconds on my feet touching the piano's pedals. Next a stage-left camera moved up close behind me and wandered aimlessly around the plaid pattern of the sports jacket I was wearing.

That started it. Thereafter almost every night that I played a solo Dwight or our crew members would add a few new tricks. On the second night somebody draped a Dali-esque limp hot water bottle over the side of the grand piano while I was playing something soulful. On the following show our stagehands moved a backstage drinking-water bottle out next to the piano. Then we started showing close-ups of a pair of novelty-shop chattering false teeth. The props got crazier and crazier. After a few weeks we were hardly showing me at all but concentrating on the quick, cartoon-like visuals.

One night Assistant Producer Nick Vanoff—later to become an enormously wealthy Hollywood studio mogul and successful Broadway producer—approached the water bottle, mopped his brow to indicate that he was perspiring, removed his jacket, straw hat, tie, and shirt, then suddenly ripped off a pair of breakaway pants, leaving him standing in his underwear enjoying a cool drink; eventually we had goldfish swimming in the water bottle.

Crazy Shots quickly became established as a staple of our comedy sketches on the show, so much so in fact that when NBC later gave me the Sunday night prime-time sketch comedy series, we incorporated the routine into that production as well. A few years later, in the mid-1960s, *Crazy Shots* came to be considered public domain by some less imaginative comedy writers, a process which culminated in its total appropriation by the *Laugh-In* show, starting with its first telecast in 1967. Dan Rowan and Dick Martin, the stars of the show, and its producer George Schlatter were personal friends, and they were always kind enough to acknowledge publicly that they had borrowed the routine from our repertoire.

Another routine I'd originated even before *Tonight* was *The Late Show Pitchman,* referred to earlier. In the Fifties, many local stations ran old films late at night. On these shows, announcer-hucksters, called pitchmen, used to hawk slicer-dicers, Broil-Quick tabletop ovens, blenders, hair tonics, or knife-sharpening sets. Our *Late Show Pitchman,* complete with coo-coo clips from actual old movies, was obviously a satire on such commercials. The routine, in toto, right down to the hairdo and mustache, would be "borrowed" several years later by another late-night host.

Because of *Tonight's* popularity, we began to receive invitations from other cities and over the next three years did particularly wild shows from Cleveland, Fort Worth, Los Angeles, Niagara Falls, and funniest of all, Miami, where we originated the program for a full week each year.

The first night down there the weather was so cold I quite sensibly wore an overcoat, muffler, and gloves since our "theater" was simply the windswept poolside area in one of the glamorous local hotels.

While this got big laughs from the people in our audience, it didn't exactly please the city officials. "For God's sake," one of them said, "tell Mr. Allen that we don't want to convey the message that it's cold in Miami in the wintertime. Please ask him tonight, no matter what the weather is, to wear sports clothes."

The next night the weather was even chillier, so I walked on and said, "Apparently last evening, ladies and gentlemen, the fact that I was wearing an overcoat, scarf, and gloves gave you an exaggerated impression of how chilly it is down here. So tonight I've agreed to wear sports clothes."

After a brief pause I said, "I'm wearing two sports *t-shirts,* a sports *sweater,* a heavy sports *shirt,* and a thick sports *jacket*—but by golly they're all sports clothes."

No matter what we did on those Miami shows, the luck of the comedy gods seemed to be with us.

On one occasion when I was rehearsing a show opening, I came up out of the sea wearing a diving mask and a pair of trunks. My monologue included a reference to the local "beauties of nature," at which point one of our people thought it would be cute to have a statuesque young woman in a two-piece bathing suit stroll casually behind me. The young lady's instructions were: "Just walk behind Mr. Allen."

Unfortunately, because of her interpretation of this simple direction, she walked up behind me and stood there, peering goofily over my shoulder into the camera.

I stopped the rehearsal and said gently, "Sweetheart, when the fellow told you to walk behind me, he didn't mean for you to just stand here. He meant for you to keep walking, okay? Just come into the picture from that side, walk over to this other side and keep going."

The young lady, who was wearing a tight leopard-patterned suit, smiled apologetically.

A few minutes later we were on the air live, and once again I came up out of the waves and approached the camera. At the appropriate moment the young woman walked behind me, following instructions perfectly. About five minutes later, when the monologue was concluded, I happened to glance to my left and saw that she was *still* following instructions. By that time she had walked about 300 yards down the beach. If one of our people had not run down to get her she might have walked all the way to Cuba.

Speaking of Cuba, one of the craziest stunts we pulled during our Florida shows was a mock military invasion of the Miami Beach area. Somehow, because of the popularity of the show, we were able to talk a local military unit equipped with a landing craft into providing about forty soldiers, fully armed, though with blank ammunition.

Because the day was particularly busy, I never did have a chance to rehearse the opening, which involved me dressed as a World War II soldier coming in on the beach as one of the assault team and running up to the camera where I was scheduled to do the monologue. At about five minutes to airtime somebody said, "We're almost on. You'd better hustle out there and climb aboard." Unfortunately by that time the tide had risen, and I almost drowned as I tried to keep afloat in the heavy surf which from time-to-time was deeper than my six-foot-three frame. I swim like a rock anyway, and the full uniform, helmet and rifle didn't help make me any more floatable. Every few seconds the water would wash up over my head. It was a scary thing. Three or four soldiers, perceiving my inability to get aboard unaided, grabbed me and hauled me on deck like a half-dead sea creature. A moment later somebody gave a flashlight signal from the shore, and we roared in precisely at 11:30 p.m. as the show started. Within a few seconds the landing craft nose was laid down on the beach and our thundering herd—firing flares and rifles wildly into the air and shouting like crazed invaders—splashed ashore.

Everything went well for about thirty seconds, at which point I stepped on a board half-hidden in the sand. It had a sharp nail in it which easily penetrated my military boot but thank God made only a small, though painful, puncture in my skin.

Since this was in the days shortly before Fidel Castro invaded Havana and defeated the reactionary forces of Fulgencio Batista, we later heard that some hotel residents in the Miami Beach area, hearing the gunfire and the wild whooping, honestly believed that a Cuban-Communist invasion of the American mainland was underway.

Far from being unusual, the mock invasion was typical of the ways in which we used to open the *Tonight* show. The trade term for the little bits of entertainment that come before the formal start of the show's opening credits is *cold opening*. The device itself goes back to the radio days of the 1940s, although it was then rarely used in a comic context. In one of those *Tonight* openings I was found frying hundreds of eggs in a thirteen-foot diameter frying pan over a stove set up on the 44th Street sidewalk outside our Hudson Theater studio.

In another instance I was a typical New York street-cart hot dog vendor selling actual frankfurters to casual passersby. One evening we filled the theater with about four hundred young men who looked remarkably like me, having announced for the previous two weeks that only Steve Allen look-alikes would be admitted to the show on that date. I then sat out in the audience and even our director had a devil of a time picking me out of the crowd.

One opening, in Fort Worth, Texas, almost injured, and might even have killed me. Because we were working in some sort of cattleman's showplace arena it occurred to our production crew that it would be visually interesting if I made my entrance on horseback. I agreed but said to one of our local hosts, "I am totally inept at horseback riding and therefore would appreciate it if you could give me the tamest, most relaxed and experienced horse in all of Texas."

The fellow laughed and reassured me. "That's exactly what we'll give you," he said.

Later that day at a quick rehearsal of the entrance, I mounted the horse, a beautiful palomino—aren't they all?— and sure enough, he seemed docile enough as I nudged him through the back door of the auditorium and onto its broad stage.

I practiced my monologue in the saddle, then turned and cantered over to one side of the stage where I dismounted. It all sounds simple enough. Unfortunately, at showtime two factors were added—both of which came as a nervous shock to the poor horse. The first was a blaring 20-piece orchestra. The second was about 5,000 screaming, hooting, hollering, whooping, stomping, frothing-at-the-mouth fans. When I urged the horse, by a gentle nudge in the ribs, to move forward into the theater he did so—but stopped almost immediately, his ears suddenly turned down and backwards. Somewhere I'd acquired the information that this was a sign that a horse was either angry or about to panic. With no further cues from me the animal suddenly dashed forward and in about three seconds I realized that he was carrying me directly toward the audience.

I saw a few terrified faces in the front row; one or two people actually got up out of their seats. As I jerked on the reins the horse did one of those classic Lone Ranger-showing-off stunts, lifting his front hoofs high into the air and teetering unsteadily on his hind legs. This was alarming enough but, even more ominous, the horse began to stagger backwards, moving sideways across the stage to the left.

Since he was in effect "standing up" I was naturally unable to remain in the saddle. Thoroughly alarmed I slid off the animal's back, luckily landed on my feet, took the cowboy hat off my head and gave the horse a thwack with it on the rump, at which he righted himself and sped off out the back door into the night.

The audience gave me the greatest ovation I've ever enjoyed, but for the peculiar reason that they thought I was a gifted horseman who had deliberately put my steed through such paces. At a dinner party later that evening, the three gentlemen who knew the realities of the situation told me that their hearts had been in their mouths.

"I just about stopped breathing when I saw the horse do that," one of them said to me. "Men have been killed by having horses fall over backwards on top of them." I needed no convincing on the point since I was already aware that songwriter Cole Porter had had the latter part of his life ruined by precisely such an accident while out riding on Long Island.

While I'm often given sole credit for devising such bits, many of them were actually dreamed up by imaginative members of our production staff. But the *Letters-to-the-Editor* routine I performed often on *Tonight*—and still do today—I did originate, actually on the radio in 1949. The letters were not ad-libbed; the overheated, angry complaints I read are real. The only thing I change is the name of the sender to make it incongruous with the message. "When people write furious letters to newspapers and magazines," I explain, "they hope that publication will induce the same sense of outrage in the reader." I thereupon slap on an old-fashioned newspaperman's fedora with the word *PRESS* on the band and read a few of the letters aloud, in a violently angry tone. If I were doing one at present, it might go: "It's an absolute disgrace the way young women are dressing these days, baring their bodies to excite men to lust!—Signed, Madonna."

Some of the bits we did on *Tonight* started simply by accident. Making put-on phone calls had actually begun while I was doing the daily CBS-TV show in 1951. On the program I'd read funny items in the newspaper, the sort of thing Jay Leno does now. One day I saw an ad that read something like: "Leiberman Brothers' third floor is now open to the public." So I said, "I wonder what's been going on on the third floor that we couldn't get in on until today?"

I called for a phone, reached the company, and asked the man who answered my simple question. The first time he hung up on me. I called back four times, and it all got screams from the audience. We realized that we'd stumbled on a funny gimmick. I've been making funny phone calls ever since, two record albums of which have been released.

Since *Tonight* emphasized comedy more than serious conversation, most recollections about it are funny. But there were straight, strange moments, too. One evening three or four minutes before showtime, a young fellow walked onstage and approached me. He was well-dressed, dark-haired, and looked about twenty-eight years old.

"Mr. Allen?" he said.

"Yes?"

"I'd like to be a guest on your program tonight, sir."

"Well," I said, "we generally book our guests a week or two in advance so I'm afraid we can't help you out tonight. What was it you had in mind to do?"

"Oh," he said, quite casually, "I'd like to kill myself."

Perceiving that he was in deadly earnest, I led him toward the side of the stage where Bill Harbach and another member of our production staff were in conversation.

"I see," I said. "Well, I wish I had more time to talk to you, but I'm just about to go on the air. However, if you'll explain your situation to our producer, Mr. Harbach, perhaps we can think of something that might be helpful."

"All right, sir," he said, again with a perfectly natural tone. "Thanks very much."

By the time the show was over the man was gone. I never found out what happened to him.

I also recall the time that one of our staff people had booked an escape artist stuntman who was prepared to defy death by hanging himself, upside down by rope, from the roof of the eight-story building across the street behind the Hudson Theater. Because in those days there were no wireless microphones, our technicians had to string assorted cables and wires up the front of the building. And, because our show was on in the middle of the night we had to install several bright floodlights on the sidewalk.

At the appointed moment I explained to our studio audience what was scheduled to happen, strode across the stage and out the large scene-dock doors, and tried to communicate with the fellow on top of the building by shouting to him. Unfortunately just about that time an old woman on the third floor, annoyed and partially blinded by the brilliant lights below, opened her window and began to shout obscenities at all of us. She finally got angry enough to use either a big shears or a kitchen knife—I don't recall which—to cut the cord that led to the stuntman's microphone. Naturally after that he could no longer be heard by any of us. This may have made him nervous because he missed a cue and instead of lowering himself to the ground by a pulley device became enmeshed in a tangle of wires and ropes and suddenly was hanging head-down at a cockeyed angle, unable to move further. This clearly does not add up to a funny story, but the combination of the angry, toothless old woman on the third floor, the general disorganization of the moment, and the klutziness of the stuntman made our studio audience hysterical.

On another unforgettable night we did the entire 90-minute show from the *New York Herald-Tribune* building, the purpose being to show what sort of work went into the creation and distribution of one single issue of a great daily newspaper. With live camera crews on several floors, I chatted with reporters, editors, writers, headline specialists, interviewed famous columnists, and just generally nosed around the paper's offices and hallways. But the newspaper show was much more than a documentary. We had our share

of laughs, as well as vocal performances by Steve and Eydie,
Pat Kirby, and Andy Williams.

The comedy high spot of the evening, completely
unplanned, came at the conclusion of the show when, back
on street-level, I walked alongside of the open truck garage,
past several paper-laden trucks roaring out into the night to
distribute the next day's edition to all parts of the city. I
suddenly saw a burly fellow approaching. He was wearing a
cap and had an enormous stack of newspapers balanced on
his shoulder. Neither of us had any idea who the other was,
the man was simply going about his appointed rounds. As I
passed him it suddenly occurred to me to ask, "What are
these?" pointing to the bundle he labored under.

"Retoins," he said, in a gruff New York voice.

I could hear immediate laughter from some of our
production people standing nearby. A moment later we were
off the air for the night.

In a relative world, humor is the most relative of things, so
it would be difficult to say which of the thousands of
interviews I have conducted was the most amusing. I can
report, however, that one particular interview got the longest
single laugh I have ever heard on radio or TV, and again I
was only the straightman.

Wandering up the theater aisle in New York one night, I
noticed three elderly women sitting together.

"Hello," I said. "Are you ladies in a group or alone?"

"Yes," said one of the ladies.

"Yes, what?" I asked.

"We are reindeer."

When something that looks like a middle-aged woman
identifies itself as a reindeer, you can be reasonably certain
that the ensuing conversation is going to be interesting. At
such moments I try to be extremely logical, for nothing will
so clearly illumine eccentricity as displaying it against a
background of common sense.

"You don't look like a reindeer to me," I said, "although
stranger things have happened. My father was an Elk."

"That's right."

"I don't see how you could have known my father," I said, "but we're already digressing, although I'm not sure from what. Let me get to the point. What makes you think you are a reindeer?"

"We just are, that's all."

"All right," I said. "I didn't come down here to argue with you. But let me ask the lady on your right a question. What do you *do* in your capacity as reindeer—pull sleds for Santa Claus or something of the sort?"

"No," said the second woman. "We does all good things."

"You does? I mean...you *do?*"

A light began to dawn. "Tell me what one of the good things is," I asked.

"We pay sick benefits."

"Ah, I think I understand. You are not really reindeer at all. You are women, just as I thought, but you belong to some sort of organization like the Order of Moose or Woodmen-of-the-World."

"That's right," the second woman beamed, not at all impatient at my denseness. "We belong to the Reindeer."

"Well, that's fine. Now tell me, what does the organization stand for?"

The three faces were blank.

"I mean," I said, "what do you do *besides* pay sick benefits?"

"Nothing, I guess."

"Have *you* ever received any sick benefits?"

"No."

"Have *any* of you ever received any sick benefits?"

At this there was a great flurry of whispered questions and craning of necks. It developed that scattered throughout the studio there were about twenty-seven other Reindeer, all of whom had come up on a chartered bus from a nearby city for a day in Manhattan. None of them, it appeared after a hasty check, had ever received any sick benefits.

"I don't wish to appear critical," I said, "but this seems to me to be a very unusual organization." Addressing the third woman I asked, "Exactly why did you become a member?"

The woman pointed a thumb at her companion. "Because she asked me to."

"And why did *you* become a member?"

The buck was passed again.

Incredibly, every woman in the room had become a Reindeer because some other woman had asked her to. None of them were able to offer any information about the aims or purposes of the club. I returned to the matter of sick benefits.

"Perhaps," I suggested, "you're not really a social club at all. Perhaps you're more of an insurance company. But then again, you all say that you have never *received* any of these benefits. That leads me to believe that either you are the healthiest group of women in the United States or your treasury must be the most bulging in financial history, or both."

They all laughed good-naturedly.

"But still, I can't conceive that not one penny has ever been paid out. And I don't see how you could all be in such perfect physical condition. There must be at least one member of your group who has been laid up with something or other. I'd like to speak with the treasurer of your club. Where is she sitting?"

"She's not here with us tonight," the lady on the aisle said.

"Oh? Where is she?"

"She's home sick."

The audience would not let me continue for almost two minutes.

On the radio I never had a problem of distractions during audience interviews but in TV there is the Waver. Wavers seem to have been spawned by television. I say seem, for the waver has actually been with us for many years. I'm sure you remember seeing him in the old movie newsreels. Sometimes his waving was more or less in keeping with the mood of the event. But often the waver was pursuing his annoying custom at scenes of great disaster. A train wreck. A long shot of railroad cars strewn in dizzy formation along a roadbed. Medium shot of one of the cars as rescue workers bend to their grim task. In the foreground, in shocking contrast to the air of tragedy that prevails, we see a couple of smiling goofs waving at the camera.

The wavers of television are, of course, usually just having a good time in more jovial surroundings, but there have been occasions when the mood of romantic musical numbers has been completely destroyed by the sight of a frantic hand waggling back and forth in an audience. Our *Tonight* show was honored one evening when Sid Caesar and his TV crew presented a satire of our program which involved Carl Reiner as "Alan Stevens" and Sid as an audience contestant. Sid performed the sketch seated in the middle of his own audience and I found it hilariously funny—for the first few minutes. After that the visitors sitting in front of Sid suddenly realized they were on camera and began waving and making faces. They proved such a distraction that neither the studio audience nor the people at home could concentrate on the professionals' performance.

Wavers break down into several categories. First there's the Rib-Poker. As soon as he sees himself on the studio TV monitors he jabs an elbow into the rib of his companion, points, and says, "Look, we're on." Then there's the Narcissist, who is so infatuated with the sight of his own face on the screen that he is completely oblivious to everything else. He does not hear the interviewer's questions, he is no longer interested in the program, and he shows a blithe disregard for those seated nearby. He just sits and smiles and waves— to himself on the TV monitor, set off-camera range. He can be deadly because often his waving is done while you are trying to interview the person sitting behind him.

Another type we will always have with us is the Sneak. He seems to realize that he really shouldn't be waving so he does it with a surreptitious air, looking in one direction and waving a seemingly disembodied hand in the other.

Lastly there is the Boy Scout, so called because he works

both arms wildly as if sending flag signals to a distant mountain top. He has been known to knock off the hats and muss the hair of women in front of him.

Audiences in general have always fascinated me. The most interesting thing about them is that they have a definite single character. Though it may be comprised of a thousand individuals, an audience has only one personality. I suppose this makes it easy for demagogues and dictators to control large masses; they are really not controlling a million entities, just one.

Part of my business is to work with individuals to create humor out of the air. But for an appreciation of this humor and a reaction to it I'm at the mercy of that sometimes "big, bad giant," the audience in toto.

Of course producers, critics, and sponsors are weary of hearing comedians complain about bad audiences. "Every time Milton Berle had a bad show," a writer I know once told me, "he blamed it on his audience."

If this is true, in my opinion Milton was right more often than wrong. An audience can be either *good* or *bad* before the curtain ever goes up and before the performer can have had any effect on it. If an audience is really unprepared to receive a particular bit of entertainment, all the writing and performing genius in the world cannot salvage the day.

I first became aware of this phenomenon while working at CBS on the West Coast, where it was my custom to peek around the curtain each evening before I walked onstage to begin the program. I gradually discovered that there were three different kinds of audiences. Sitting out there waiting for me might be the average expectant but calm assemblage, and when I turned in a poor performance in front of such a group I had no one to blame but myself. Secondly there was the *good* audience; a glance from the wings would reveal a mob rippling with carnival atmosphere, laughing, craning necks, whispering, talking, making a great deal of noise and ready to have a good time, no matter what. And no matter

what, they did. I could do no wrong for such an audience.
The man who could function before such crowds day in and
day out could rule the world.

Then there would be the occasional *bad* audience. Peeking
through the curtain at them one would think they had come
to attend a funeral. There would be no laughter, no talk—
just polite, resigned attention. Every man in the theater
looked as if he had just had an argument with his wife. They
sat silently and listlessly, even before the curtain had gone up
and before the performer could have been held responsible
in any way for their collective mood.

For a period of several years I conducted a haphazard
research into what mysterious factors so clearly determine
the character of an audience the moment it has come in off
the street (or even before). For a time I thought it was
something as simple as rainy weather, but I soon discovered
that one rainy night reaction would be wonderful, the next
disastrous. Next I considered the matter of the national or
local emotional climate as dictated by important news events
of the day, but I was eventually obliged to discard that
possibility too.

A friend said, "I'll bet it's nothing more than the day of the
week. Good shows on Saturday when people are out to have
a high time and bad shows on Monday when they're feeling
let down after the weekend." Again the hypothesis didn't
hold up.

I finally pinned down a secondary reason for the moodi-
ness of audiences: air conditioning and room temperature.
Often an out-of-whack air-conditioning system makes an
audience hot, restless, and preoccupied with its own physical
discomfort. This is an obstacle the entertainer has to sur-
mount. But just when I thought I discovered ingredient X, I
found out that there were too many exceptions: too many
good shows on hot, sticky nights and too many bad shows on
comfortable evenings.

Currently I assume that changes in atmospheric pressure,
sunspots, cosmic radiation, or something of the sort may be

responsible. Statistics show that suicides do not occur in equal numbers every day but tend to cluster in certain peak periods. We all are familiar with days when things just get off to a bad start and stay that way; frequently we learn that we are not alone in feeling out of sorts. Some investigators feel that sudden changes in atmospheric pressure may have peculiar and as yet little understood effects on our emotional or glandular equipment. I leave it to science to confirm or disprove my theories but in passing will submit one bit of evidence.

Many actors are aware that on some nights things are bad all over town. Performers in one play will complain or enthuse about an audience only to discover that players in another company share their sentiments. In the 1950s my wife, Jayne Meadows, would report that the studio audience at her *I've Got A Secret* panel show were especially receptive on the same evening that I had had a good audience. David Wayne and Tom Ewell, two of Broadway's most popular leading men, decided to put this theory to a test years ago when they were appearing in *Teahouse of the August Moon* and *Seven Year Itch* respectively. Each evening after final curtain they would call each other and compare notes on audience response. They discovered that their audiences were identical in mood far more often than mere chance would have allowed. Obviously something external was responsible.

I always find the study of audience psychology fascinating. Man is the most wondrous of animals; considered as a social creature he seems even more peculiar. For example, people who'd never dream of jumping up from their chairs and whistling shrilly at a cocktail party if someone happened to mention the name of their hometown will often give vent to semimaniacal outbursts of enthusiasm at any passing geographical reference that is part of a broadcast.

"What is your hometown?" I ask a guest. "Chicago," he says—and the walls fall down. One night I became so intrigued at this behavior on the part of an audience that I called a halt to the regularly scheduled entertainment, reached into my pocket, withdrew a bulky wallet and, pretending it was a pocket atlas, "read" the names of various cities, states, and nations aloud. At words like *Brooklyn, Kansas City, Texas, Canada, Ireland,* and *Gary, Indiana,* the audience exploded with meaningless applause.

To have purpose, applause must be directed towards an object that can be aware of its existence, such as a speaker, pianist, tap dancer, or at the very least a performing seal. But a city is something geographical and inanimate, if not abstract. One does not applaud a statue; one applauds the sculptor. At any rate, the audience got the point after a few minutes of this exercise and finally lost interest, but the routine must have appealed to one of my Hollywood comedy-writer friends because shortly thereafter it was incorporated into the screenplay of a Dean Martin and Jerry Lewis picture.

Some sort of an ultimate was achieved one time when I was interviewing a Mrs. Ryan, who had come to the studio accompanied by four children. "So these are your youngsters?" I observed.

"Yes," she said. "And I have eight more at home."

"You mean you have twelve children?"

"That's right."

I paused momentarily, waiting for the expected demonstration from the studio audience. None was forthcoming. "Where do you live, Mrs. Ryan?" I asked.

"Brooklyn." At the word the mob erupted in a mighty burst of applause. Which means, I suppose, that as far as studio audiences are concerned it isn't what you do, it's where you do it.

For all their peculiarities, however, radio and television audiences are much better behaved than those that frequent nightclubs or theaters. In fact, I have an urgent message for the theatergoers of America: *Sssssshhhhhh!* Stereophonic sound has its attractions, but my enjoyment of a play is not enhanced when the sounds coming from the stage are drowned out by those coming from the right, left, and rear.

Undoubtedly the present sorry state of American audience behavior can be related to larger ills affecting our
society, but it's not my purpose here to make subtle analyses;
I just want everybody to please shut up so I can hear the
people on the stage. To say *anything* during a performance
(short of "I believe I smell smoke," or "Usher, the man next
to me seems to have dropped dead") is criminal enough, but
the content of the remarks that from time-to-time float out
of the darkness renders them doubly objectionable. Boors
boastfully predict the outcome of the plot, comment on an
actor's appearance ("He looks older than I thought he was"),
the scenery ("That wallpaper reminds me of the kitchen at
Margaret's"), or the private lives of the performers involved.
In the second act of Alec Coppel's Broadway comedy *The
Gazebo,* Walter Slezak nightly planted a firm, husbandly kiss
on the lips of my wife Jayne. One evening when he did so a
woman in the audience cried out angrily, "I wonder what
Steve Allen thinks of *that!*"

Mrs. Allen, in fact, reported frequent visits of The Talker
(who is usually, but not always, female). One night at a tense
moment in the third act when Jayne slowly lifted a glass to
her lips, a woman seated in the middle of the house said with
great admiration, "My, hasn't she lovely hands!" Grateful as
actresses are for compliments, Jayne would have been glad to
forego this particular one.

From time-to-time one hears of incidents involving A
Talker versus A Sensitive Soul. Actor James Mason, attend-
ing a showing of the motion picture *The Red Badge of
Courage,* once participated in such a drama. As he told it:

> This guy a few rows ahead of me was talking so loud I
> couldn't hear the dialogue. This went on for about fifteen
> minutes. Finally I couldn't stand it any more. I got out of
> my seat and walked down to where the man was sitting and
> said, 'Damn it, shut up, will you? I can't hear the movie!'
> Then I slapped him.

As it happened, Mason's lid-blowing was especially embarrassing because he suddenly recognized his foe as William

Saroyan. But he stood firmly on principle: "I said, 'Oh, hello, Bill. Shut up, will you?' Then I went back to my seat."

Although I doubt if I could be so goaded into slapping a man's face, I do recall a night when I leaped to my feet in exploded frustration, prepared to lick any man in the house. It happened during a showing of the film classic *If I Had a Million,* which includes one of the most touching scenes in motion picture annals. The star of this particular vignette was May Robson and the action took place in an old people's home where once a day Miss Robson would read a letter from her son to a roomful of her sisters in despair. The tragic faces of the lonely, forgotten old women glowed as she read them her letters in the hope of bringing them a flicker of vicarious happiness. A stab of poignancy was introduced by a camera shot revealing that the "letter" from which she was drawing such happy pictures was in reality only a laundry advertisement.

All during the picture I had been disturbed and had tried to shush the raucous, vulgar chatter of a group of teenaged toughs several rows behind me. At this moment on the screen, a particularly aged woman, suffering from an ailment that gave her withered hands a noticeable tremor, rose from her bed and shuffled toward Miss Robson. As I was attempting to stifle the tears that this pathetic spectacle aroused, I suddenly heard one of the boors behind me say, quite loudly, "Shake it, baby!" The next thing I knew I was on my feet shouting, "Shut your God-damned mouth!"

Immediately I was surprised by three reactions. First, there was applause from the audience; secondly, the teenagers were frightened into immediate silence (who would not have been at the sight of an apparent madman screaming at the top of his lungs?); and thirdly, my ferocious courage suddenly vanished, leaving me unnerved, breathing heavily, and ashamed at having made a spectacle of myself. To the charge that in speaking aloud I had committed the very crime against which I am inveighing I plead not guilty because of temporary insanity.

CHAPTER TEN

The *Tonight* Show: Wider in Scope, With Political Debates

lthough the current *Tonight Show* format is all show-biz, originally it had considerably more scope. On certain nights the now-standard talk formula would be followed, but on others the program might consist largely of jazz music, a political debate, a scripted drama, an opening night party—almost anything. Once I requested and was granted an extra thirty minutes on the air for a special program: a two-hour documentary on the subject of Organized Crime and its influence in New York.

One of the first instances where I felt compelled to take some sort of action about Mafia and other criminal control of urban America occurred early in the 1950s. I remember opening an issue of *Life* magazine and being brought up short by a dramatic photograph. The picture was that of a man lying in a hospital bed swathed in bandages head-to-toe. He had been savagely beaten, left on the vergè of death by a couple of Organized Crime "enforcers." Why? Simply because he'd spoken out at a Lutheran church meeting against the installation of pinball games in a candy store near a neighborhood school.

The photograph angered me so much that I took a public stand that very day. I propped the *Life* picture up and told our camera director to hold a close-up on it while I spoke my unscripted feelings on the matter. I explained that professional gamblers with ·mob connections were not merely genial Damon Runyon types but animals willing to resort to arson, terror, atrocity, and murder. We received a considerable amount of congratulatory mail afterwards.

So now, in 1954, I was pleased that the New York station was allowing me to do an entire show about this type of hoodlum and giving me an extra half-hour of TV time to boot.

Certain journalists have a tendency to assume that anything noteworthy an entertainer does is motivated by a desire for publicity. Unfortunately some reactions to this important documentary were a glaring example of this jaundiced attitude. For my part I was doing this show for no other reason than that, as a private citizen, I'd become so fed up with the brazen activities of the top-level mobsters in New York City that I had to express my indignation in the most public manner available to me—a television documentary.

Working for many weeks with William Keating and John O'Mara of the New York City Anti-Crime Committee, I wrote a script, dug up pictures of the top gangsters, found film clips on them, lined up a panel of experts that included people like labor columnist Victor Reisel and narcotics agent George White, and prepared to put on the broadcast.

As the date of the program approached, strange obstacles were thrown in my path. One of the members of the panel telephoned after reading the script to say that he wouldn't be able to participate in the show.

"Why not?" I asked. "You've written a book yourself, covering a lot of this same territory."

"I know," he said, "but that was when I was working for the state. Now I'm an attorney in private practice. You're talking about an awful lot of people, and I have to face the fact that as an attorney I can't afford to antagonize so many men in positions of power."

I told him that I understood his predicament and hung

up. Later that day I received a call from one of the biggest men in the clothing industry. His telephone manner was charming.

"Steve," he said, "I've just seen a copy of this script you want to broadcast next week and although we've never met I just wanted to offer you a little friendly advice."

I didn't ask him how he'd gotten a copy of the script, but it seemed that the most likely source was the attorney who had just begged off.

"What's your advice?"

"Don't do it."

"I'm sorry," I said, "I'm committed. The show has been mentioned around town. I couldn't cancel it now even if I wanted to, and I don't want to."

"Well," the man continued, "don't misunderstand me. I have no personal axe to grind, but I've been around this town a long time and I think I know it better than a young fellow like yourself. I wonder if you realize that you can do yourself a great deal of harm doing a thing like this?"

"I realize it."

There was a pause. "Well, if you can't cancel the whole show perhaps you could make some changes in the script. I've been looking at it here and I think you go a little too far."

"What do you mean?"

"Well," he said genially, "there's one man you mention here and I want you to know that although it's true he was in with bad company in his younger years he's straight now. A thing like this would do him a great deal of harm."

"Who do you mean?"

"Benny Levine. Believe me, he's a fine man. He's got children and a position in the community. A program like this would be a terrible blow to him."

"The Anti-Crime Committee has a different opinion of him," I said. "I'll check back with them to make absolutely certain that they gave me the straight dope. If you're right and they're wrong I certainly wouldn't want to injure the man or attack him unfairly. But if he's still in with the boys then I'll have to go ahead with the program as planned."

"Look, Steve," my caller asked, "what do you want?"

"What?" I didn't understand his question.

"What is it you want out of this town? You want money? You want some special business contacts? You interested in a new car or something like that?"

I couldn't answer him. The conversation suddenly seemed unreal, like the dialogue in a bad motion picture. I was being offered a bribe.

"I don't want anything, except a better city," I said. "I'm working steady, thank you."

"I know, but it's a great help, to anybody, to have powerful friends. You could have them if you just follow my advice."

We went around again on the same track. The man said he would call me back later after I checked with Keating and O'Mara.

I called them. "Levine," Keating told me, "is now a wealthy and powerful garment manufacturer, but he was an important member of the Lepke-Gurrah gang and went to jail for extortion. He was an advance man for the mob back in the thirties, the guy who could make the proper labor contract when a strike was getting too rough. He's also mixed up in the Algam Corporation which owns the land and buildings at Yonkers Raceway. Don't believe the stories that he's now sweet as a rose."

When the clothing executive called back I said, "I'm sorry. I checked the facts on Levine and was told they are accurate."

"Listen," the man said, "what do I have to say to make it clear to you that you're making a big mistake? Believe me, you should make the decision yourself to take Levine's name out of your script. Otherwise you might have trouble even getting the show on the air."

Again we talked at great length, saying the same things to each other over and over.

Still later that day I got a call from a Mack Gray, who at the time worked for my friend Milton Berle. "Steve," he said, "I've just heard about this show you're planning to do and I wanted you to know that I think you're placing yourself in danger. This sort of thing just isn't smart."

"Maybe you're right," I said, "but it's too late to change my plans now. I think it's time somebody said these things out loud anyway. That's one reason the mob is so powerful in New York—people are afraid to speak up."

"But why you? You're an entertainer. Why don't you leave this stuff to the newspapers? Please understand, I'm not calling for myself, but I understand you've got one guy's name in there that shouldn't be."

"Who's that?"

"Mr. L." Apparently he was afraid to say the name on the phone. "I hear that if you just took his name out that there wouldn't be any other trouble."

I thanked him but refused. I didn't hold his call against him; his motives on my behalf were entirely friendly and I realized that he'd been pressured by Levine's friends. I later heard that he knew nothing personally about Levine and believed the stories that Benny was "a good guy." But now even darker clouds were gathering.

The next day I was called to the executive offices of WNBT, the NBC television station over which I was to broadcast the show. An eminent lawyer who said he'd been sent by ILGWU Union President David Dubinsky was there.

After the introductions he got right to the point: "Mr. Dubinsky has heard reports that you're planning to put on a show that has an anti-labor slant. We hold no brief for gangsters, but naturally we *are* interested that any references to labor be factually correct."

"I'm glad to hear that," I said. "There's not one word of anti-labor propaganda in my script. But there's plenty of criticism about the thugs who infest the labor movement."

The lawyer asked to be allowed to study a copy of the script and said he would get in touch with us in a day or two.

Although I felt reasonably sure that he was honest, I now began to worry. The close tie-ups between mobsters, politicians and union leaders in New York are notorious, and I was afraid that pressure was going to be exerted upon the station to prevent the show's broadcast. I had twice criticized the infamous teamster labor leader Jimmy Hoffa on the air, and it occurred to me that he or one of his unsavory associates might be able to intimidate the station or my sponsor with threats of slow truck deliveries or something of that sort. Indeed, Ham Shea, the station manager, told me he'd been receiving inquiries and "suggestions" about the forthcoming broadcast. Though he said not one critical word, I got the impression that he wished I'd never started this ball rolling. I heard, too, that our regular sponsors, the Ruppert Knickerbocker Beer people, had received calls. Since it was my impression that all the pressure to suppress the broadcast was coming from Levine and his friends I finally had to face the question: Should I insist on keeping his name in the script and risk having the station cancel the show, or should I agree to delete his name in order to be certain that the rest of the program would be broadcast? When the calls from Levine's business associate continued and his arguments became even blunter, I decided to sacrifice one trick in order to win the rest of the game. But I had a high card in my hand that I did not reveal to Levine's man.

"All right," I agreed. "Take off the pressure and I'll take Levine's name out of the script."

The night I put the show on the air, when I reached that part of the script that referred to Levine I looked away from the TelePrompTer and spoke from separate notes. "Ladies and gentlemen," I said, "for reasons that I will not go into I have deleted from tonight's script the name of a very powerful man in the garment industry. But even though I will not mention his name I think you ought to know about his evil influence. So I will tell you his story but will refer to him only as Mr. X."

It was my hope that by this device public interest in the

case would be greatly increased. It worked. The day after the broadcast Jack O'Brian of the *New York Journal-American* broke the story that Mr. X was Levine—but by that time all hell had broken loose. The Ruppert people called to report that even though they had not sponsored the program on the Tuesday night of the special broadcast hundreds of saloons in Brooklyn and along the water front had refused to accept deliveries of their beer. The tires on my car, parked right outside our theater, were slashed. A few nights later the mob sent thugs to the show who mingled with the audience. Shortly after the program started they released stink bombs in the balcony and then ran out. The smell immediately became apparent, of course, but oddly-enough the incident resulted in one of the funniest shows we had done in months. However, the theater had to be fumigated, and for weeks the terrible odor lingered in the upholstery, curtains, and walls.

When news of this attack got to the District Attorney's office I was called in and questioned about the pressures before the broadcast. Assistant District Attorney Alfred Scotti, Chief of the District Attorney's Rackets Bureau, talked to me at great length and assured me that I would be given adequate police protection until it was felt I no longer required it. For the next two weeks I was accompanied by a pair of detectives wherever I went. Victor Reisel wrote an article about the incident and Bill Keating, in his excellent book, *The Man Who Rocked the Boat,* also mentioned it.

All of the foregoing is by way of leading up to the fact that after all the smoke had cleared away a number of news-papermen dismissed the entire incident as "just another publicity stunt."

A day or two later, WNBT—perhaps thinking publicity, and thus increased public attention, might be helpful in ensuring my personal safety—called to ask if I would be willing to appear at a press conference. I agreed.

When I showed up at the meeting room, a number of cordial journalists immediately began to put intelligent questions to me. After a moment I noticed that one reporter was simply sitting silently in his chair, an undisguised sneer on his face. After listening to several questions and answers, he finally stood up as if to leave and said contemptuously, "Frankly, I don't know why we were called here." I knew I didn't deserve his contempt, but as of that moment he deserved mine; looking directly at him I said, "I wasn't aware that attendance was compulsory."

It was, of course, incredible that this dunce would assume I worked for weeks on a story, tackling nothing less than the murderous Mafia itself, placed myself in serious physical danger and my career in jeopardy as well, purely for the purpose of getting publicity.

The career dangers, incidentally, were not merely hypothetical. To this day there are certain clubs and theaters around the country where I'm not bookable because the owners and proprietors have connections with organized crime. It's an easy way, in fact, to identify them, although government anti-mob specialists already know who they are.

There are two fascinating postscripts to the story. Four years after the incident—on June 5, 1958—the *New York Times,* under the headline "Seventeen Arrested Here in Narcotics Raid; Top Racketeers Among Those Held on High Bail," related a follow-up to the Levine element in the story:

> Racketeers and hoodlums were among seventeen persons arrested yesterday as members of a reputed multimillion-dollar-a-year narcotics ring. Also held on $35,000 bail was *Benjamin Levine,* 63, who owns a $150,000 home at Atlantic Beach, Long Island. Levine, a one-time confederate of the garment racketeers Louis "Lepke" Buchalter and Jacob "Gurrah" Shapiro, was said to have *planned the financing of the narcotics traffic.* (IA)

I sent a clipping of the *Times* story to Levine's clothier friend, among others.

And even later—just a few years ago as a matter of fact—Jayne and I were invited to a small Hollywood gathering at the home of a well-known film producer where the classic film *The Godfather* was to be shown. Certain other guests, I noticed, had Las Vegas and business connections that had long been of quite justified interest to federal law-enforcement agencies. The morning after the gathering, in a moment straight out of the horrifying scene in the movie where the head of a horse is found in a producer's blood-soaked bed, one of my secretaries was shocked to find the enormous severed leg and shoulder of a horse on my doorstep. Angered, I sent an equally unmistakable message to one of the party's guests; within 24 hours he found the forequarter of the animal on *his* front doorstep.

Parenthetically, when the comedy film *My Favorite Year,* which starred Joe Bologna as a character obviously based on TV comedian Sid Caesar, came out, friends told me they thought I would be particularly interested in seeing it. Part of the humor of the film was based on the real-life story of what happened when Caesar's producers booked the aging film actor Errol Flynn, with emphasis on the problem of keeping him sober long enough to make an actual appearance. Peter O'Toole played Flynn in the picture. But another element of the storyline puzzled me. It pitted New York Mafia gangsters against Bologna's character, and to my knowledge nothing of the sort had ever happened to Sid. The mystery was resolved when, a few months later, I happened to attend a benefit dinner in Los Angeles and met one of the two authors of the screenplay. "I'm glad to see you tonight," he said. "It gives me a chance to tell you that a good part of the story of *My Favorite Year* was based on your trouble with the mob back in the early '50s. None of that happened to Sid, but we thought it would be too confusing to deal with two comedians so we just took the story about you and the Mafia and put the two separate elements together."

In any event, favorable public reaction to the *Tonight* show anti-crime telecast encouraged us to devote other programs to serious problems in American society. Early in 1955, for example, long before the drug culture was a topic for the Sunday supplements, our staff put together a production that included interviews with addicts, displays of equipment used by junkies, films on withdrawal, and an interview with the Commissioner from the New York City Health Department.

And long before the popular interest in political "blacklisting" highlighted by the memoirs of Lillian Hellman, the film *The Front*, starring Woody Allen, and the recent *Guilty By Suspicion* with Robert DeNiro, we did a program on AWARE, an organization which existed to "expose Communists and other leftist members of the acting profession."

Actress Faye Emerson and newspaper columnist John Crosby took part in a lively debate with Godfrey P. Schmidt, president of AWARE, and Vincent W. Hartnett, one of the authors of *Red Channels,* the directory that promoted the 1950s' blacklist. By putting the story on the air we had done some good.

In broadcasting such programs I was encouraged to know that NBC's Program Director Pat Weaver was in favor of incorporating a certain amount of instruction, or moral exhortation in network programs. He even sent around a memo to all of us connected with production which not only gave us the freedom to include thought-provoking material in our fare, but actually encouraged us to do so. It was marvelous. That memo ought to be reprinted and sent to everybody in the business about once a week.

The *Tonight* show's interview guest list was long and varied, but when we first considered having people from the world of sports, I foresaw a problem. Some athletes are fascinating, outgoing characters, but they are exceptions. Most sports figures are likable, reserved fellows who, though they may be ferocious and aggressive when it counts, are generally lamb-like in social contexts. This may make them endearing husbands, fathers, and fishing buddies, but unless they've just hit a crucially important home run in the World Series, scored the winning point in the Super Bowl, or something of the sort, they're not much in demand as talk-show guests. In ruminating about this, it occurred to me that it would be more amusing to interview sportsmen while they were in action on our stage. Consequently, I chatted with Willie Mays while the two of us tossed a baseball back and forth, tried to dribble a basketball around Bill Russell while interviewing him, and so on. We sometimes used to book whole teams—the Harlem Globetrotters, the New York Rangers—and put on a mock game with the pros against the ungainly "Allen All-Stars," the latter usually consisting of Gene Rayburn, Steve Lawrence or Andy Williams, Skitch Henderson, Jules Green, myself, my aunt, or whoever else could be coaxed into a purposely ill-fitting uniform.

I never understood why Johnny Carson took so many and such extended vacations from what is actually quite an easy job. During the years our gang was in the studio, the easiest part of the day was the ninety minutes we were on the air since, as I've said before, it was very much like attending a party. There were sometimes pressures, of course, but this was usually because of my outside activities, such as filming *The Benny Goodman Story.*

Appearing in the picture was an adventure, chiefly be-cause it gave me the pleasure of spending time with jazz musicians I had idolized as a schoolboy—Gene Krupa, Lionel Hampton, Teddy Wilson, Harry James, and Ziggy Elman, as well as my contemporary Stan Getz. But what made the experience truly unique was that I fulfilled the eight-week shooting schedule without missing a single broadcast of the *Tonight* show.

At the time I saw nothing unusual about this. But if God had wanted man to be able to do a 90-minute telecast at night and keep a busy motion picture filming schedule by day, he would've made him a sleepless creature. I was so young and naive it never occurred to me to ask NBC if I might have a few weeks off while making the film. I suppose they figured that if I was too stupid to make such a reasonable request, they would take advantage of my inexperience.

Anyway, I rose about 4:30 every morning in a suite which Jayne and I occupied at the old Ambassador Hotel on Wilshire Boulevard. At 5:30 a limousine driver would arrive to take me to Universal Studios in the Valley, where I would sit staring heavy-lidded at my sleepy countenance in the makeup mirrors while technicians and hairdressers made me somewhat more closely resemble Benny Goodman than I actually do. At the end of the day, generally around 6:00, I would be driven back to the Ambassador where I would have time for a quick dinner before being rushed to the NBC studios in Burbank where, at 8:30 p.m. I would start the nightly live telecast.

After about three weeks of this schedule I was in a somewhat vegetative state disguised to the public because I'm rather a low-key creature anyway. The last few weeks on the film, understandably enough, I had trouble remembering lines and took to pasting little scraps of dialogue on the upstage side of walls, pianos, between the shoulder blades of other actors, wherever.

Somehow I survived the ordeal, but I don't think I ever *have* made up for the loss of sleep.

Our band on the old *Tonight* show was marvelous, and it played a much broader role than does the current program's orchestra. Skitch Henderson—as noted—was the leader; the musicians were, in large part, NBC studio personnel. Doc Severinson, years later conductor for Johnny Carson, was one of the trumpet players. Another was Yank Lawson, a fine old Dixieland blower who in recent years has been one of the leaders of "The World's Greatest Jazz Band." The great Harry "Sweets" Edison was also in the trumpet section, as was Buck Clayton. Lou McGarrity, who'd worked earlier with Benny Goodman and other name bands, played trombone, and Bobby Rosengarten—later to serve as Dick Cavett's conductor—was our drummer.

The band members had considerably more fun in those days than they do presently, when their primary function is to play the opening and closing themes and to offer a few musical flourishes coming out of filmed or videotaped commercials. One night when I was filling in for Johnny, I said facetiously, "You folks at home think that you're missing two-minute numbers by the band during our commercial breaks. Actually you're not. The band just plays seven-second arrangements as we come out of commercials, so you're not missing much."

In reality the orchestra does play exciting material—mostly of the traditional big-band swing sort—during breaks, for the pleasure of the studio audience, but oddly enough, rarely with the attention of the program's hosts or guests. These worthies are usually too preoccupied to attend to the magnificent musicianship being displayed on the other side of the stage.

Today the *Tonight* show orchestra seldom gets to perform a full number except when accompanying a guest singer. In the old days they'd occasionally do numbers of their own. They would accompany me at the piano, play for our regular singers, or behind guest vocalists such as Peggy Lee, Tony Bennett, Ella Fitzgerald and Joe Williams.

One form of musical entertainment that originated on the old program involved an in-person appearance by one of the world's leading songwriters. The visiting writer—say Harold Arlen, Hoagy Carmichael, Richard Rodgers, Johnny Mercer—Skitch, and I would take turns at the piano and Steve and Eydie would sit on barstools beside us. With sheet music strewn about, we would reminisce, running through as many of the composer's hits as time permitted. And since on such nights we'd forget about doing a "talk" show, time permitted quite a few tunes.

Shortly after Steve and Eydie were hired as singers on the show, Bill Harbach and I thought we should set up another boy-girl team to give the program a little wider variety, so in 1954 we hired Andy Williams, who looked somewhat like a teenaged Noel Coward, along with pretty Pat Kirby, another fine singer.

The first thing I liked about Andy in those days—besides his voice of course—was his taste in music. Influenced by vocal arranger Kay Thompson, he liked the good, New Yorky, sophisticated special-material or show-tune sort of thing. I assumed that because his musical tastes were so elevated, he would never become a truly popular singer. He employed no vocal tricks nor performance gimmicks. He didn't move much while singing. While I highly approved of his performances on the show, I felt that his style would probably result in great critical respect but deny him wide popularity. A third reason I didn't anticipate the marvelous success that Andy would ultimately enjoy was that both on and off stage he was a quiet, low-key, unassuming sort of fellow.

Other singers might project the image of a swinger, a drunk, a man-of-the-world, a hillbilly, a rebel confidante of Mafia murderers and heroin-sellers, a child molester, or God-knows-what, but Andy's image was that of the gentlemanly boy next door. It says something good about the musical taste of the 1950s' American public that, despite his nice-guy image, Andy nevertheless became a singing star of the first magnitude.

Although there's a common assumption that singers become famous from TV, that's rarely the case. They really make it big through the medium of recordings. Andy's true success—and the success of Steve and Eydie too—came after they left the *Tonight* show and began to have a few hit records.

I think one reason for Andy's long success on television, with his variety show series and specials, is because he *is* quiet and introverted. Television is such an intimate medium

that it poses a problem to those entertainers who overpower
you with their talent or personality. While such extroverted
artists as Sammy Davis Jr., Alan King, Jerry Lewis and Joan
Rivers have worked successfully in television, the medium
has proven much more congenial to lower-key performers
like Arthur Godfrey, Dave Garroway, Johnny Carson, Perry
Como, David Letterman, and myself.

The TV audience possibly prefers to stare at the set with
lids half-lowered and brain working at low-idle, all other
things being equal.

Public figures, because their image changes very gradually in the absence of sudden dramatic developments, constantly hear the same questions. Perhaps the most common
put to me during the last thirty years is: "The *Tonight* show
seems always to have been a success—under you, Jack Paar,
and Johnny Carson. Why did you ever walk away from it?"

The answer is that of almost everyone who changes jobs—
I got a much better offer, though the employer was the same
(NBC). Because of the popularity of the late-night program,
the network thought I might be of help with their long-
unsolved problem of how to do better in the ratings race
against the CBS institution—*The Ed Sullivan Show*—that
aired at 8:00 p.m. Sunday nights. Inasmuch as the new
proposal was for a major league, early-evening series, which
meant a vastly larger audience and a great deal more money,
it would've been idiotic to say, "No, I'm having so much fun
with the late show, I think I'll just stick to that and forget
about the big time."

Both the network and I at first thought that I could add
the new show without greatly increasing my workload since I
was already working five nights a week, live, for a full ninety
minutes without undue strain.

Although the *Tonight* show is now perceived by the media
and public as of great importance simply because it has
lasted for some thirty-five years, none of us connected with it
in the beginning saw it as of major cultural significance at all.

Certainly I didn't. In the world I came from most people were sound asleep by 11:00 at night, except on Fridays and Saturdays; and for that matter, even now, on any given night, the overwhelming majority of the American people are *not* watching *The Tonight Show*. Given the evidence of all those magazine covers and extended newspaper features about me at the time, you might think that I'd have had the importance of the show in better focus, but the fact is I did not.

After a few weeks of working on the new Sunday night program I came to realize that, although hosting a talk show is so easy a job that it's almost like stealing money, by no means could the same be said for our weekly prime-time sketch-comedy presentation. Putting together a solid hour of comedy and music in only six days is a remarkable feat. Many a Broadway producer has spent a year or more developing a musical comedy revue and seen it close in one night. Our crew was creating a damned good production week after week with only a few days of lead time.

Of course, if I'd elected to do a show in the Sullivan formula—hiring several acts and presenting them one after another—there would've been no such problem. But we created fresh sketches for our guest stars and the members of our regular company, and this required hard work morning, noon and night, with no days off.

After several weeks I sent word to the NBC program people that I had to give up the *Tonight* show because I could hardly spend the daytime hours writing, booking, and rehearsing the Sunday program and still be on the air live from 11:30 until 1:00 in the morning and do justice to both programs. To my surprise, the network's reaction was semi-panic, which I suppose is understandable since both shows were being well-received and bringing in enormous profits.

NBC suggested that the matter ought not to be decided on an either-or basis so we compromised: I would continue with the *Tonight* show for three nights a week. I suggested that Jack Paar or Ernie Kovacs, both comedians, would do quite an acceptable job on the other two nights. NBC agreed and tried Jack twice and Ernie more often. Unfortunately for the network's interests, I soon tired of the three-night obligation and again told them that I would have to be relieved of it as early as might be convenient.

Our last *Tonight* show was telecast on January 25, 1957, six months after the start of the prime-time Sunday night series.

When I left *Tonight*, NBC unwisely decided to replace the show with an entirely new late-night program called *Tonight: America After Dark*. Magazine-like in format, it featured a number of coast-to-coast correspondents who reported on what was happening in the country during the late hours. As an abstract idea there was nothing wrong with the concept. Quite an entertaining show, in fact, could have been constructed on such a basis. The reality, unfortunately, was otherwise. *America After Dark* turned out to be one of the most inept programs in television history, partly because some of its spokesmen in the various cities were not even public speakers much less entertainers. They were journalists and columnists. Jack Lescoulie was the original host. Jack was a genial fellow but he was only an announcer, not in any sense an entertainer and certainly not a comedian. The ratings plummeted, NBC affiliates around the country began to drop the show on their own initiative, and after a 26-week run the whole experiment was scrapped. It was then that NBC, unable to think of a third alternative, decided to resurrect *Tonight*.

As for the Paar-or-Kovacs decision to host the revived show, NBC had seemed to favor Ernie during the trial period but finally went back to Paar. So while it is correct to refer to Kovacs as one of the interim hosts of *Tonight*, he did not in fact make his mark as a talk-show host since he preferred to do his own creative camera tricks and off-beat visual comedy on his own early-evening TV show.

(Above) We offered Jayne every single woman's role on the four-year *Meeting of Minds* series, so versatile an actress is she. Here she is as Marie Antoinette—or Zsa Zsa Gabor with a swelled head.

(Right) Mickey Mouse has been a hit for years. I wish I could say the same for my character, Schticky Mouse.

(Left) **Our Westinghouse show announcer, Johnny Jacobs, laughs it up as I arrive at the studio with my chauffeur "Smokey."**

(Below) **On our NBC prime-time comedy series Johnny Carson shows me how to make a gesture with his right hand, and I give him a good long "Oohhh" in response.**

(Above) **Don't ask me why, but I've occasionally interviewed studio audiences while flying over them Peter Pan style.**

(Right) **Sure, it was fun doing** *The Benny Goodman Story,* **but I would have made a more dramatic Superman than did Christopher Reeve.**

(Right) **This isn't trick photography. I'm actually broadcasting "from high-atop" Vine Street on one of our Westinghouse shows.**

(Below) **Jazz was always an important part of my programs. Here I am on the NBC Sunday night series with (left to right) Sol Yaged, Lou McGarrity, Urbie Green, Benny Goodman, Buck Clayton, and Sid Caesar.**

(Above) Steve Jr., today a success-ful doctor and comic lecturer, meets Elvis and Imogene at one of our rehearsals.

(Left) This was probably the first truly dangerous stunt in what turned out to be a long series of them. (CBS)

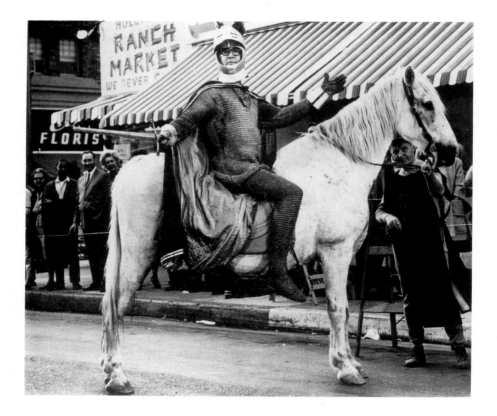

(Above) The now long-gone Hollywood Ranch Market, on Vine Street, served as a backdrop for a lot of our wilder sketches and show openings.

(Below) This is a rehearsal of our famous NBC ultra-modern group, The Unidentified Flying Objects. Producer Nick Vanoff checks the shot, with the help of Louis Nye (who played *water* that night), Don Knotts and Pat Harrington, Jr.

(Left) Liberace and me in rehearsal. The man actually dressed like that before the show went on the air. (NBC)

(Below) Two of the most talented gentleman of our time, Sammy Davis Jr. and Orson Welles, amaze me with a bit of card magic. (NBC)

(Right) It was always fun working with probably the second most beloved comedian—after Will Rogers—in show business, the great Jimmy Durante. (NBC)

(Below) Jayne starred in this production of "Bride of Frankenstein." I, as the proverbial mad scientist, encourage Louis Nye, as the monster, to—well, need I say more? (NBC)

CHAPTER ELEVEN

The Sunday Night Prime-time Show:

Man-on-the-Street Interviews/
Characters and Hoaxes

Slotted opposite Ed Sullivan, I predicted that our program would eventually come to be recognized as the better show but that Ed's would remain the more popular. My guess was correct. Although there were many weeks when we had the higher rating, he won the race more often.

The *Tonight* show had been five percent scripted and 95 percent ad lib. But our live Sunday evening comedy hour, which ran four seasons (1956-1960), reversed this proportion. Starting with only Stan, Herb and myself, it eventually had a staff of seven writers.

The program won a Peabody Award in 1960 as Best Comedy Show on TV; I give much of the credit not only to our writers—Stan Burns, Herb Sargent, Leonard Stern, Don Hinkley, Arne Sultan, Marvin Worth, and later Hal Goodman and Larry Klein (A friend named Ray Seery also submitted occasional useful ideas by mail.)—but also to our production-direction team, Bill Harbach, Nick Vanoff, Dwight Hemion, and Jules Green, and—for damned sure—the great cast of supporting comics who worked with me: Bill Dana (who also doubled as a writer), Louis Nye, Don

Knotts, Tom Poston, Gabe Dell, Pat Harrington Jr., and Dayton "Why Not?" Allen.

Don, who was born in Morgantown, West Virginia, enrolled as a speech major at West Virginia State University, with the intention of becoming a teacher. A little thing called World War II intervened, however, as a result of which Don spent two years touring the South Pacific handling assorted comedy assignments in a show called *Stars And Gripes.*

After the war, he headed for New York and landed a juicy role in the Broadway comedy, *No Time For Sergeants.* I hired him for two appearances on the *Tonight* show, on which he did monologues of his own creation that I at once recognized as classics in the Benchley tradition. One was an impression of a last-minute replacement for a TV weatherman; the other had the same last-minute gimmick, but the speaker this time had to address a convention of doctors in his capacity as representative of a pharmaceutical company that had just introduced a new tranquilizer. After his four hilarious years with me, Don would, of course, go on to the delightful *Andy Griffith Show.*

Tom Poston, oddly enough, also got his post-high school education in West Virginia, although at that state's Bethany College, majoring in chemistry. At the outbreak of World War II, Tom and his brother Richard enlisted in the Air Force and served as pilots. Considering that Tom's well-deserved reputation has been achieved in comedy, it is interesting that his first intentions directed him to the Broadway theater and serious acting. Although he had worked in television in the early 1950s, I knew nothing of that.

For a few weeks he hung around our offices, chiefly in the company of Stan Burns and Herb Sargent, and so favorably impressed the fellows that they recommended him for an assignment in our then-emerging *Man On The Street* sketches, where he quickly became a fixture with his wonderful Stan Laurel-like portrayal of a man so confused he couldn't remember his own name.

Happily for Tom's original ambitions his new-found fame enabled him to work in a number of Broadway plays, while continuing in TV. During the 1980s he would enjoy great success as the goofola handyman on Bob Newhart's series. People are always asking me where I discovered one performer or another. Well, I discovered Bill Dana working on my show as a writer. He had first come to my attention as creator of some brilliant comedy monologues, for comedian Don Adams, who combined a marvelous impression of film actor William Powell with an impeccable sense of timing. "Are these the legs of a homicidal maniac?"

To this day people still use the stock line, "Would you believe —?" that Bill created for Don's character.

Considering that Bill would later—in his characterization of Jose Jimenez—become widely popular, it's interesting that he had had difficulty establishing himself as a nightclub stand-up comic or a partner with performer Gene Wood. When I would interview Jose, usually in *Man On The Street*, it never particularly mattered what his alleged job was, but when he finally claimed to be an astronaut, the timing could not have been better. In the late '50s and early '60s the nation was fascinated by the space program and Bill apparently had become the only comedian dealing chiefly with that subject matter.

More recently Bill has made occasional appearances on *Golden Girls* as Father Angelo, the aged Sicilian priest and older brother of the character Sophia.

It's a minor annoyance that, like other TV viewers, critics don't always correctly interpret or appreciate what they see on regularly broadcast programs. For instance, I don't feel that our direction-production team has gotten the credit it deserves for the often wildly creative innovations it has introduced. One time while doing some shows from Hollywood, we decided to have me play a piano solo with the entire panorama of the area's mountains for a background.

To accomplish this innovation, it was necessary to hoist a

heavy concert grand piano up the outside of the Capitol Records Building on Vine Street and place it on the wind-swept roof. During a commercial, I ran across the street, was whisked to the twelfth floor in a waiting elevator, ran up a couple of flights of stairs, and arrived on the roof just in time to go back on the air. As I spoke to the audience, I walked completely around the building's circular top, describing the beauties of the city as the camera's eye looked past me at distant Los Angeles, with Hollywood in the foreground and the hills behind. Then I played the piano while hundreds of automobiles, looking like tiny toys, could be seen scurrying along the freeway that winds through the area. To my knowledge, no TV columnist in the country even mentioned the routine, although if it had appeared on a one-shot special they might have devoted several paragraphs to it. While critics have generously always given me more credit than I deserve, it does not often enough occur to them to credit imaginative production and direction on a regular series.

I should also mention that several people with whom I later discussed the rooftop piano solo number assumed the whole thing was a camera trick.

Another illustration of imaginative production occurred during our last year in New York. I'd played the first eight bars of a piano solo when suddenly my piano began to rise slowly in the air. It continued to rise, as I played, until it was about ten feet above the floor; then in rapid succession it turned over completely so that I did three "outside loops" while playing. To make sure that no one thought this was a camera trick, we filled the stage with singers and dancing girls, to one of whom I threw a flower as I whirled about. We also placed on top of the piano a shawl and small vase, which naturally fell off as the instrument turned over. The studio audience was flabbergasted by the whole stunt, but I saw not a word of comment about it in any TV column during the following week. Since the routine was prepared for us by professional magician Bob McCarthy, I can't divulge how it was accomplished, but the fact remains that had it happened on a Fred Astaire or Ethel Merman special, their directors would've been nominated for the Congressional Medal of Honor. Our own production people, Dwight Hemion, Bill Harbach and Nick Vanoff, were granted nary a nod.

In any event, several of the regular routines we had done on the *Tonight* show—like *Crazy Shots* and *Letters to the Editor*—we now transferred to prime-time. As an added attraction we also featured top guest stars each week.

When the program premiered—on Sunday, June 24, 1956—we broadcast from the Hudson Theatre on 45th Street in New York. Bob Hope, Jerry Lewis, Sammy Davis Jr., Kim Novak, Vincent Price, Dane Clark, and Wally Cox were our guests.

When our announcer Gene Rayburn first introduced me, I was led out onstage by a pretty young model. I said, "You're probably wondering why that young lady had to lead me out here. At least I *hope* you're wondering. Every time I see those $64,000 and $100,000 quiz programs I always think: Here are people brilliant enough to answer questions that would throw a genius and they can't even find their way to the middle of the stage without help." It was the very first joke I had written for the new show.

I next explained that one of the features of the new series would involve my doing an occasional impersonation. "For example," I said, "here's my impression of Bob Hope." I turned my back to the camera, removed my glasses, and pretended to adjust my hair in the manner of impressionists from time immemorial. But as I started to turn back to the audience, the camera dissolved to Bob himself, who was turning around simultaneously with my movements. His appearance involved just that quick cameo. The underlying purpose, of course, was to throw a superstar into the picture right at the outset, but in a funny way. Since our opposition was Ed Sullivan, who, though he knew close to nothing about the nuts-and-bolts details of creating entertainment, nevertheless had a superb journalistic sense of the human fascination with celebrities. NBC felt—and we agreed—that although Ed's was a true variety show and ours was comedy, we still could not ignore the booking of box-office names if we were to compete. The difference on our part was that we always used them in funny and creative ways rather than simply having them take a bow from the audience in the Sullivan show manner.

Although the media would quickly refer to the Sullivan-Allen competition in terms more appropriate to a heavy-weight title fight, there was no ill-will between us personally that first night. In fact, Ed sent me a telegram: "Dear Steve, Having a wonderful time tonight—wish you were here."

After the Bob Hope walk-on, I proceeded to show "Ed's guest list" for that night—on an exceedingly long roll of paper. Then I held up a copy of *Look* magazine with Sullivan's picture on the cover. "If any of you want to read while our program is on..."

The first actual routine we did was *Crazy Shots* from the *Tonight* show. With our prime-time budget, we could now afford actors, props, and scenery that made possible even funnier sight gags.

The routine was always introduced by my saying, "One of the things I do regularly on television is play the piano, but I know that many viewers get bored watching a man playing piano on TV because you see the same pictures each time—close-ups of fingers on the keyboards, profile shots, etc. Well, we're going to do something about that tonight. I'm going to be at the piano, but we've arranged for you to have something more interesting to look at while I'm playing." We then ran through a number of quick visual jokes as I played. One of the funniest was a close-up of one of our staff secretaries, Marilyn Jacobs, who yawned and closed her eyes, to reveal another set of wide-open eyes painted on her lids.

Actor Dane Clark was shown sipping soup, but as the camera panned down to the bowl it discovered a pair of chattering false teeth slopping soup on the tablecloth. The next shot opened on a tombstone. The camera pulled back to reveal two empty milk bottles next to the stone, one with a note sticking up. A milkman entered, looked at the note and replaced the empty bottles with full ones. The following scene showed actor Vincent Price in a dining room, napkin under his chin, ready to eat. The waiter removed a silver cover from the platter in front of Vincent to reveal not an entree but bandleader Skitch Henderson's head, his eyes darting fearfully about. For the next shot we cut to an exterior of 45th Street where two cars—driven by stunt-men—crashed in an actual head-on collision.

The camera then panned up from the confrontation between the two angry drivers to a window of the run-down hotel across the street where a man appeared to be slapping a woman (actually a dummy) around. The last *Crazy Shot* started on a close-up of Jerry Lewis eating a large slice of watermelon. As he spit several pits off-camera, we concluded by cutting to a close-up of me with watermelon seeds attached to my face and eyeglasses.

The next sketch was related to the then-common television commercial based on a testimonial in which an individual tells us why we should buy a product he happens to be using. In the first segment we found Dane Clark in a saloon starting an argument with the bartender.

A man on the next stool tells Clark to shut up, that he's had enough to drink. After another word or two, Dane takes a wild swing at the fellow, misses, and for his pains is belted over the head by a breaking bottle, at which he turns to the camera and very pleasantly says, "Oh, hello there. When headache strikes, as it often does, I get instant pain relief with—*Boffo*. (He *takes one with a jigger of liquor*.) And I always have this little bottle of Boffo handy because these head-aches strike *me* at least once every night. You see, to be really effective, a painkiller has to get right into your blood ...and when your blood is 100-proof like mine, that ain't easy.

"But Boffo gets in there because it acts twice as fast as aspirin—and three times as fast as straight alcohol."

The next scene opened on actor Vincent Price lying in the street, his clothes tattered, half-buried under the debris from a just-happened auto accident. He pushes a few pieces of wreckage off his body, looks into the camera, and says, "Oh, hello there. I've just been hit by a new 1956 Crashmobile. Man, what a thrill! The 1956 Crashmobile has everything! What pick-up! It picked *me* up and threw me 65 feet. The crashmobile has all the latest features, too. Look at this double-duty, triple-thick balloon tire. These treads really gripped my body—with no danger of skidding off. And the new pinpoint-beam headlights—why, they picked me out from a mile-and-a-half away. The Crashmobile also has the new clear-view wraparound windshield. I personally had a very clear view of the driver as he wrapped the car around me."

Next comedian Wally Cox, wearing old-fashioned prison garb, looked up as a guard appeared with the proverbial last meal on a tray. Cox checked the items—fried chicken, dumplings, brown gravy, a pork chop—then looked into the camera and said, "Oh, hello there. You know, whenever I have a last meal, with rich, hard-to-digest food, I never worry about it because... I always carry *Stummos* for the stomach. I know I can eat anything I want, take a Stummo, and an hour later I won't feel a thing. I used to lie awake nights with indigestion, but after tonight I'll say good-bye to indigestion. In fact, after tonight I'll say good-bye to everything. Pick up a package of Stummos and always keep them handy—because your next meal may be your last."

To add a bit of glamour and movie-star name-value to the show we had booked the lovely Kim Novak and decided to repeat a sketch that had worked wonderfully well several months earlier on the *Tonight* show. In introducing the routine I explained that a recent survey had revealed that school children were now spending many more hours watching television each week than they spent doing homework. This, I insisted, was another argument in favor of putting more educational value into TV programming. The sketch was our tongue-in-cheek solution to the problem. Our cameras found the beautiful Kim looking distraught as she waited for my arrival. After a moment I rushed in wearing a hat and coat and carrying a small suitcase. I slammed the door and leaned against it, panting.

"You're late," Kim said. "What happened?"

"The cops got wise," I said. "I have to leave the country."

"Oh, Gus," Kim said. "I knew this would happen. This is no good—running—always running. Why don't you give up?"

"Give up?" I said. "Never! Not as long as I have this!"—and I pulled a revolver from my pocket.

"A revolver!" Kim cried, apparently in shock. Then, turning to the camera, she lifted up my arm with the gun in it and very deadpan said, "Revolver. R-E-V-O-L-V-E-R. Noun. A firearm, commonly a pistol, with a cylinder of several chambers so arranged as to revolve on an axis and be discharged in succession by the same lock."

The sketch was going well until a few minutes later when Kim was supposed to say, "Well, you're going to leave without me. Why should I get involved in this mess? You started out like a big shot, but you're just like all the rest of them. And I thought you had a brain." She was then supposed to turn to the camera and say, "Brain. B-R-A-I-N. Noun. The large central mass of nerve tissue enclosed in the skull." Unfortunately she forgot her lines at that point and had to make several attempts before she could say the line, "And I thought you had a brain." I made the best of the awkward situation by ad-libbing to her, "and I thought *you* had a brain."

From that very first show on, we often worked comedy into our musical numbers (as we would a week later with Elvis Presley). Sammy Davis Jr. and I did a parody I had just written on the famous jazz number, "The Birth of the Blues," called "The Death of the Blues." Oddly enough, it was a satirical put-down of the very sort of music that Presley would perform the following Sunday.

Looking back at both the script and warm media comment about our second show is an illuminating experience. The press, partly whipped up, I suppose, by the publicity engines at the two rival networks, was treating the Sullivan-Allen confrontation as if it were equal in importance to a Presidential race. Primary concentration, of course, was on my booking of Elvis. Consequently, although again the critics were generous in their assessments—they said the second show was even better than the first—they generally ignored the other segments of the show and focused on the controversial new country-rock singer.

I started the program by walking onstage dragging a loaded mailbag. "We received a great deal of mail after our first show last week," I said. "I thought I'd read some of it to you. Let's see what's in here—it's pretty heavy." At that I loosened the bag, whereupon singer Steve Lawrence climbed out wearing a mailman's uniform. He handed me the one postcard that was in the bag, smiled at the camera, and exited.

Sullivan had a custom of introducing celebrities—actual and alleged—in his studio audience. The previous week, in his typical competitive style, he had booked seemingly a thousand-and-one stars to counteract our opening broadcast. To poke fun at this situation, the next thing I said on our second outing was, "Before going on with the show, I'd like to introduce some famous guests in our audience. First a man who flew in from the West Coast just to be on our show tonight—Mr. Fred Garber of Hollywood, California. (applause) Mr. Garber is the only person in Hollywood who was *not* on *The Ed Sullivan Show* last week."

I next introduced comedian Ernie Kovacs, with a joke referring to a now-forgotten television commercial. Then came Milton Berle. During the applause and the fanfare, Milton and I exchanged vigorous handshakes, hugs, shoulder-pats, and warm smiles, after which I said, "Milton, did you notice what we just went through? When an emcee calls out a guest star they always shake hands, pat each other on the back, smile and talk; but all this goes on during the applause, so the audience never gets a chance to hear what they're actually saying."

Then I suggested that we repeat exactly the same business but this time without applause and music so that the audience could hear what was being said. At that I introduced Milton again. He walked on to total silence, and the audience heard the following exchange as we shook hands and embraced:

MILTON: Steve, that was the worst introduction I ever heard.
STEVE: What do you expect for nothing?
MILTON: *(hugging Steve)* I'll never come on your stupid show again.
STEVE: *(hugging Berle)* Is that a promise?
MILTON: *(with a big grin)* Drop dead. *(He kisses me.)* You're a phony! *(He walks offstage.)*

That portion of Milton's appearance was written by Stan and Herb. At that point Milton returned, and we did a routine I had written for the occasion.

MILTON: Seriously, Steve, I'm on my summer vacation and I know you have a big show lined up for the folks tonight—Imogene Coca, Elvis Presley, Andy Griffith—but there's one thing I want to do right now.
STEVE: What's that, Milton?
MILTON: Well, last week Bob Hope gave you a special award. Then the other night on your *Tonight* show you received the Optimists Club Award. And just a few weeks ago you were given the Junior Chamber of Commerce plaque. In fact, I've had my people check, and I've discovered that during the past year you've received fourteen plaques, three citations, five silver cups, four gold cups, and seven certificates of merit.
STEVE: Well, that's television, Milton. Organizations like to give all of us plaques and awards as long as we're willing to receive them in front of a camera. You've been given a great many yourself.

MILTON: That's true, Steve. Sid Caesar, George Gobel—we've all received plenty of them. But you've received the most, Steve; and so at this time it gives me great pleasure to present you with *this* award: As the comedian who has received the most awards during the past year, here it is...the *Award* Award!

After I thanked Milton, he added a P.S. written by Burns and Sargent: "Wait! That's not all. Because this makes a total of 237 awards, it gives me great pleasure now to present you with something I know you need—a bare wall." He then quickly moved an enormous section of wall, complete with wallpaper and small curtained window, to center stage, took the plaque he had just given me, and hung it up for display.

This routine was based on something I had observed shortly after coming to New York in 1951 (and something I had already addressed in essay form, in an article for *TV Guide*)—that practically anybody on television can win all the awards he wants, if he is willing to publicize the presenters.

For many people the Sunday night show is best remembered for our *Man-on-the-Street* routines. I created the sketch simply as a satire of the ancient and still popular journalistic cliché called *Man on the Street* or *Vox Populi*, where a question-of-the-day is asked and the answers, along with close-up headshots of those responding, are printed. We photographed the routine in the same way, using a series of close-ups of our regulars, or whoever else was performing in the sketch. As the inquiring reporter, I played straight for everyone. There was very little ad-libbing; all the bits were written—mostly by Herb and Stan—and rehearsed. The regulars always appeared as the same characters:

Louis Nye was Gordon Hathaway, the fey advertising man: "My name is Gordon Hathaway and I'm from Manhattan. Hi-ho, Steverino! Move over, Big Ben, I'm clanging tonight!"

Don Knotts was the trembling nervous little guy:

KNOTTS: My name is B. F. Morrison. I'm from New York and I'm a carnival show knife-thrower...retired.
STEVE: What does the B.F. stand for?
KNOTTS: Butter fingers!
STEVE: Are you nervous?
KNOTTS: Noop!

Tom Poston played the guy who could never remember his name. And Bill Dana later got huge laughs just by uttering his character's name in that "foreign man" accent of his: "My name—Jose Jimenez." *(laugh)* "I'm glad you like my name."

The zany Dayton Allen, who joined us in 1958, had previously been a puppeteer on the *Howdy Doody* show, doing the voices of Mr. Bluster and Flubadub, among others. His invariable response to our weekly question became something of a national catchphrase:

STEVE: Do you plan to vote in this week's election?
DAYTON: *(finger pointing skyward)*: Whyyyyyy not!!!!

Occasionally we used guests in this spot—Skitch Henderson, our secretary Marilyn Jacobs, who proved to be hysterical on camera, and my mother, to whom we gave the name Mag Haggerty because she used to call herself that when I was a child. She'd sometimes look in the mirror after a rough night and say, "My God, I look like Mag Haggerty's Revenge," as if the last three words were the title of an old play.

It's ironic that today memories of Louis Nye, Tom Poston, and Don Knotts on the Sunday night show are of the *Man-on-the-Street* sequences when these roles are arguably the least funny of the many in which the fellows distinguished themselves. The reason they are remembered as men-on-the-street, of course, is that those sketches were a regular feature, seen on almost every show of the series, but Don, Louis, and Tom were brilliant in countless other characterizations, playing an endless assortment of Mafia gangsters, German soldiers, fuzzy-brained scientists and technical experts, movie stars, matinee idols, members of Senate investigating committees, quiz-show contestants, and so forth. There was really nothing those gifted gentlemen couldn't play. Fortunately the reader doesn't have to take my word for this; the evidence became once again available in late 1990 when the all-comedy cable channel—Ha!-TV, now called Comedy Central—began rerunning our show. Though it might sound odd, I'd forgotten myself how really good they were. In that day—the 1950s—strong sketch comedy was a TV staple, but thereafter the networks actually had such performers as Sonny and Cher, and Marie and Donny Osmond doing comedy sketches.

Another character I did on the show was sportscaster "Big Bill" Allen, who read the sports results: "Final score on that big game between Harvard and William and Mary. The score—Harvard 14, William 12, Mary 6." One night, I suddenly started laughing so hysterically while I was doing this bit that I couldn't stop. Before the show, I had put some greasy tonic on my hair to make it stay down; the reverse occurred. Having no time to fix it, I grabbed the fedora I always wore for the routine and hurried onstage. When I glanced at myself in the monitor as I started the bit, the way I looked—like Mark Twain's Injun Joe in *Tom Sawyer*—struck me so funny that I began to laugh. Forty million people were watching and that was part of the problem. Once I was over the edge, everything I did struck me funny. The fact that it was striking me funny struck me funny. I knew I shouldn't be laughing, but it was the old laughing-in-church syndrome.

"Oh, if only the script were this good," I said, falling back in my chair in hysterics.

Another reason I kept laughing was that the always funny rotund comedian Jack E. Leonard, the next guest scheduled to appear, was yelling lines at me from the wings. I was eating into his time by laughing for so long. "Come on, goddammit," he bellowed. "I've only got five minutes, and you've blown three of them already!" He had a point, since live shows had to be strictly timed and controlled so that at the end of an hour you didn't find yourself with either three minutes to fill with absolutely nothing planned, or else go off the air before you had completed the scheduled entertainment. But I laughed away anyway.

To this day, the segment is the most-requested clip from the whole Sunday night series.

From time-to-time over the years I've had another kind of fun pulling hoaxes. For example, I made two record albums under phony names and fooled a few dozen disk jockeys, some jazz critics, and a number of record-buyers. I even published a book of poetry under another name. But the hoax that attracted the widest audience was the one we played on Louis Nye on one of our Sunday night shows. It was actually a risky proposition all around because we were on the air live, with millions of people watching.

As I've already mentioned, once in awhile in the days of live TV, something would go wrong. An actor would forget his lines, a piece of scenery would fall down, somebody would hold up the wrong cue-card. Since you couldn't yell "Stop the tape!" the performers had to do some nimble ad-libbing around the problem.

In any event, the plot line of this particular stunt involved setting Louis up as the patsy. From the first day of rehearsal that week Tom Poston pretended to be having a drinking problem. So far as I know, in reality, Tom wasn't drinking at all. But when the fellows would take their lunch break, he would go to a neighborhood bar, order a shot of bourbon and, when Louis wasn't looking, rub a little of the liquid on his lapel. Now Tom does a great drunk. Every comedian in the world, of course, knows how to act drunk, although many of us are no better at it than your neighborhood class clown, but some—Foster Brooks is probably the best example—are masterful at it. Tom is one of them.

By Wednesday he had not only totally convinced Louis that he was a semi-alcoholic, but, with the help of Don Knotts, had added the twist that "No matter what happens we have to be sure Steve doesn't find out about this because you know how he feels about people who drink." Everyone familiar with the gifted Don Knotts, of course, knows that his specialty is acting nervous, so it was not surprising that by Saturday poor Louis was convinced that Don's jitters were for real and consequently actually thought Tom's job might be in jeopardy.

In reality, everyone on the show was in on the gag except Louis.

All week, in addition to their participation in other segments of the show, Louis and Don had been rehearsing a sketch which was supposed to take place in a seedy waterfront saloon. Louis played the part of a Mafia gangster, and Don played one of his flunkies.

Before I go further I should mention another necessary ingredient of the hoax—that the audience be in on it. To accomplish this, just before the sketch started, I signaled for the boom microphone to be lowered right into the picture so that I could speak just an inch or two away from it, in a semi-whisper that could not be heard backstage. As extra insurance, Bill Harbach, our producer, engaged Louis in conversation at the same time so Louis' attention would be diverted.

So the sketch began. Don and Louis, in character, walk into this dive and stand at the bar. While they're waiting for service, Don says, "Big Al, I gotta go make a phone call. I'll be right back." At that he walks a few feet to a phone booth, sits down, drops a coin in the slot, and pretends to forget his lines—totally—in such a way that, had they not known better, everyone in the studio audience, and the millions watching around the country, would not have had the slightest doubt that his memory had failed him completely. And at this point there was no way Louis could help him by ad-libbing, because he was about twelve feet away, at the bar.

Naturally Dwight Hemion, the camera director, was taking close-up reaction shots of Louis as he listened, with growing consternation, to Don talking gibberish in the phone booth.

The script next called for Louis to say to the bartender, Gabe Dell, "Give me a double." All week long he had been served ginger ale, which has the color of liquor. But now— need I say it?—he got the real thing—a double scotch. Naturally, we had set it up in the script that "he downs the drink in one gulp." When Louis did that with the actual booze, his eyes practically crossed.

The audience, knowing what was going on, howled. Louis, of course, began to be puzzled by the laughter because ostensibly nothing funny had happened in the sketch as he perceived it.

At this point, Don continued to deliberately garble his lines. Now, if you're in a scene and another actor doesn't give you the right cue, you can hardly just go ahead as if nothing had happened because your next line may not make sense. Consequently, Louis had to keep revising the text, which he did quite well, although still puzzled by all the hysterical laughter.

Then Tom came in. The scene, as rehearsed, called for him to confront Louis, call him a squealer and a fink, and finally pull a gun and shoot him. But from the moment of Tom's entrance, he appeared to be high as a kite. His speeches were partly unintelligible and when he reached inside his pocket to pull out a gun, there was no gun. So he pulled out what he did find, a pack of cigarettes, which he pointed, with a goofy smile, at Louis. Louis was then supposed to pull his own gun and fire first. But when Louis pulled the trigger, the gun would not fire. He thereupon proceeded to pantomime that he had a knife, with which he "stabbed" Tom. Needless to say, it broke the audience up.

On another of our shows that year, something happened that Stan Burns still says is his favorite coo-coo moment of television history, although there was supposed to be nothing funny whatever about the visit to our show of The Oldest Man in The World. He was a very short, wrinkled but reasonably alert gentleman from Colombia, brought in by a representative of the syndicated *Believe It or Not* newspaper feature, who touted the man as being 167 years of age. The little fellow spoke no English so it was impossible to carry on a conversation.

When the old man was brought onstage to a tremendous ovation, I smiled, approached him, and extended my hand, which I naturally assumed he would shake. To my great surprise, he did indeed accept my hand, lifted it close to his face, examined it briefly as if it were some artifact of special interest, pulled it to his mouth, and gave it quite a strong bite. Stan Burns is probably right—that's got to be one of the nuttiest things that ever happened on our show.

One of my favorite series of sketches, although I usually did nothing more in them than play straight for Tom, Louis, and Don was called *The Allen Bureau of Standards.* The three colleagues usually wore laboratory smocks and were introduced as technical experts, well-qualified to analyze one new product or another.

In *The Allen Report to the Nation,* our "far-flung correspondents"—Tom, Louis, Don, Gabe Dell, Pat Harrington, or Bill Dana—would cover some timely issue, in the manner of *60 Minutes.*

And as I've mentioned before, long before the idea of doing *Karnac the Great* ever occurred to Johnny Carson, *The Question Man* was a regular feature on our Sunday night program. We would explain: "In this day of startling scientific accomplishments and fully solved mysteries, we've reached the point where there are more answers than questions."

As the Question Man I wore a goofy hair-comb and mustache, an old-fashioned swallow-tail coat, and baggy pants, and provided questions for answers fed to me, usually by Tom Poston.

TOM: The answer is 'The Bounding She-Monster, the Viking Woman vs. The Great Sea-Serpent and The Fantastic Puppet-People.' May we have the question, Mr. Question Man?

STEVE: Yes. The question is: You tell me your dream and I'll tell you mine.

TOM: Here's another one, sir. 'Butterfield 8-5000.'

STEVE: The question is: How many hamburgers did Butterfield eat?

No sooner had we introduced *The Question Man* than we began to receive Question-Man jokes from all over, even from our writers. A high school girl sent us a couple and a Los Angeles radio funnyman by the name of Bob Arbogast not only contributed a number of jokes but also provided us with the somewhat unnerving information that he had thought of the Question-Man idea itself several years before we did. When I satisfied myself that this was indeed the case, I promptly told Arbogast that I would be quite willing to either immediately stop doing the routine or else give him both money and public credit every time we did it. He voted for the latter option, and I have continued to refer to his originality in this context to the present day. I understand that periodically Arbogast tried, some years later, to stop Johnny Carson's *Tonight Show* group from doing the routine but never received any acknowledgement from the show of his attempt to protect his creation.

CHAPTER TWELVE

The Sunday Night Show: Hot Box Office Stars

I generally concentrated my writing and performing efforts for the Sunday show on the comedy although—because we were on opposite Sullivan—we were under constant pressure by NBC to book guests who were "hot box office."

One instance stands out in my memory, not only because of the star we booked, but because her appearance resulted in the creation of a sketch-form that is still in common use, having been much appropriated in the ensuing years. It is the technique by which new, funny questions are created to fit already-existing answers. I devised the idea as a way of getting around a problem connected with the appearance of film star Ingrid Bergman.

After confirming the booking we were told by 20th Century-Fox publicists that Ms. Bergman would not actually be available in person but that she would be glad to film an interview about a picture she was making at the time in England. We were not happy about the prospect of doing a straight interview in the middle of a comedy show, but I went through with it for the obvious reason that, as a superstar, Ingrid would guarantee us a good rating. But after the film had run as agreed, we sprang a new twist on

Fox. Here, first, is part of the original interview, a stilted exercise in which I, in New York, talked to the pre-filmed Ms. Bergman, on-location in England, wearing a Chinese peasant's conical straw hat and smiling at the camera:

INGRID: Hello, Steve.

STEVE: Good evening, Ingrid. It's a pleasure to have you back with us on the show.

INGRID: It's nice to *be* back.

STEVE: Tell me, what are you doing filming in London? Doesn't the story of your picture take place in China?

INGRID: Yes, it does. But we discovered that the weather in China this time of year is very difficult, and we found a place right here in Britain which we're going to use.

STEVE: China in Britain?

INGRID: Yes. In Wales.

STEVE: Isn't the movie based on the true experiences of Gladys Ayleswood?

INGRID: Yes, it's based on a book about her called *The Small Woman.*

STEVE: I hear the film is quite good.

INGRID: Yes, it's wonderful. I wish you could see it.

The rest of the exchange didn't get much more interesting or less blatantly commercial than that. I then said to the at-home audience, "As you know, the interview with Miss Bergman was on film. The technique used in the making of these interviews is quite interesting. Since it was impossible for me to be in England, someone else stood off-camera and asked the same questions that I've just asked Ingrid here tonight in New York. Though her answers were on film, however, there's no control over what questions I might have asked. This will now allow us to change the whole meaning of the original interview by putting new questions in front of Ingrid's same answers."

Ingrid's responses now elicited hysterical laughter from our studio audience.

INGRID: Hello, Steve.

STEVE: Ingrid, how do you say 'It's nice to be back' in Chinese?

INGRID: It's nice to *be* back.

STEVE: Oh, the accent is on the *be*....That's a lovely hat you're wearing, Ingrid. I understand it costs about $400 at Hattie Carnegie's.

INGRID: Yes, it does.

STEVE: By the way, is it true that you and your film unit had trouble booking passage on ships and crossed the ocean in a novel way?

INGRID: Yes. In whales. [Wales]

STEVE: I hear you're reading a movie scenario based on the life of Elsa Maxwell [an overweight hostess of the day]. Is that true at all?

INGRID: Yes, it's based on a book about her called *The Small Woman.*

STEVE: I'm glad to hear that. Ingrid, what do you think of the TV show *Maverick?* Do you like it?

INGRID: Yes, it's wonderful. I wish you could see it. [*Maverick* was slotted on ABC-TV at the same time as my show.]

The first offender who "borrowed" this sketch idea was a gentleman named Earl Doud, a member of our staff at the time the solution to the Ingrid Bergman interview problem occurred to me. Not long thereafter he created quite a funny comedy album by acquiring audiotapes of public figures (such as Lyndon Johnson speaking at press conferences) and replacing the actual questions that had been put to them with fresh questions that made their answers funny, as we had done with Ms. Bergman. Years later a cable comedy series, *Not Necessarily The News,* now depends heavily on precisely this idea.

The star who generated the most attention on our Sunday night series—Elvis Presley—was a rising young singer at the

time, unknown to most of the nation but soon to become
The King of Rock'n'Roll.

In the 1930s and '40s, when singing stars were rarely seen,
the factors of personal appearance and physical charisma
were not especially important. The two avenues to success
were recordings and radio, both of which are nonvisual. Had
Elvis gotten into the business at that time he might not have
succeeded at all because his basic vocal sound wasn't particularly attractive. Some popular entertainers are born with
the ability to make a naturally pleasing noise with their vocal
equipment—Perry Como, Sarah Vaughn, Frank Sinatra,
Bing Crosby, Russ Colombo, Andy Williams, Ella Fitzgerald.
Elvis was not. But his lack of a good "instrument" turned out
not to matter.

What his millions of young fans responded to was Elvis
himself. The young women who constituted 90 percent of
his early following were reacting to him in precisely the same
way that young women have, for decades, reacted to handsome film stars, talented or not. Initially Elvis had no mature
adult fans at all. Most Americans over forty, in fact, were
strongly critical of him, as was Ed Sullivan until he realized
Presley's power to attract TV viewers. Such is television's
attachment to principle.

That demographic fact has now changed, obviously, for
the simple reason that the 17-year-olds of 1956 are now
middle-aged. Today's 17-year-olds don't especially care that
much about Elvis.

I frequently read that Ed Sullivan introduced Elvis Presley
to television.

Wrong.

Almost as frequently I read reports that I did.

Wrong again.

While Elvis appeared on my program before he performed on Ed's, I had seen him a few months earlier on
Jackie Gleason's summer replacement *Stage Show*, which
featured bandleaders Jimmy and Tommy Dorsey. I didn't
catch his name that night and have no recollection now as to

what he sang, but I found his strange, gangly, country-boy charisma, his hard-to-define cuteness, and his charming eccentricity intriguing. The next day I typed a memo to my staff people to find out who he was, and to book him for our new Sunday night show.

Between the date of the memo and when he appeared—July 1, 1956—his recently released recordings had made him an important attraction, as a result of which our program that evening far surpassed Sullivan's in the ratings race.

When I booked Elvis, I naturally had no interest in just presenting him vaudeville-style and letting him do his spot as he might in concert. Instead we worked him into the comedy fabric of our program. I asked him to sing "Hound Dog" (which he had recorded just the day before) dressed in a classy Fred Astaire wardrobe—white tie and tails—and surrounded him with graceful Greek columns and hanging draperies that would have been suitable for Sir Laurence Olivier reciting Shakespeare. For added laughs, I had him sing the number to a sad-faced basset hound that sat on a low column and also wore a little top hat. (I learned not long ago that small ceramic statues of the dog-and-top-hat are now among the more popular items of Presley memorabilia. I think somebody owes me royalties.) We certainly didn't inhibit Elvis' then-notorious pelvic gyrations, but I think the fact that he had on formal evening attire made him, purely on his own, slightly alter his presentation.

For his other spot, I wrote a spoof of a typical country-and-western TV or radio show. Presley played my sidekick and the two of us were well supported by Andy Griffith, who in those days was a comedian, and the always delightful Imogene Coca.

Inasmuch as Elvis later made appearances on *The Ed Sullivan Show,* I've often been asked why I didn't make the same arrangements with him myself. Here's the reason: Before we even left the studio the night Elvis appeared on our show, Ed telephoned Presley's manager, Colonel Tom Parker, backstage at our own theatre. So desperate was he to make the booking, in fact, that he broke what had until that moment been a $7,500 price ceiling on star-guests, offering the Colonel $10,000 per shot. Parker told Sullivan he'd get back to him, walked over to us, shared the news of Sullivan's offer, and said, "I feel a sense of loyalty to you fellows because you booked Elvis first, when we needed the booking; so if you'll meet Sullivan's terms we'll be happy to continue to work on your program."

I thanked him for his frankness but told him I thought he should accept Ed's offer. The reason, primarily, was that I didn't think it reasonable to continue to have to construct sketches and comic gimmicks in which Presley, a noncomic, could appear. Ed's program, having a vaudeville-variety format, was a more appropriate showcase for Elvis' type of performance.

For his own part, Elvis had a terrific time with us and lent himself willingly to our brand of craziness. He was an easygoing, likeable, and accommodating performer. He quickly became the biggest star in the country; but when I ran into him from time-to-time over the years it was clear that he had never let his enormous success go to his head.

I later wrote, in my regular *Cosmopolitan* magazine column:

In the national furor about Elvis Presley I should like to inject a note that I'm sure will horrify his detractors, who are legion and leather-lunged. Before using Elvis on my Sunday evening program back in July, I went up to the offices of Paramount Pictures in New York City and viewed his screen test, filmed under the guidance of producer Hal Wallis. To get right to the point, the boy has it. I'm not talking about his singing or about that hard-to-definite factor, *talent;* I'm talking about an even harder to define something—that mysterious quality that has distinguished most of Hollywood's major stars, very few of whom were true acting talents. There are people like Marlon Brando, Paul Muni, or Frederic March who are both stars and actors, but most of moviedom's luminaries have been freak

174 ☆ STEVE ALLEN

personalities, people like Marilyn Monroe or Gary Cooper, who were just off-beat enough to be fascinating. It's not just a matter of looks either. Hollywood gas stations and drive-ins are full of beautiful people who have nothing more to offer than their good looks. Rather, it's the extra electric-plus that makes all the difference, granted the breaks. And Presley has it. On the screen, with the words of writers in his mouth, he exudes a sort of sleepy-eyed, Robert Mitchumish, bloodhound-puppy appeal, with just the hint of an evil glint in the eye for added spice. I hasten to advise his followers, however, that the evil glint is no more indicative of his true personality than would be freckles on his nose or bowed-legs. In person Elvis is soft-spoken, polite, and a bit withdrawn; he becomes a wild man only when he sings. The glint is nothing more than a matter of droopy eyelids over pale blue eyes, but it could do as much for Elvis on the screen as Chevalier's lower lip, Bette Davis' eccentric diction, or Jack Palance's murderous glare did for those stars.

Since it's long been established that audiences enjoy looking at beautiful women, our producers naturally booked a great many of them. In one such instance I suffered a painful injury. We'd constructed a sketch on romance-in-a-supermarket in which I played an aproned clerk and the statuesque blonde actress Marie MacDonald was a shopper. Ms. MacDonald was one of those women who seems to drift through show business and popular culture with increasing frequency in recent years. It would not be correct to call them talented, but because they are often strikingly beautiful and sometimes become involved in personal scandal, the media pay them a good deal of attention.

At any rate, Ms. MacDonald and I had reached a moment in our sketch where we were supposed to give each other a kiss. Nothing particularly passionate but a bit more than a quick peck. Everything had gone simply enough during rehearsals, but when I now kissed Ms. MacDonald—with about 25 million witnesses—she suddenly startled me by biting down, hard, on my lower lip. I'm not talking about a playful love-nibble; the pain was so severe that, had the show not been live, I would have given voice to a good loud "Ouch!" When I drew back in shock and looked into Marie's eyes, there was no clue as to why she had bitten me. She seemed as mischievous and playful as ever. After the show we went our separate ways, the little mystery never solved.

I have frequently been asked over the years if doing love scenes with glamorous actresses ever involves the emotions. The answer is yes, sometimes it does. I do not suggest that every onscreen kiss leads inevitably to a romantic relationship, adulterous or otherwise. In the great majority of such cases I'm sure that nothing of the sort results.

Nevertheless, problems can arise for the simple biological reason that at such moments not all of your body is aware that you are in a let's-pretend situation. Beauty is beauty and the closeness of a warm, attractive woman can lead to precisely those reactions to which all animal species, including the human, have been conditioned by millions of years of evolutionary development.

In one such instance actress Anita Ekberg, possibly the most beautiful woman on earth at the time, was playing a scene in which I was dressed as a Bogart-like private eye with trench coat and fedora (my favorite prop). The script called for Anita to enter in a tight-fitting gown, seat herself on my lap, and give me a kiss. (It's just occurred to me to wonder why the writers were forever writing all those steamy kisses into our comedy sketches. I never complained, but I must ask about it the next time I run into any of them.)

In any event, Ms. Ekberg's kiss, though it had been impersonal enough in rehearsals, suddenly turned out to be considerably warmer than one of those just-for-the-camera gestures. Even with the best of intentions it was difficult to keep my mind on the script work for the next few minutes, although the awareness that millions are watching is a great aid to virtue.

Some of the best sketches we did during the four years of the show's run, however, involved my wife Jayne. Most were in the situation-comedy form, with the two of us essentially playing ourselves. On one occasion Jayne had to jump in at the last minute when Ava Gardner, who'd been booked to appear with her gentleman friend of the moment, Italian comedian Walter Chiari, backed out the day before the show for reasons never made clear. Jayne filled in like the trouper she is, even though, because she was five months pregnant at the time, we had to photograph her carefully in the flirtatious love scene in which she played Chiari's girlfriend.

Occasionally something odd happened with one of our guests. There was, for instance, the day at a rehearsal when dear Zsa Zsa Gabor made a grand entrance, spent the next twenty minutes complaining loudly about the very funny sketch we had written for her, and finally succeeded in annoying me so much by her display of hubris that for the first and only time in my professional career I simply walked out of a rehearsal, telling a member of our staff to call me if and when Zsa Zsa's tantrum subsided.

I was eventually reached at a nearby restaurant; when I returned Miss Gabor was as good as gold. With the exception of that one instance, we've been friends for many years.

One of our funniest celebrity sketches on the Sunday show involved setting film actor Errol Flynn into the context of a satire on the popular panel show, *To Tell The Truth,* in which the participants would try to determine which of three contestants was the actual person all three claimed to be. As host I welcomed our viewers to "America's favorite panel show—*To Tell A Lie.*"

When the camera went to the routine shot of three contestants standing in silhouette, I asked the first one— Louis Nye—for his name. Just something about seeing that familiar and always funny face saying, "My name is Errol Flynn" sent the audience into gales of laughter.

Contestant Number Two was Errol himself, looking extremely confused about the whole situation.

Don Knotts also claimed to be the real Errol Flynn.

The contestants were seated and I began:

STEVE: I have here a sworn affidavit which I'd like to read to you. *(As Steve begins to read, a camera shows Louis' face.)* 'I have been in motion pictures since 1935. My first movie, *Captain Blood,* made me a star overnight. I was under contract to Warner Brothers for many years and was voted one of the top ten moneymakers in the industry. *(Camera pans to Errol's face.)*

'I have led an adventurous and dangerous life. I've been married three times. I've sailed the seven seas on my yacht and have written two books and many magazine articles. *(Camera pans to Don Knotts.)*

'At one time I was a light-heavyweight boxer and made the semi-finals of the Olympics. I am best known as a swash-buckling lover and am famous throughout the world as a ladies' man. Signed, Errol Flynn.'

All three claim to be Errol Flynn. Two of these gentlemen are impostors. All right, panel, let's see how sharp you are. It's up to you to figure out...who is the *real* Errol Flynn.

(Camera goes to close-ups as each panelist is introduced.) Our panelists today are that famous actor *Ralph Bellboy* (Tom Poston), who just came in from Philadelphia where his new hit show closed in rehearsal; lovely singer and actress, *Kitty Carlot* (Martha Raye)— you no doubt remember her perfor-mance in that stirring horror musical—*Dr. Jekyll Meets the Carioca;* and last but not least, columnist and man-about-town—*Hy Gargoyle. (Camera goes to Don Adams wearing glasses on top of his head, former Broadway columnist-TV show business commentator Hy Gardner-style.)*

All right, we'll begin our questions with Ralph Bellboy. What would you like to ask, Ralph?

TOM: Number Two, who is your publicity man?
ERROL: I don't need any. I get into trouble on my own

time. I need a publicity man like Yul Brynner needs a haircut.

TOM: If you're really a movie star, you'd know this. When you make a picture in Europe, do you get paid in American dollars or in foreign currency?

ERROL: I really don't know. My salary is generally attached.

TOM: Number Three. The real Errol Flynn was a good light-heavyweight boxer. Is that right?

DON: Yes.

TOM: Could you take a punch on the chin?

DON: Yes. I was very rugged.

TOM: Could you take it in the stomach?

DON: Oh, yes. I liked it all over.

TOM: Number One. Being a seafaring man, you ought to know this. What's the difference between port and starboard?

LOUIS: I know port. But I never drank starboard.

STEVE: And now we continue the questioning with Miss Kitty Carlot.

MARTHA: Can I kiss the contestants?

STEVE: No, no. That's another game. On this show we just ask questions.

MARTHA: Contestant Number Three, since you claim to have had experience as a pearl-fisherman, how do you tell which oysters have pearls in them?

DON: That's easy. You look for the married ones; they're already irritated.

MARTHA: Number Two.

ERROL: Yes.

MARTHA: What are you doing tonight?

ERROL: I'm going home early to read a good book.

MARTHA: Well, *he's* not Errol Flynn! Number One, how many Warner brothers are there?

LOUIS: One.

MARTHA: I thought I had him there. Number One. When you're in New York, what hotel do you stay at?

LOUIS: Park South Hotel.

MARTHA: *(leans forward)* Number Two, what's your room number?

ERROL: Fourteen twenty-five. *(Martha writes down number.)*

MARTHA: Number Three, in *The Adventures of Don Juan,* how many women do you make love to?

DON: Twenty-two. It got so bad I had to use a stunt man for the kissing.

MARTHA: Number Two. What's your latest picture?

ERROL: Darryl Zanuck's latest hit, *The Sun Also Rises,* now playing at your neighborhood theater at popular prices. It's an exciting movie, brilliantly acted. And right now, I'm making the movie version of Diana Barrymore's book, *Too Much Too Soon.* I play the part of John Barrymore.

MARTHA: Geeez! What a blabbermouth!

STEVE: Your time is running out, Miss Carlot.

MARTHA: Just one more question. I think I've got it! Number Two, let me hear you say, 'Darling, I love you. I can't live without you. Kiss me.'

ERROL: Darling, I love you. I can't live without you. Kiss me.

(Martha reacts by flipping over backwards and disappearing from view.)

STEVE: And now our last panelist, Hy Gargoyle.

ADAMS: Thank you, Steve. *(Now wearing three pairs of glasses on his forehead, he stares at the three Errols.)* I've been studying you, and I've come to this conclusion—all three of you are lying!...Now, according to my deductions, the real Errol Flynn is an athlete. He moves with the grace of a cat. Number Two, let me hear you say 'meow.'

ERROL: Meow.

ADAMS: *(thinks)* Mmmmmm. Not bad for a man—but lousy for a cat. Number One, did you ever cut yourself while dueling?

LOUIS: Yes. Once in a duel with Basil Rathbone I was doing this—*(he flexes an imaginary sword over his head.)* I cut my whole hand. *(He indicates on palm.)*

ADAMS: Did it hold up the picture?

LOUIS: No. I have a stand-in who does nothing but bleed for me.

STEVE: Panel, your time is up. It's time to vote. We'll find out right now which of these distinguished gentlemen is the real Errol Flynn. Ralph?

TOM: *(holding up card with Roman numeral two on it)* I voted for Number Two. He seems so bored with it all.

STEVE: And you, Kitty?

MARTHA: I vote for Number Three. *(holds up card with Roman numeral three)* He's been giving me the eye all evening...you fool you! *(waves at Don Knotts)*

STEVE: How about you, Hy?

ADAMS: I vote for Number One. *(holds up card with Roman numeral number one)* I *have* to. That's the card they gave me.

STEVE: Thank you, panel. Now, will the real Errol Flynn...please stand up?

(Short pause, then Don Knotts stands)

STEVE: Number One, would you please tell us what you do and who you really are?

LOUIS: My name is Gordon Hathaway and I'm from Manhattan. I don't do anything, really. I'm just a man-on-the-street.

STEVE: Number Two, would you please tell us who you are and what you do?

ERROL: My name is Herman Krupmeyer, and I'm a truck driver from the Bronx.

STEVE: Well, gentlemen, we certainly enjoyed having you here tonight. And to you, Mr. Flynn...*(turns to Don)*

DON: Call me Errol.

STEVE: Good night.

The sketch was written chiefly by Arne Sultan and Marvin Worth.

Errol performed creditably during rehearsal and was, as always, personally charming backstage, but by the time we were on the air—live—he was so spaced out on God-knows-what that he offered a very poor impression of himself, and in fact, came creatively alive for only one brief moment when he mentioned playing the role of the famous actor, John Barrymore and arched a remarkably Barrymore-like eyebrow.

Not long ago I was reminiscing with Louis Nye about the experience and he said:

> What I remember about that was a very sad moment. Errol's son came backstage to see him. He was a young fellow, looked about twenty-three. Anyway, he came back to see his father and I just happened to be standing there as Errol walked over to say hello to his son. Apparently he hadn't seen him in some time. We were there in the hallway, in front of the dressing rooms, and it was really sad. The two just looked at each other, almost as though they were strangers. Then they shook hands, sort of formally. At one point the boy put one arm out, as if to indicate that he was willing to embrace his father, but Flynn just fumbled the moment and talked, a little incoherently. I'm afraid he was stoned out of his mind. It was such a sad thing, seeing a failure of communication like that between a young man and his famous father.

CHAPTER THIRTEEN

The Sunday Night Show: Top and Unknown Comedians

B ecause our program was first and foremost a comedy show, we naturally invited as many top comedians as possible to appear with us. Over the course of our run there were guest appearances by Groucho Marx, Red Skelton, Jimmy Durante, Abbott and Costello (doing their routine *Who's On First?*), Bob Hope, Mel Brooks, Carl Reiner, the Three Stooges, Joe E. Brown, Bert Lahr, and Martha Raye (who did a series of twelve brilliant sketches we specifically wrote for her after NBC had canceled her own weekly show).

With most of the Raye sketches we'd first present a straight noncomic dramatic version, then a second take showing what could happen if everything went wrong. Martha displayed her typical enthusiasm and professional discipline and once even left her bed in Doctors' Hospital to both rehearse and do the show that night. A few days earlier she had been rushed to the emergency room by ambulance at 4:30 in the morning. A hospital spokesman said she had been brought in for "a check-up."

Many of the young unknown comedians we had on the Sunday show received their first or most important early exposure there: Shelley Berman, Mort Sahl, Don Adams,

Mike Nichols and Elaine May, Jackie Mason, Jackie Vernon, the team of Vic Grecco and Fred Willard, and Lenny Bruce.

Lenny was a brilliant and original comedian who was considered too outrageous for his time and was, in fact, arrested more than once on obscenity charges. There are not many comedians to whom I would apply the word *genius,* but I would in the case of Bruce. He was certainly more than just a successful nightclub stand-up comedian; he was like Jackie Mason, a comic philosopher. Since it's known that I'm prejudiced against off-color humor, I'm frequently asked why I not only was the first to praise Bruce lavishly but hired him for three national television appearances.

The explanation is simple. It is true that as a general rule I am not amused by vulgarity, particularly the scatological—jokes about outhouses, toilet-paper, constipation and diarrhea—I am quite prepared to laugh at a well-constructed line in a Broadway theater or in a nightclub that I might find objectionable on television. But there was an enormous difference in Lenny's use of four-letter words and the work of today's comedians. Lenny was never simply trying for a cheap laugh but was invariably making a philosophical point. This clearly makes all the difference.

An illustration: For reasons that are not clear to me and of no importance to the reader, I have a somewhat negative reaction to the word *ass.* It is not part of my personal vocabulary, and I inwardly wince in most situations when I hear it. But Lenny, poetically perceptive observer of human behavior that he was, once noted that in certain stock eight-by-ten glossy publicity photographs handed out by all the Flamenco dancers in the world—the fellows in the flat black Spanish hats, short jackets, tight-fitting black pants—they all seemed to pose in the same position, with hands up over their heads, eyes turned back down over their shoulders. The pictures always looked to him, Lenny observed, as if the dancer was applauding his own ass.

The brilliance of this perception quite overcame my conditioned revulsion to the key word.

In speaking of the kind of vaudeville and nightclub acts
that one sees in small-time theaters and clubs, Lenny also
mentioned the specialty dance acts, those that usually involve
a man and a woman. He said:

> The woman, to make herself look sexy, will usually wear
> black net stockings. But if you looked closely, it was usually
> possible to spot small tears and rips—some repaired, some
> not—high on the backs of the stockings.

It will be seen immediately that neither of these lines are
jokes. They are the kind of perceptive observations about a
small, usually unnoticed aspect of the human predicament,
the sort that customarily come from novelists or poets, not
nightclub comics.

The network went over Bruce's material with a fine-tooth
comb since it was leery about our booking him. Despite the
censors' efforts, however, they entirely overlooked a routine
he did about a teenaged boy getting high by sniffing
airplane glue, for the quite understandable reason that they
had never heard of the practice and thought it was just
something silly, like sniffing a catcher's mitt or a screwdriver.

Bring up the subject of practical jokes and you'll usually
discover two sharply opposed attitudes. Some people regard
the practical joke as the highest, most satisfying form of
humor, others insist it is a sadistic, or at least juvenile, type of
comedy.

Whatever the reader's position, he must at least admit that
the practical joke was responsible for bringing to humor-
hungry American TV audiences a brilliant new funnyman
who became a regular member of our cast, Pat Harrington,
Jr.

Discovered at the bar of Toots Shor's restaurant by
Jonathan Winters one winter afternoon in 1958, Pat (as
Guido Panzini, Italian golf pro) was introduced by Jonathan
to television night owls, fooled them completely, and, in fact,

did such remarkable sleight-of-tongue Italian dialect that within a few weeks NBC received a telephone call from a representative of the United States Immigration Service, who asked, "Where can we find this guy Panzini? We've got no record of his port of entry."

That Pat could so completely trick millions of people (including myself, by the way) is doubly remarkable when you realize that he does not speak one word of Italian and has never been closer to Italy than Manhattan's West Side, where he spent most of his childhood. The gag that started him on a show business career had come about as a spur-of-the moment bit of tomfoolery at Toot Shor's (again) back in 1956, one day when Pat and a good friend, Lynn Phillips, were taking a breather from their jobs as time-salesmen for NBC television.

The ocean-liner *Andrea Doria's* collision with a Swedish vessel was the big news of the day and, spying a CBS man at the bar, Phillips decided to put Pat's talent for mimicry to work. "This is Guido Panzini," Phillips said, manufacturing the name on the spot. "He's a survivor of the *Andrea Doria*. He was on the bridge when it happened."

"What was it like up there?" the CBS man asked, all ears.

Guido had great difficulty explaining but at last managed to blurt out, "Well, it was-a dark. Verra dark. But we knew we were-a close when-a Captain Calamai ask-a a question, an' somebody answer in Swidish."

In a few minutes the funny little Italian was the center of attention as intrigued barflies clustered around, peppering him with questions. The stunt was such a success that it was taken on the road—to another bar down the street where some Italian waiters got into a vehement argument with Guido about rumors that the *Andrea Doria* crew had headed for the lifeboats well ahead of some of the passengers. When Pat realized the Guido could fool even Italians, he knew he was home. He and Lynn expanded the routine in the course of time and gradually Guido became a golf pro. But this practical joke, momentous as it was, is not Pat's sole experiment with the form. He personally is prouder of another stunt. As he tells it:

> This friend of mine and I were in a bistro one day when we happened to see a little guy who looked exactly like General Sarnoff, the boss of RCA and NBC. We gave him twenty bucks and told him to show up at our office the next morning right after our weekly sales meeting. Well, he did, and by golly he looked more like the General than Sarnoff himself. I had cued him to walk up to me and ask my name. He did. I told him, and then, as rehearsed, he asked me what I did in the department. Everybody just stood around with their mouths hanging open.
>
> 'I'm a time salesman,' I said. 'And why don't you just get back upstairs and tend to your electrons? I'll take care of the sales, if it's all the same to you.'
>
> Well, my fellow workers practically fell through the floor, but my friend, the General, stuck out his hand and shook mine. He said, 'Good for you, young man. That's the spirit.' And then he walked out. And I walked over to the head of the department and said, 'Look, I'll be out for the rest of the day, okay?' Before he could think of an answer, I was gone.

Pat comes by his talent naturally, since his father was a popular nightclub comedian of the 1930s, but the young Harrington never actually had his sights set on show business. Even after he was working regularly in television, he looked on acting as a sideline. "Some guys play golf as a hobby," he said. "Me, I do *The Steve Allen Show*." It was only when our program moved to Hollywood and Pat received a call from Danny Thomas to do a series of guest appearances on his program that he began to realize he might never again sell a piece of TV or radio time.

From his first "celebrity" appearance, Pat became invaluable to our program. Oddly enough, his talent at submerging himself in a role was so great that frequently he did not get the credit he deserved simply because, although people would enjoy his characterizations (a famous jockey, a former boxing champ, an Italian busboy, a Scottish laird, etc.), they often didn't realize it was the same man playing all those parts.

In a comedy album recorded in 1960, Pat worked with a man who is also richly talented—Bill Dana, a former nightclub comedian who was on my writing staff for four years. Like Pat, he is a gifted dialectician with a quick mind and a delicate sense of the ridiculous.

My friendship with Pat and Bill led, that same year, to one of the funniest experiences of my life, although I didn't think so at the time. The incident began when officers of UNICO, an Italian-American organization, decided to arrange an important banquet in Los Angeles to honor the great songwriter Harry Warren, composer of such hits as "I Only Have Eyes For You," "You're Getting to be a Habit with Me," "42nd Street," "You're My Everything," "The Lullaby of Broadway," "Jeepers Creepers," and "Chattanooga Choo Choo."

I was first alerted to the forthcoming event when I received a call from my good friend Gus Bivona, a clarinetist and bandleader who had just been hired to provide the orchestra for the affair.

"The whole thing will be to honor Harry Warren," Gus said. "Some of the UNICO guys said that because you're a composer yourself and you love good music, you'd be right to emcee the show."

"I'd love to," I said, and asked to be provided with further details.

A few days later a letter arrived giving the names of speakers, entertainers, and local dignitaries who would be participating. I was asked if I could recommend any suitable entertainment. The only idea that occurred to me was to book my dear friends, Pat Harrington and Bill Dana. The reason these particular names came to mind—as opposed to, for example, those of Louis Nye and Don Knotts, who also worked for our show at the time—was because they had just

completed recording the album that included the Guido
Panzini routine.

In retrospect, it was easy to see that recommending to Pat
and Bill that they do the *Andrea Doria* bit at an all-Italian
dinner was not the wisest suggestion I ever made. It occurred to me, nevertheless, because when one is putting a
show together pre-existing comedy routines or monologues
that have some relation to the subject matter at hand are
often the first straws for which one clutches. If one were
booking attractions for a football banquet, for example, it
would be natural to ask Andy Griffith to do his famous
football monologue, to ask Don Adams if he would do his
funny routine about football cheers, or to ask Tim Conway if
he would perform his marvelous comedy interview in which
he plays a harebrained road manager for a professional
football team.

In this case my reasoning was simple: It's an Italian
dinner; let's see, who do I know who does an Italian routine?

The banquet was held in the large ballroom of the then-
new and glamorous Beverly Hilton Hotel in Beverly Hills,
California. As I mingled with the crowd during the cocktail
hour, I began to pick up comments that indicated there
might be some confusion about the evening. A number of
people were overheard to ask just who Harry Warren was,
and two or three who knew him fairly well still seemed
puzzled that he'd been chosen to be the guest of honor at an
Italian dinner; they thought he was Jewish.

Eventually the audience assumed dinner places and the
waiters began to serve a sumptuous meal. The first indication that the evening had already taken a peculiar turn was
when it suddenly occurred to me that the dinner serenade I
had been listening to for perhaps half an hour consisted, not
of Harry Warren's music, but of my own.

During the orchestra's first intermission I excused myself
from the head table and sauntered over to Gus, who was just
stepping off the bandstand.

"Thanks a million for playing my tunes, man," I said, "but do you plan to play anything by Harry Warren?"

"Well," he said, "not during the dinner hour. I just brought charts of those twelve songs of yours that we did in the new album. To tell you the truth, I didn't give the thing much thought."

Bivona had indeed recorded a dozen of my songs a few weeks earlier, the arrangements having been done by Henry Mancini and Skip Martin, an arranger for the Les Brown orchestra. Gus and I both assumed, of course, that during the formal entertainment later in the evening heavy emphasis would be put on Warren's music. I returned to the head table, and for the next-forty-five minutes or so continued to enjoy the orchestra's melodious and spirited renditions of my own compositions. The exclusive playing of them must, I suppose, have greatly puzzled Harry Warren, who had been assured that every part of the evening's festivities was intended as a tribute to him that was not only well deserved but for which the poor man had been waiting during some thirty years of general obscurity.

At last the dinner had been served, the waiters had removed the dishes, and it was time to get to the program itself.

When one serves as a master of ceremonies for an affair of this sort, one is provided with cards on which are typed introductions to the various program participants. The order in which the various ladies and gentlemen appear, either to speak or to entertain, is predetermined; the introductions therefore are rendered in the appropriate order. The first gentleman I was called upon to introduce was a Catholic priest. His name escapes me, but he was a pastor at a local church, perhaps the one attended by Mr. Warren, who—contrary to common assumption, even in the music business—was not Jewish but Italian Catholic.

The priest was seated about a dozen chairs to my left, and when I introduced him I naturally assumed that he would take over my microphone at the center of the head table, offer the customary brief invocation, and return to his seat. To this day I haven't the slightest idea why he kept on walking when he reached the podium. He did not stop until, a good two minutes later, he reached a microphone at the far side of the room—out in right field, so to speak—in front of the orchestra, on a small dance floor. Two thousand pairs of eyes followed his long and peculiar journey through the room, which he accomplished by curving around tables, bumping a shoulder or two, and all in all having a bit of difficulty wending his way to the distant mike. Perhaps the good father had had a drink or two.

Eventually he reached it and, one assumes, muttered a suitable prayer. I say "assumes," because the microphone was not turned on, nor is there any reason why it should have been; the audio engineer had expected that the priest would speak into the mike designated for his use. No one in the room, with the possible exception of a few people standing very close to him, will ever know what he said. There would be no evidence that he said anything at all except that his lips were observed to move. His prayer made such a faint impression that I would not be surprised to learn that God himself, no doubt being otherwise occupied at the time, overlooked it.

And, of course, after the pastor had finished his mumbled remarks, all guests—still standing respectfully—had then to wait while he retraced his long, rambling course back to his chair. A number of witty comments occurred to me, but I held my tongue.

When the priest had returned to his starting place, I made the traditional announcement, "And now, ladies and gentlemen, the national anthem." At this point dazzling spotlights, properly enough, focused on an American flag behind the dais down to my right. As it happened, a short, thin gentleman named Ned Washington, himself the lyricist of a number of fine popular songs over the years, was standing directly in front of the flag. Washington had no idea, however, that Old Glory was behind him. All he knew was that he alone, out of two thousand people, was suddenly illuminated by two of the brightest spotlights he had ever seen. His face, as he tried to fathom why this might be so, was a study. He blinked, smiled, looked from side to side in embarrassment, frowned, looked at me, raised his eyebrows, and blinked once more into the lights. Most of us, of course, were singing, but a number of people, observing Washington's puzzlement, blew a few notes, and there was a bit of elbowing and giggling, I regret to say, during the singing of the anthem.

Pat Harrington has recalled, "I was next to Ned and also partly blinded by the spot on the flag. I estimate the flag and stand at five-feet-three-inches, and Ned is about five-feet-five-inches, so he covered it completely. He hadn't been paying attention to the announcements and just stood up perfunctorily when everyone else did. When the spot hit the flag—or him—he froze, thinking he had been singled out for some momentary praise. When he heard the first words of the anthem coming up from the crowd, he side-mouthed to me, 'I didn't write this.'"

After the anthem I formally welcomed the audience and opened the evening with a few jokes.

Another tip-off that things were not going to go well came after I had introduced the first of several civic dignitaries representing, respectively, the county and city of Los Angeles and the state of California. Two of these gentlemen, in fulsomely praising Mr. Warren, and asserting the enormous respect in which he was held by millions of Californians, referred to him quite distinctly as Harry Warner.

The first time this happened the audience gasped, then laughed. I leaped to my feet, stepped briefly to the microphone, and said, "No, no, Mr. Simpkins. The dinner for Harry Warner is taking place in the ballroom on the *other* side of the lobby."

This saved the moment, in a sense, although I'm sure it did not relieve the speaker's embarrassment. It seemed to put him, in fact, in something of a panic, so that a moment or two later he concluded his remarks by saying, "And therefore it gives me great pleasure indeed to present this handsome plaque, from the people of Los Angeles and the mayor personally, to that great American composer Harry Warner."

It was the coliseum roar of laughter that greeted the second gaffe that probably unsettled the nerves of the following speaker. I can think of no other explanation as to why he would get up and commit exactly the same offense, but he did.

It was then time to introduce the first entertainer of the evening, a young gentleman of whom I had never heard before, nor since. His name was Joe Vina. I said something to the effect that it was remarkable how many of America's greatest singers over the years were Italian and that I had every confidence that young Joe Vina was going to join the distinguished company of Frank Sinatra, Dean Martin, Enrico Caruso, Perry Como, Russ Columbo, et al.

Just as I was about to call for the usual "nice big hand" for Vina, my eyes drifted to the orchestra. Far from being on the qui vive, instruments poised, the musicians were lounging about in their chairs. Most of them were not holding instruments at all, and were clearly in a state of non-attention. While I had no idea what the explanation of this mysterious circumstance might be, neither did I have the luxury of speculating about it, so I simply introduced Vina. He promptly ran out, smiled broadly, waited until the applause died down, spread his arms wide as if he were about to leap off a rocky cliff on the west coast of Mexico, and then—believe it or not—just stood there with his mouth open, not making a sound.

Two thousand people stared at this puzzling spectacle for a few seconds. My eyes went again to Bivona and his orchestra, none of whom yet gave any indication that they were expected to accompany Mr. Vina. In an instant I solved the mystery and rose to my feet.

"Joe," I said, "by the fact that the orchestra hasn't snapped to attention may I assume that you had planned to do a record-synch?"

"Yes, Mr. Allen," he called out gratefully. "They're supposed to play my record now."

"Well, thank you, Joe," I said. "I guess whoever the engineer is now knows what he's supposed to do, so don't you worry about a thing, Joe. We're all with you, and I'm sure we'll enjoy hearing your recording, whatever it turns out to be. We'll also be impressed, I'm sure, by your singing live right along with it, if that's part of your plan."

Inasmuch as I had already made it clear that we were gathered for the purpose of honoring Harry Warren and his truly incredible contributions to American music, it was naturally assumed that whatever number Vina had recorded was one written by Harry. No such luck, of course. The record finally started—much too loud, as I recall. Vina had a bit of trouble synchronizing his motions with it, but finally he and the record were on the same track. The number had a faintly Italian flavor, as I recall, but naturally fell strangely on the ears of Harry Warren, who no doubt also had assumed that Vina was there to accord him the honor of performing one of *his* songs.

After Vina had retired from the stage-dance floor, I introduced a young lady named Pat Healy who, it was anticipated, would regale us with not one, but a medley of songs by Harry Warren. The spotlight illuminated the location where it was reasonable to look for Miss Healy, but she did not appear. I jumped up again to the dais mike and began a verbal search for the missing singer. The light roamed around a bit while again Bivona and the orchestra sat with the same degree of interest and curiosity as the audience, not preparing to play their instruments but simply craning their necks to locate Miss Healy. She was finally found, oddly enough, lost in thought, seated at a nearby table, from which dreamily—and quite unsteadily—she arose and moved to the microphone.

I never had the pleasure of getting to know Miss Healy well, so to this day I do not know whether she had a few drinks too many or whether she simply had one of those loose, off-the-cuff personalities that, a few years later, were to become associated with the hippie demeanor.

"Oh, wow," she said, running a hand through her already disordered hair. "I'm not really dressed for the occasion and I'm sorry to say I-I—haven't prepared a particular song. In fact, I don't know what to sing at *all.*"

Two thousand jaws dropped.

I looked at Harry Warren and groaned inwardly.

"Please, God," I said to myself, "whatever the hell she sings let it be something written by this great composer."

"Well," Miss Healy continued, "I mean, I didn't bring any arrangements with me—as a matter of fact, I don't *have* any arrangements of anything written by Mr. Warren, so maybe the piano player and drummer and I can, you know, just *fake* a little something here, to pay our respects to Harry—er—Warren."

Miss Healy's approach might have been defensible if she had not the slightest warning that she was about to be called upon, but to my knowledge she had had a good many days' warning.

"What would you folks like to hear?" she said, not very wisely.

I felt like shouting, "Ella Fitzgerald" but bit my tongue.

Somebody called out, "How about 'Lullaby of Broadway'?" one of Warren's great standards.

"All right," she said, at which she turned to the drummer and indicated, by languidly waving her hand, at what tempo she wanted to do the number.

As anyone over twenty will know, "Lullaby of Broadway" is one of the best up-tempo numbers ever written, very much on a par with the best of Gershwin, Porter, or Berlin. It is peppy, original, harmonically complex, and yet eminently singable. Nevertheless, although you may find it hard to believe, Miss Healy indicated to the drummer and pianist a tempo that would have been more suitable for "Someone to Watch Over Me." Perhaps the word *lullaby* had confused her.

The musicians had no alternative but to play an introduction in her snaillike tempo. She sang—not precisely on key, either—"Come..on...along...and...listen...tooo...the ...lull...ah...by...of...Broad...way."

Mercifully, considering possible alternatives, she proceeded at once to forget the rest of the lyric and then said, "Oh, God, I forget the words. Mr. Warren, can you ever *forgive* me?"

We all know the answer to that question.

"God," she said, "I'm so sorry. This is really embarrassing. I'll tell you what—I'll make up for it, Mr. Warren, by doing *another* of your great songs. This is one my *mother* used to sing to me. Actually my mother should be here tonight, because she was a lot better singer than I am. She was really *great,* my mother was. Let's see now...what was it I was going to sing, anyway? Harry Warren, please *help* me!"

By this time the audience had lost control and was laughing. It was not purposely a cruel laughter and was not really directed at Miss Healy herself. The object of the hilarity was simply the astounding incongruity of the situation. On the one hand was one of America's greatest composers; on the other, incredible, long-playing chaos that was supposed to have been a tribute to him.

I stepped to the dais microphone and said, "Well, Miss Healy, just relax. Perhaps a little later in the evening the full lyrics to some Harry Warren songs will occur to you."

She left the floor and, I would not be surprised to learn, show business.

I felt that since the audience was already laughing hysterically, this might be a suitable time to introduce Pat Harrington and Bill Dana.

"Ladies and gentlemen," I said, "we are very honored to have with us tonight a gentleman who is the cultural attache to the United States from the Italian government. He has recently come here from Rome, and I know that you will want to hear his comments on this marvelous evening staged under the auspices of UNICO.

At this point Pat and Bill launched into the *Andrea Doria* routine.

They had gotten about to the point where they talked about the crew abandoning ship first when, far down to the left side of the dais, perhaps a dozen seats or so away from the lectern, a short, dark-complexioned man suddenly stood up and began walking toward us, face red with fury and brows knotted in a fierce scowl.

During the five or six seconds before he reached the lectern my mental computer began to range over a number of possible explanations for the intrusion. Did he perhaps wish to announce a medical emergency? Could it be that— but at this point the man stomped angrily past us, muttering furiously under his breath in what, as I recall, was half-Italian and half-English. The only phrase I remember clearly was "You think-a it's-a funny, eh?"

Continuing his rightward progress he approached a middle-aged woman seated far down to the other side, grabbed her by the wrist, pulled her to her feet, and, one assumes, said to her, "We're getting the hell out of here right now."

By this time Pat and Bill had, understandably, fallen into stupefied silence. The three of us joined the audience in simply staring at this peculiar demonstration, which now continued as the man and woman—he still furious, she looking puzzled and embarrassed—came back toward us. I thought that perhaps this time he might explain to us what was going on.

No such luck.

Pat Harrington recalls, "The guy stopped on the way back—with wife in tow—shouldered in between Bill and me and said, 'This is not funny. People died, men were killed. This was a bad thing and you should not laugh.' He left, and when he got perhaps twenty feet away—still pulling his wife—Bill said, 'Boy, you know, you give a guy one line— one small line—and he thinks he's the whole act.'"

It got a laugh. I, of course, was frozen; the *Doria* was my piece, and for it to provoke this kind of reaction meant an unpardonable lack of sensibility on my part.

The intruder now continued off to the left and then through a dozen or so tables, whose puzzled occupants stared at him open-mouthed.

The single oddest event in this whole crazy sequence occurred now. The lighting man was responsible for it. Apparently, observing from his distant perch at the other end of the great hall that three popular television comedians named Dana, Harrington and Allen were at the lectern, he must have assumed that the stranger and his woman companion were simply part of the act. Accordingly he had hit the man with a brilliant spotlight almost as soon as he had started to walk, and he and his assistant continued to illuminate the two strangers, with separate spots, as they departed. This left Bill, Pat and me in relative darkness, a factor for which we were at the moment profoundly grateful.

While the audience's attention was still focused on the man and his hapless wife I leaned over to one of the UNICO executives at the dais and said, "Who the hell were those people?"

"I'm sorry to tell you," the man said, "that he is what you said Bill Dana was. He's connected with the Italian Embassy—either here or in Washington, I'm not sure which."

The mystery about the man's anger was thereby explained. Although jokes about the *Andrea Doria* were funny to Americans, even those of Italian descent, to a representative of the Italian government the humor was not so readily apparent, particularly since some of the funniest lines dealt with the cowardice of a few of the ship's crew.

It was, of course, out of the question for Bill and Pat to continue with the routine. Bill turned to me—speaking now without an accent—and said, "Steve, Pat and I would like to thank you very much for getting us into this thing tonight. Believe me, we'll remember this for a *long* time."

In a daze myself, I rose, thanked the fellows for being "good sports," whatever that meant, and explained, in case there were any other native Italians in the room, that there had been no intention to malign the Italian people nor to transgress the bounds of good taste in any way.

The next of several performers on the program—not a single one of them celebrities, by the way—where were Frank Sinatra, Dean Martin and Vic Damone?—was a then young chap named Johnny Holiday. He is a fine singer, but I do think it would have been more appropriate if the dais had been graced by Tony Bennett or Perry Como, not to mention an Italian comedian or two. But the singers present were all largely unknown to the public and mostly non-Italians.

As for Mr. Holiday, he at least did a Harry Warren song— "I Only Have Eyes For You"—with the assistance of Gus Bivona and the orchestra. Few in the audience had eyes or ears for Johnny's fine performance, however, for the reason that the entire room was in noisy consternation over the dramatic walkout of the Italian diplomat and his wife.

A sotto-voce explanation of the incident started out from the dais, and as of five or six minutes later had reached the back of the room. This was accompanied, of course, by a rushing wave of whispers, hoarse cries, laughter and catcalls. At any given moment hundreds of people were saying, "Who *was* that? What the hell's going on?" while those who had already absorbed the news were explaining the situation.

Frequently, when audiences get a little out of hand, the master of ceremonies takes over the microphone and either pleasantly or sharply calls for order. In this case I couldn't do that, since Holiday was singing, even though both music and lyrics were totally drowned out, from start to finish.

At staggeringly long last, the evening drew to a close. The President of UNICO himself stepped to the lectern to make a presentation of the Italian-American group's most prestigious honor, called the Columbus Award. In presenting it the gentleman said, "It gives me great pleasure to present this handsome plaque to Harry Warner—er, *Warren*—because we are very proud of what he has accomplished in the world of music. And therefore, on behalf of UNICO, I present him the Columbus Award. Although it's not Columbus Day now, it will be next year."

More hysterical laughter.

I wouldn't be surprised to learn that at least one of the handsome plaques that the guest of honor received that night is inscribed in bronze to Harry Warner.

One more thing: A couple of weeks later Gus Bivona and the members of his orchestra received their checks for playing at the event.

They bounced.

Since *The Steve Allen Show* ran for five seasons, four on NBC and one on ABC, not even a book of formidable dimensions could do justice to the hundreds of individual productions and talented performers involved. But because to many of our readers any scrap of information about a rock performer such as Jerry Lee Lewis will be of great value, I shall merely say that although I'm often publicly described as loathing rock music (a bum rap), the fact remains that an impressive number of rock performers have appeared on my shows over the years. Lewis was certainly one of the more unusual. In the definitive history of today's music—*Rock of Ages* by Ed Ward, Geoffrey Strokes, and Ken Tucker—there is a reference to one instance in which Jerry Lee's path crossed mine:

> His success was sealed with his midsummer stint on *The Steve Allen Show*. Stuck on at the very end, he got five minutes, and he took full advantage of them. Swinging into "Whole Lotta Shakin'," he slowly stood, riding the piano like a madman, kicking the piano stool out of his way so he could get a better purchase on the keyboard. Caught up in the spirit of the moment, Steve Allen threw the stool back at him and then sent a hail of other objects after it. Undaunted, Jerry Lee started playing with his foot. It was scandalous, and it gave Jerry Lee his big break. Recognizing the debut, he later named his son Steve Allen Lewis.

In 1988 I had the pleasure of traveling to Memphis to repeat this scene in the film biography of Jerry Lee's difficult life, *Great Balls of Fire.*

CHAPTER FOURTEEN

More Sunday Night Show: Jack Kerouac & James Dean

As with all my comedy programs, we sometimes turned away from fun and music on the Sunday night show to focus on serious topics.

One of our most interesting noncomic guests was my friend Jack Kerouac, author of *On The Road*, lavishly praised by the first wave of reviewers and then, after it'd become a best-seller, criticized severely. While the novelist wasn't on the level of Hemingway, Faulkner, or Fitzgerald, Jack was no pop-freak literary success either. In *On the Road*, he talked about leading a life free of middle-class values. Kerouac was a spokesman for the so-called "Beat Generation." One of the most beautiful examples of nature-writing I've ever encountered was his account, published I believe in either *Vogue* or *Mademoiselle*, of his several months spent alone in the forests of the Northwest, living in those tall look-out towers from which forest fires are first sighted.

Jack appeared with us, leaning somewhat nervously on our grand piano and simply reading aloud some colorful passages from his novel while I played unobtrusive jazz-piano background. This idea was not specifically created for our program but grew out of a record album Jack and I had then recently recorded as a result of a casual suggestion by *New*

York Times critic Gilbert Millstein, who had favorably reviewed *On The Road*.

Millstein believed that the book could be compared to
Hemingway's examination of the "Lost Generation" in *The
Sun Also Rises*. Like others who met Jack, Gilbert felt that
Kerouac's personality was an appealing combination of
visionary and worldling:

> There was a sort of uninformed innocence about him, as
> when he wrote a friend, 'I am an awful storyteller, a writer
> in the great French narrative tradition, not a spokesman
> for a million hoods.' His voice turned out to have a
> childlike timbre to it, oddly at variance with the regularity
> and physical strength of his features, and it was also a
> nervous and compelling voice.

It occurred to Millstein that since the combination of
poetry and jazz had been successful in small San Francisco
clubs, the trick might also be turned in New York. He got in
touch with Max Gordon, owner of the Village Vanguard,
who was receptive to the suggestion and engaged Kerouac
for a week during late December. I went down to the
Vanguard to see him and immediately felt that his poetry
should have musical accompaniment. When I mentioned
this to Millstein, he asked whether I would be willing to
provide the accompaniment myself, for the second show that
evening. Jack was agreeable, so when he went on again about
an hour later, he introduced me. I went to the piano and,
playing as softly as I could, laced a few jazz licks and chords
in and around his words, in effect "scoring" them rather
than simply playing jazz as an unrelated background color.
Also present was a friend named Bob Thiele, producer for
Dot Records at the time. He suggested that Jack and I repeat
our performance for posterity. Jack later described the
recording session as follows:

> I came up to New York from Florida for the date, which
> was arranged by mail, and went into the studio to meet

Steve at 11:00 p.m. He was there. I was carrying a huge suitcaseful of untyped manuscripts of prose and poetry. I said, 'What'll I read?' He said, 'Anything you want.' He sat down and started to stroke chords on the piano. They were pretty. I reached into my suitcase as if blindfolded and picked out something and showed it to Steve, who glanced at it briefly and said, 'Okay.' He started to play the piano, making a sign to the engineer. They turned on the tape. I started to read. Between cuts I kept giving Steve some of my pint of Thunderbird, which he drank with a charitable gaiety. He was nice. We finished the session in an hour. The engineers came out and said, 'Great, that was a great first take.' I said, 'It's the only take.' Steve said, 'That's right,' and we all packed up and went home.

This agrees with my own recollection except for the minor detail that Jack's suitcase was more of the under-the-seat variety and looked as if it might have been picked up at an Army-Navy store. It was indeed full of a jumble of papers, almost all handwritten by Jack, some on long rolls rather than separate pages. Since I tend to doze off after even one glass of beer, I do not drink while working; but in this case I accepted the cheap wine simply so as not to make Jack feel uncomfortable about drinking alone.

Later, after I got to know him better, I realized that he wouldn't have been in the least embarrassed had I declined his offer. He had, in fact, a serious drinking problem.

Some months thereafter, just before he appeared on my TV show, Jack came up to our apartment for dinner, arriving at about 5:30 in the afternoon. When asked if he wished anything to drink before dinner, he said, "Do you have any brandy?" I produced a bottle and a glass, setting them on the coffee table in front of him. He had several drinks of brandy before, during, and after dinner, and by midnight had finished the whole bottle, our total supply of the moment. As I recall he then switched to something else—perhaps scotch—and continued to drink.

The incredible thing is that the astounding amount of alcohol he'd consumed seemed to have practically no visible effect on him. His normal manner of speaking was soft, loose, and rather musicianlike anyway. But his mind raced on at a great pace, as did mine, as the two of us talked for hours. I learned about the gifted French writer Celine that night. Kerouac said that Celine had had a powerful effect on his own work; I thereafter read some of that author's work and could see why Jack had admired it.

Some time after midnight I began yawning and finally was quite prepared—despite Jack's boyish charm—to call it a day and have him go home. Jayne, too, although she thought him amusing, had to work the following day so she did what she could, with casual yawns and references to clocks, to tactfully suggest that the evening might profitably be considered at an end. But Jack refused to acknowledge such hints, and our conversation rambled on into the night. And he continued to drink. Finally at about 2:30 a.m., I said, "Man, it's been the kick of all time, but I'm really wiped out."

"I'm not goin' home," he said. "Oh, don't worry, I'll split, but I ain't goin' home: I'll find somebody else who's up. Can I use your phone?"

He made several calls, finally found someone willing to take him in, and left shortly after three a.m.

After the album was released, it attracted a certain notoriety because Randy Wood, the president of Dot, suddenly called a halt to both its pressing and continued distribution, explaining that certain passages were "in bad taste," several lines "offensive," and that he would not permit his children to listen to it. His record company, Wood added, would never distribute a product that wasn't clean family entertainment.

Wood's vice-president, Bob Thiele, who had commissioned the album, was naturally surprised by Randy's comments. Bob agreed that some of Jack's poetry was too sophisticated for the ears of small children but pointed out that such great poets as Walt Whitman and e.e. cummings, too, had written passages that could be similarly described. Millstein, who'd written the liner notes for the album, said that if Wood intended to set the standards of his record company according to the taste of his own children—or those of any children—he was afraid that the standards of the record industry might fall to an even lower level than they already had. Millstein also bristled at the suggestion that there was something tasteless about his own participation in the project, adding, "I am not accustomed to writing liner notes in defense of pornography."

By the standards of the 1980s and 1990s, even Kerouac's blunter lines seem very tame indeed, so greatly has our world changed in the last thirty years.

The last time I ever saw Jack was in Hollywood sometime in, I think, 1961. I can't remember what it was that had brought us together, but we were saying good-bye to each other on the street late at night, and I told him sincerely that I hoped to see him soon. We walked our separate ways and then I heard his voice distantly calling my name. I turned and saw him now almost a block away. When he could see that he had my attention, he twisted his mouth into an imitation of comedian Dayton Allen, of our show's cast, pointed one finger to the sky, and called out, "Whyyyyy *not*?!!!"

I laughed, waved and walked away smiling, not knowing I would never see Jack again. He would die young not long thereafter.

The nation was shocked by another death, that of the brilliant young actor, James Dean several weeks after the Sunday program started. I at once announced plans to devote a segment of one show to an analysis of the Dean phenomenon. For this project we made arrangements with Warner Brothers to televise a clip from one of Dean's pictures. We also got in touch with Dean's aunt and uncle in his hometown Fairmount, Indiana, to book them for an interview. Just when we were all set to go, we received a call from a publicity man at Warner's.

"I'm terribly sorry," he said, "but we can't deliver that film clip to you. Somebody higher up has just taken the thing out of my hands."

"Where is the clip going?" we asked.

"To Ed Sullivan," the man from Warner's said.

Then we learned that the people in Fairmount had also been grabbed from under our noses. I suppose that from Ed's viewpoint this was simply a matter of scooping the competition. But as a performer, not a newspaperman, I didn't see it that way. It seemed unethical; I complained, loudly, and, I now realize, somewhat naively. Within twenty-four hours I was surprised to discover that the argument was headline news across the nation. Unfortunately, because there were charges and countercharges almost immediately, the argument became muddled. I wanted to forget the whole thing, but the papers had tacked the word feud to the exchanges between Ed and myself, and they kept blowing on the coals as long as it would sell copies.

Lord knows I have no desire to rehash the issue at this late date. Ed and I had an argument but no feud. It was just another example of the media getting involved and blowing things out of proportion. And to this day there are people who say the whole thing was a publicity stunt.

In any event, we still proceeded with our James Dean feature, even without the film clip. I traveled alone to Fairmount and conducted interviews with Dean's friends and family. The show was well-received and we got many laudatory letters from the James Dean fans who watched the tribute.

CHAPTER FIFTEEN

The Show Moves West

The Sunday show remained in its 8 p.m. position for three productive years. The critics were even kinder than the public; there was very little negative commentary. Every few weeks our show got a higher rating than Ed Sullivan's. Since I hadn't anticipated doing that at all, the experience was gratifying. One critic's account of the so-called ratings battle said that during the first season, although Sullivan started out with "a healthy lead, as the year went on Allen whittled down the advantage until the race was virtually a tie." This was a tremendous improvement for NBC, which, noted Harry Castleman and Walter J. Podrazik in their book *Watching TV*, "for several seasons had been decimated on Sunday night running its moribund comedy-variety hour."

During the second season of our competition, *both* Ed and I ran into serious rating difficulties because ABC, the then-upstart network, had introduced *Maverick*, an entertaining western with a comic factor which starred on alternate weeks James Garner and Jack Kelly, as Bret and Bart Maverick respectively. This program shortly became so popular that, as I recall, there were certain Sunday nights when *Maverick* had a higher rating than Ed's and mine together.

Neither CBS nor NBC did the incredibly stupid thing networks often do when they find that an obviously high-quality program is getting only modest ratings. The usual solution is to cancel the program, its artistic merits notwithstanding. A more rational alternative is to move the program to another night or time slot where its rating fate might be better. NBC did just this in taking our program, in the fall of 1959, out of the Sunday night line-up and putting it into a spot on Monday at 10 p.m. This slot had long been a ratings graveyard, but we were grateful that the network had not simply scrapped our project.

At this point we made another change: the show moved west, to Hollywood. My own reason for the westward move was entirely personal. I have three wonderful sons by my first marriage who lived most of the year with their mother in California; I wanted to enjoy them every few days rather than every few weeks or months.

During the remainder of the season, after the program finally ended, while I appeared frequently on television as a guest on other people's shows, I was for the first time in a good many years not involved with a regular series of my own. The new luxury of time afforded me the opportunity to do concert appearances, as well as song and book writing.

In 1961, the year following our removal from NBC's line-up, the program moved over to ABC, thanks largely to Dan Melnick. Dan had worked for me as cue-card holder way back in 1951 but in the ten ensuing years had moved up to become one of the top programming executives of ABC and president of one of that network's divisions.

I suppose ABC's reasoning was something like NBC's had been earlier. Putting me opposite Ed Sullivan had worked out well, but ABC now set our program into an hour that had been low-rated for quite a long time: Wednesday nights at 8 p.m. It was also our misfortune to again run into my nemesis: The Western. This time it was NBC's juggernaut, *Wagon Train,* which for three previous years had been the second-highest rated program in the country. By 1961, it had climbed to the Number One spot.

Not only was NBC riding high, but CBS's fare in the time slot was also successful. With such competition so firmly entrenched, we naturally opened at the low end of the rating spectrum. Additionally, ABC kept promotion of the show to an almost unprecedented minimum, perhaps reflecting a division of opinion in their programming department about the merits of putting the series on the air in the first place.

Opposing Dan Melnick was a pleasant gentleman who just happened to be his superior. His name was Tom Moore, and he'd come newly to his job as ABC's arbiter of America's taste in television programming from his prior distinguished service as *Chief Executive Officer of the world-famous Forest Lawn Mortuary.*

I am not joking.

Mr. Moore grasped the obvious in recognizing that the rating of our opening show was depressingly low. I think it was something like seven. We crept up another point or two in our second week since word-of-mouth on the first show was favorable. But then came the brain-numbing announcement that the network was going to take the show off after a run of thirteen weeks, even though we had been given a guarantee of twenty-six. This meant that if the program did indeed conclude after half that time, ABC would owe me an enormous amount of money for doing nothing.

When my business manager first told me the news I thought he was kidding.

"No," he said. "It's true. They've already decided to drop the show."

"Do you mean," I said, "that we all just go home today and they pay us off the rest of the twenty-six shows?"

"No," he said. "They want us to do a total of thirteen."

"What about the rest of the guarantee?"

"They don't want to pay us for that."

"I see," I said. "Well then, would you be good enough to remind them that they're contractually obligated to pay us?"

Oddly enough, corporate employers who so casually disregard contractual agreements invariably try, in one way or another, to avoid paying what they're clearly legally and morally obligated to pay. A surprisingly common procedure is to settle for some figure less than contractually called for but large enough to assuage the canceled performer's or producer's wounded sensibilities. Inasmuch as (a) our program was very good, and (b) was increasing its ratings each week by modest increments, I decided to insist on full payment. This, the network, in due course, turned over to me. It wasn't too surprising, however, that quite a few years passed before I was again employed by ABC.

A good deal of television, that visible on the nation's home-viewing screens, is evident to the mass audience. Other aspects of the medium are either totally unrecognized or generally misunderstood. But even within the industry itself not everything is clear at all times to all participants. Consider, for example, the commonplace observation that if a program is rejected by the mass-audience it goes off the air. That seems a simple enough assertion and indeed there are boxcars full of evidence to support it. The general reality of the situation, however, is more complex than it at first appears. The simple fact that a given program has either low or middling ratings by no means necessarily establishes that it has been rejected by the mass audience. This is clear from the many instances of series that ultimately enjoyed fabulous success but which nevertheless had such low ratings in their initial season that they were canceled.

Can the American viewing public be so fickle, or stupid, that in September it consciously rejects a new series and then, only months later, rushes it to Top Ten status? Of course not. Those early weak ratings for such series are the result of the new show's introduction in a difficult position on a network's schedule. Any program that has the misfortune to be telecast at the same time as an already established hit—as we did—will inevitably have rough going initially, simply because a large segment of the audience, in the habit of watching the successful program, does not even notice that there is something new about the competition.

As for the ingredients of our ABC show, I constructed them partly out of pre-existing factors and partly of new material. Louis Nye, Pat Harrington, Gabe Dell, and Dayton Allen participated; we also introduced such then-new faces as Jim Nabors, Tim Conway, and the Smothers Brothers. Conway I had heard about from comedienne Rose Marie who'd just returned from a visit to Cleveland where she'd seen him performing on a local station where he was also serving as a producer. After seeing only about thirty seconds of Tim on videotape, I realized I was watching a very funny fellow and immediately instructed our people to hire him for the new show.

Writer and sometimes-performer Buck Henry worked with us that season. So did a young comic named Don Penny, who gave up the funny business not long after and eventually occupied an office in the White House, that of public speaking advisor to President Gerald Ford. I've always thought there was a nucleus of a situation comedy, perhaps even a Broadway musical, in that bit of historical reality. Today Don is a well-established figure in official Washington.

Bill Dana was our head writer that year, and the team of Arne Sultan and Marvin Worth provided strong creative help. Leonard Stern served ably as comedy director. One of the best sketches of the season was a satire on the then enormously popular dramatic series *Ben Casey*. I played the good doctor, and Joey Foreman, a very reliable and funny actor, appeared as Dr. Zorba (who was portrayed by the venerable Sam Jaffe on the actual *Casey* show). The clever Mitzi McCall was a nurse. Most of the sketch was written by Bill Persky and Sam Denoff. In recent years Bill served as producer on the successful *Kate and Allie* series.

I interpolated a funny visual joke into the sketch which worked wonderfully well. On practically all hospital series and real-life medical documentaries, I'd noticed that a directorial-cliché had been introduced in which the camera moved swiftly behind a gurney as it was rushed down a hospital corridor by anxious doctors, nurses, and other medical personnel. It occurred to me that it would be hysterically funny if two gurneys were seen hustling through two separate halls which, at the point of intersection, would naturally lead to a tremendous crash. In our sketch, Tom Smothers was the patient on one of the rolling beds. Since he was already heavily bandaged, the sight of him badly rattled by the accident was very funny. I stood next to him, as Dr. Casey, shouting, "There's been a terrible accident here! We've got to get this man to a hospital!"

Another of the better sketches on the series was a remarkably realistic takeoff on the then-top-rated *Sing Along With Mitch* program that featured the goateed maestro Mitch Miller. I'd noted that, unlike other conductors, Mitch moved his arms in a remarkably puppet-like, mechanical manner, a bit of physical business easy to imitate and exaggerate. Another comedy component of the sketch was based on the part of Mitch's show where the singers would line the stage in a large horse-shoe pattern, a curve which would be followed by an enormous boom-camera as it moved along the rows of singing faces.

In our version—Pat Harrington, the Smothers Brothers, and Tim Conway were among the stripe-jacketed, straw-hatted vocalists—the camera moved in much too quickly toward their smiling faces, converting the smiles to looks of horror as they perceived, at the last possible moment, that the giant camera was going to run right into them and knock them all down. In a moment a dozen bodies were writhing on the studio floor in apparent pain, having been knocked off their pins by the rolling juggernaut of the camera and its platform. This somehow led to a combination revolution and mutiny during which I, as the mechanical Miller, was chased up the aisle, out of the studio, and towards the ABC parking lot below, where I was finally trapped and apparently beaten to a pulp by an angry mob of singers, ushers, network executives, studio-audience participants, and anybody else who felt like jumping up and joining the melee.

My favorite show of that ABC season was taped, in its entirety, at Jayne's and my home in the Valley. Tim, the Smothers Brothers, Bill Dana, my sons Brian, Steve, David, and Bill, Jayne, a line of bathing beauties doing Esther Williams shtick in our pool, and a number of stuntmen all combined to make it a truly funny show. To demonstrate that we lived in what was then a rural neighborhood—Royal Oaks, California—we had what appeared to be real bare-chested Indians riding on painted ponies around the perimeter of our property, firing rifles and bows-and-arrows in our direction. For our part, we manned rifles and knelt behind our concrete block fence, defending our enclave as bravely as Randolph Scott or Gary Cooper ever held off a band of marauding Indians.

Part of the funniness of the day never got put on camera. First I should explain that (a) because this was a Christmas show we'd invited the children of dozens of people connected with the production to it, (b) a slight drizzle kept most of them indoors, though only after their little feet had picked up a good deal of mud, and (c) to keep them happy we had to ply them with candy, popcorn, and ice cream bars as well as more nourishing fare all day long, a good part of which they promptly smeared on every chair, sofa, and rug in the house.

A few technical taping delays made the day drag on interminably so that by the time we were scheduled to shoot the last segment, in which I, disguised as Santa Claus, took a number of kids on my lap one at a time and ad-libbed with them concerning what they wanted for Christmas, I was in a state of complete physical exhaustion. My condition contributed to making Santa Claus's conversations with the children so disorganized and sideways that at one point four-year-old Bill, who had no idea that I was his father, looked up at me and blurted, "Santa Claus, you're all mixed up!"

By the time the ABC series went off the air, to the great lamentation of critics, our ratings were a good deal higher than they had been initially. It was a pity the network had not allowed us to play out our hand.

CHAPTER SIXTEEN

The Westinghouse Show

In June of 1962, after having done network sketch-comedy work in prime-time for five years, I returned to the talk-and-comedy format in a syndicated ninety-minute program for Westinghouse Broadcasting, producing the show in Hollywood. Ironically, the nightly series, also seen in Canada and Australia, was scheduled opposite the *Tonight* show in a number of U.S. cities.

Once again viewers were watching me from a horizontal position, although this time I didn't have to stay up late to do a live program since the new series was prerecorded on videotape. We did one program a night in front of a studio audience, never stopping for retakes.

Once I'd accepted the offer from Westinghouse, I arranged to hire a creatively gifted friend named Allan Sherman as my producer. Allan—who'd labored in obscurity for years on the CBS-TV *I've Got A Secret* panel show—would, not long after working on this program, achieve instant stardom through the success of his brilliant song parodies such as "Hello Mudda, Hello Fadda," a kid's letter from camp done to the tune of "Dance of the Hours."

During the weeks immediately preceding our first taping, it became apparent, however, that organization and administration were not among Allan's skills. The result almost from the start was something of a backstage shambles. He was still aboard during our first week on the air, but the Westinghouse executives were becoming ever more insistent in their demands that he be replaced. After another few days of defending Allan I unfortunately had to bend to their will, since it was their money and their syndication service. Milt Hoffman was hired in Allan's place.

The new series was similar to the old *Tonight* show but what distinguished it from the original was that it was even wilder and more experimental, relying more heavily on visual, physical comedy and crazy stunts. I was seen nightly in bizarre situations, sometimes athletic in nature, other times downright dangerous. On one program I might clumsily walk a tightrope high above Vine Street and La Mirada Avenue outside the studio. The next night I might drive sixty miles-an-hour into a wall of ice, be attacked by giant tarantulas, or play the piano while swinging in midair from a construction crane high above Vine Street traffic.

Since the writers—chiefly Stan Burns and Mike Marmer—loved putting me into spots that I'd have to ad-lib my way out of, they'd routinely create these strange and sometimes perilous circumstances and then stand at the side of the studio laughing hysterically while I suffered through whatever it was they'd planned.

The staff would come into my office every few days and ask me things like: "Would you object to being shot out of a cannon?" I'd tell them that of course I objected; but somehow they'd order the cannon—or whatever—anyway.

There was very little time for conjecture—or worrying about what could go wrong. When you're doing a nightly comedy show you're too busy creating ninety minutes of new material every day. One evening, though, when silent-screen comedian Harold Lloyd was a guest, he and I discovered that we had something in common: Just before the camera would start to roll for our stunts, we would—quite reasonably—feel afraid of being physically injured. But once we were on-camera somehow our fear would dissipate, and we would obligingly go through with the stunt.

Of course there *were* times when the fear would not go away, and rightly so. The most frightening predicaments, for me at least, were those connected with fire or heights. Once I was to open the show by emerging from a sarcophagus dressed as a mummy, to the accompaniment of spooky music. A few minutes before airtime, Johnny Wilson, our irrepressible floor manager, thought it would be funny to set me on fire, after which I was to run down La Mirada Avenue and jump into an enormous plastic swimming pool that had been erected near the stage door of the theater. My mummy wrappings, accordingly, were somehow treated with a fire retardant substance, except for a few dangling pieces of cloth that hung down behind me like old-fashioned trapdoor long underwear.

At the time this seemed to me at least as amusing and nutty as most of our other death-defying stunts...until we were on the air and I saw Wilson approaching with a flaming torch with which he proposed to set fire to the back of my garments. The moment posed a classic confrontation between the intellect on the one hand and the combination of instinct and emotion on the other. Intellectually I was perfectly willing to submit to being partially ignited, reasoning that it would take only a few seconds to run down the street and leap into the water should anything go wrong. But when I actually saw Wilson sneaking up behind me, smelled the smoke and felt the intense heat of the flames, the instinct of self-preservation told me: "To hell with your agreement—run like a deer from that flame, as would any intelligent animal!"

My concern was obvious to our studio audience, if not to at-home viewers. They howled with laughter as I tried—really tried—to remain motionless long enough for Wilson to ignite the tatters behind me. But I literally could not stop jogging in place like Bugs Bunny in the cartoons, as if I could somehow get off to a faster start if I were already running. When Wilson finally touched his torch to the back of the mummy suit, I raced down the street in genuine fear until I'd thrown myself into the cold water.

In another stunt involving fire, one of my staff people suggested it might be fun if I went across the street to the pool behind the Elaine Apartments and jumped off the diving board into a ring of fire. At first I expressed very little enthusiasm for the idea since I'd seen those daredevil carnival acts where a stunt diver leaped from a high perch into a pool covered with flaming gasoline. Actually, dangerous as this looks, it's apparently safe because the diver's body passes through the flames in less than a second and the enormous splash either dampens the fire totally or at least creates a large area of water that is not covered by flaming gasoline. When I discussed this point, one of the writers said, "Oh, no, we wouldn't expect you to dive into a whole pool that was on fire. There's a guy who has a metal ring which sits an inch or two below the surface of the water. It's got a lot of holes for gas jets, and it's only the gas that's lighted."

Since this meant that the flames could not actually touch me so long as I jumped within the ring and swam under it to safety, I agreed to go through with the stunt. But once again, in the doing, my body's internal wisdom proved to be totally unhooked from my rational processes. When I got out to the end of the diving board, wearing only a pair of trunks and feeling the waves of heat from the flames on my bare skin, I had fearful second thoughts. I suppose some men have become heroes in wartime, and others have been killed performing some courageous act while under hostile fire, partly because they were afraid to reveal their terror to their fellow soldiers. That is somewhat how I felt. The fact that the audience was watching made me feel that I had to go through with the routine purely because I was too embarrassed to back out.

In another fiery trick I felt a strong enough pang of fear that, without realizing it, I muttered a fervent "Oh, Jesus" as the stunt started. Here, I was spread-eagled on the hood of a car, with only loose protective straps around my arms and ankles so that I would not slide off. The car was to be driven at top speed—straight through a wooden fence that had been set afire.

Once again, reason told me that the car's bumper would collapse the fence and the vehicle's speed would carry me through the danger zone in a fraction of a second. But then we were on the air and the driver stepped on the gas. The wheels spun rubber and I looked up at the wall of fire we were approaching at about sixty miles an hour. I was, frankly, petrified. As I'd assumed, I suffered no harm, but again the addition of fire had added an element of fear to the proceedings.

Whether my reaction is purely normal and wisely self-protective I do not know. It may be that my fear of fire is somewhat in excess of the norm because I burned myself once in early childhood; and another time, when I was four and refused to stop fiddling with a book of matches on the table of a restaurant where we were dining, my mother deliberately burned my hand to teach me that playing with matches was dangerous. So I have that fear.

Another perfectly normal fear I have is of extreme height, and many of the show's stunts indeed placed me in such danger. One night we opened with a close shot of me in a tub sudsing up with a soapy sponge and rubbing my back with a long-handled brush. When the camera pulled back, our at-home viewers could see that I was not in a backstage bathroom but suspended on a tiny platform high above Vine Street while busy nighttime traffic passed beneath me.

After several minutes of monologue jokes and ad-libbed comments, I pulled the plug in the tub, which sprayed the water down to the street below.

Another night a guest and I—I can't remember who—played a vigorous game of table tennis while suspended by thin wires high in the air over the same street corner. In one of the nuttiest midair stunts of all, I dangled from a construction crane, addressing our cameras from inside a specially built wrecking ball which—after my opening ex- planatory remarks—was repeatedly dashed against the wall of the Hollywood Ranch Market across the street from our theater.

Oddly enough, one stunt that I suppose should have scared me to death did not. It was actually quite exhilarating. We taped the segment at a small private airport in the Los Angeles area, from which I took off in the old World War I-type biplane that had been made famous in the film *It's a Mad, Mad, Mad, Mad World.* The unusual factor, however, was that I was not seated in the plane but stood on its upper wing. There was a small safety harness, of course, but otherwise there I was. As to why I didn't feel much fear, the chief reason was that in those days I was riding motorcycles. When the possibility of doing the airplane stunt was first discussed, my only question was, "At what speed does the craft take off?" When I was told that it was airborne at fifty or sixty miles an hour, my fear dissipated because I was already used to moving faster than that on my motorcycle.

As the plane took off, Jayne and our son Bill—who was about four at the time—stood mournfully at the side of the airstrip wondering why I was crazy enough to do such a stunt. The staff had dressed me in World War I aviator's gear—putties, riding pants, an old leather jacket, a flowing white silk scarf, and a goofy-looking helmet. The only emotion I was conscious of during the ten-minute flight was annoyance because the wardrobe man had forgotten to fasten the two flaps of the helmet under my chin. As a result of this oversight, I had to keep one hand on my head while airborne to avoid losing not only the hat but my eyeglasses.

There was one other stunt that was extremely frightening, even though it did not involve fire or great height. This one had me squeezing myself into a wooden box filled with about ten small bags of dynamite, which was literally blown up outside on La Mirada Avenue. When the explosives went off, pieces of the box were sent about eighty feet into the air. Even though I was covered by a couple of piano movers' pads, when the box exploded I felt as if I was being simultaneously kicked by about eight people wearing army boots. When I later watched the show on the air, I got nervous again; the powerful explosion shook the whole neighborhood.

Compared to being confronted with the above dangers, some of the routines we did with animals and insects seemed relatively mild. One night I entered a cage filled with bees; on another show I was swarmed over by hundreds of large, vicious red ants; and over the series' three and one half years I was growled at by assorted wild beasts, including a tiger and a bear.

And I shall never forget the night when a luckless animal trainer was suddenly attacked by an enormous alligator right on our stage. I was playing a jazz piano solo just prior to introducing the fellow, who was from a nearby alligator farm. Suddenly I heard a commotion offstage. Glancing over I saw two or three bodies thrashing around, after which one man lay on his back with his right arm firmly gripped in the jaws of the enormous creature. Two of his co-workers immediately came to his rescue, poking the eyes of the animal until it relaxed its jaws just enough for them to stick a block of wood into the maw. When the man's arm was finally worked free, several deep tooth-holes were discovered on its upper part.

I could usually tell when a planned stunt was going to be messy because the producers would come to my dressing room before the show and recommend that I underdress. This meant that at some point in the program my clothes would be ripped off. So as not to be left standing in my Jockey shorts, I would immediately don a pair of tight-fitting swim trunks under whatever other clothing I put on.

One night propmen painstakingly attached scores of tea bags to my clothing, hoisted me aloft, and then dipped me down into an enormous transparent plastic vat of hot water into which stage manager Johnny Wilson had thrown a few lemon halves. After I had steeped a few moments, the audience was invited onstage to partake of a freshly brewed cup of tea. Years later David Letterman would do the same stunt, replacing the tea bags with little packets of Alka-Seltzer. On another occasion I jumped feet first into the plastic tank, which this time was filled with Jell-O, after which some of our crew sprayed me with whipped cream.

James Wolcott once wrote in the *New York Times:*

> Allen had the true spirit of a comic anarchist fluttering like a red flag in his soul. His crackling laugh really did seem torn from all inhibition.

Wolcott was right about that, I suppose; but the reason I laughed so heartily on those old shows was that I was just as amused as anyone else over the wildness and unpredictability of many of the stunts and experiments on our nightly melee.

Maybe the Westinghouse series' popularity had something to do with America's mood. The early '60s were a powerfully emotional time. With 43-year-old Jack Kennedy moving into the White House in 1961, the country was infused with a spirit of youth and vitality. Then the Beatles came over from Britain and began to revolutionize pop music. The satirical Pop Art movement was in full bloom. JFK had his idealized *Camelot,* but he also had the Cuban Missile Crisis. And in 1963 he would be killed. Through all of this, perhaps, our crazy show somehow psychologically filled an audience need.

It was on the Westinghouse series that we quite accidentally created a brand new form of comedy sketch. The basic draft of the scene would be written, in the conventional method, accompanied by scenery, wardrobe and rehearsals. But once in front of an audience I would roam far outside the boundaries of the plot, sometimes even running into the audience and, staying in character, incorporating some of its members into the sketch.

In one of the first instances of this, Louis Nye and I were doing *Mutiny on the Bounty* on a mock-up of a sailing vessel out in the street. Suddenly I raced into the audience and began to shout insane orders in sea lingo to the people seated

there: "And you, sir, you call yourself an able-bodied sea-
man? Why you ought to be Shanghaied to Tokyo, and
Tokyoed to Shanghai! Either you do as ordered or I'll hang
you from the highest yardarm! And those of you seated over
on the starboard side—there are no stars on board tonight,
but tell the boatswain's mate that I have issued an order to
man the women! Ahoy, there; jib the mains'l! Swab your
tonsils! Save your tinsel!"

In one of the wildest examples of this sort, I was doing a
Superman sketch, starring as the mild-mannered reporter
Clark Kent in the newsroom of the *Daily Planet*. I got a
telephone message that Lois Lane (played by singer Molly
Bee) was in danger, so I rushed out onto La Mirada Avenue,
zipped into a phone booth, and attempted to remove my
street clothes so as to be left wearing Superman garb.
Unfortunately, this turned out to be difficult in an actual
phone booth, due chiefly to the limited elbow room and the
fact that I am a tall man. I was able to remove my jacket and
shirt, but the pants were impossible to get off. At that
moment a shopper came out of the nearby Hollywood
Ranch Market, carrying a large grocery bag.

As he passed the booth, I called out, "Hey, chief!"

"Yes?" he said, turning to me.

"I'm having a little trouble changing my clothes here.
Could you give me a hand?"

Believe it or not, the fellow set his grocery bag down on
the ground, came over and helped me pull my pants off,
then nodded, picked up his bag and continued on down the
street.

At that point of the sketch the camera went to a tight
close-up of me doing some joke about my x-ray vision while
an unseen stagehand attached a metal hook to my back. I
was then hoisted into the air—the better to "fly." The
procedure worked pretty well except that the question of my
center-of-gravity had not been given enough forethought so
that when I attempted to come in for a landing I came down
headfirst. This suddenly struck me as so hysterically funny
that I laughed helplessly while I hung suspended about two

feet off the ground and tried to get the damned hook off my back so that I could save Lois, who had been tied to the trunk of a curbside tree.

It was on this nightly series, too, that a routine I'd occasionally done on the original *Tonight* show—taking camera shots of people out on the street—became a more important regular feature. The sidewalk camera, of course, could photograph people who did not know they were being televised. I would sit at my studio desk ad-libbing hopefully witty remarks about the assorted tourists, gawkers, and neighbors who strolled past. The conductor/pianist and members of the orchestra would also watch the studio monitors and ad-lib appropriate musical scoring, which greatly enhanced the funniness of it all.

Since so many of our stunts were performed outdoors, our crew was a constant source of irritation to residents of the area. The police were frequently called, but because of the popularity of our show, they invariably treated us kindly. In all honesty, I could understand the reason for the grumpiness of some of our neighbors. After all, almost every night along La Mirada Avenue we would have, say, a basketball game against a team of striptease dancers, midget car races, motorcycle-gang invasions, and other outlandish stunts. One time, attached to an enormous kite, I tried to loft myself up into the air by running as fast as I could straight into the blast from a giant wind-machine used in films to create the illusion of a hurricane. Unfortunately, I was never able to rise above an altitude of something like eighteen inches.

Finally, a group of sixty-five angry neighborhood residents complained formally to the Los Angeles City Council, citing obstruction hazards—temporarily stored scenery, furniture, cables, floodlights, sandbags, caged animals, ladders, baggage—that blocked the street and impeded access to homes and apartments. A spokeswoman for the complaining group said, "How would you like to go into your backyard and find Steve Allen sitting up in a tree, and a chimpanzee picking blossoms in your flower garden?"

When a newspaperman asked for my response to this

statement, I said, "Can I help it if they happened to send us a chimp that likes flowers? If that lady wants to even up matters, I hereby give her permission to come to my house and climb one of our trees."

The woman was right, of course. I'd been sitting in one of her trees during an out-of-control sketch in which I was dressed as Tarzan with the typical off-the-shoulder leopard-skin and loincloth. What I hadn't known until I later saw the show at home was that when the camera shot a from-the-ground picture it was possible for viewers to see my droopy-drawered white Jockey shorts hanging down below the macho Tarzan loincloth.

On another night our crazy crew and I had a tug-of-war with an elephant which, suddenly losing interest in the fray, rambled off down La Mirada Avenue scaring assorted drivers to death as he loomed into their headlights.

Eventually the nearby residents became more-or-less blasé about our nightly nonsense. Once comedian Gabe Dell and I did a burlesquey take-off on the World War II movie *The Longest Day* in which we converted the street outside the studio into a battleground complete with sandbags, barbed wire, smoke pots, machine gun emplacements, and explosions. As the sketch neared its conclusion, I ordered our troops "over the top," at which we ran across the street like madmen and attacked not a German pillbox but the Hollywood Ranch Market. Rounding the Vine Street corner, Gabe and I shot our way into the produce department, firing blanks at the ceiling, shouting commands, and hurling green peppers stiff-armed as if they were grenades. But the funniest element of the routine was that regular customers in the 24-hour grocery store looked at us only briefly before shrugging and going back to their shopping.

Ad-libbing jokes with the studio audience remained an important part of my work. But one night I ran into a visitor who, like the man who was prepared to kill himself during the *Tonight* show, had absolutely no interest in the comic elements of the program. The young man, apparently in his mid-twenties, told me that he had a gift he wanted to present to me personally.

"All right," I said. "Come on up and bring it with you, whatever it is."

A moment later he stood facing me at center-stage, at which point he carefully withdrew an egg from the pocket of his jacket. I spent a moment or two making joking references to his generosity, the oddity of the gift he had chosen, and so forth. But when we then cut to a commercial, the man leaned in close and whispered in my ear, "I'm not kidding— this isn't a regular egg. I emptied it out and filled it with nitroglycerine."

I gave the young fellow careful study and could see that his eyes were blank, level, and noncomic. Whether the eggshell was indeed full of nitroglycerine or the man was insane—or both—I had no way of knowing. Oddly enough, at such times I often am not conscious of fear, though I did realize that the situation required careful handling. Speaking softly to him so that the audience could not hear, I led the man to the side of the stage and spoke to some of our staff people standing there.

"Guys," I said calmly, "this gentleman says he has an egg here with explosives in it—nitroglycerine. You might want to take him outside the theater and check that out."

Our crew did indeed take the man out of the theater, very gingerly. When the show was over he was gone—no joke intended.

Obviously you can never predict what strange situations you'll run into winging it with an audience.

Sometimes local hosts or hostesses of certain telecast public events can be quite insistent that you spend time with them socially. The worst experience of this sort happened when we took the Westinghouse show to Minneapolis-St. Paul for five days of broadcasting during the famous annual St. Paul Winter Carnival. Before we arrived, one local socialite was kind enough to extend an invitation to a midday cocktail party. After checking our production schedule for that day and finding it hopelessly busy, I instructed a staff member to thank the woman profusely but to explain, in detail, why it was impossible for me to have the pleasure of joining her and her guests.

A few days later, while we were still in Los Angeles, somewhat more pressure was applied. The woman, apparently of some standing in Twin Cities society, sent back a message that made her invitation seem almost like a Command Performance.

Again I told our production people to outline—this time by letter—the reasons it was not possible for me to attend the party. One was that we were scheduled to pretape a segment of our show from a small lake nearby during that afternoon. The plan was for me to don a wet suit and breathing apparatus and plunge through a hole in the ice into the water below.

By the time the day came I had quite forgotten about the invitation. I changed out of my own clothing and into a wet suit at some sort of Elks or American Legion lodge close to the lake. The vice president in charge of acquiring wet suits had unfortunately neglected to get the proper size. The suit in question was so short that I literally had to walk stooped-over since it was impossible to straighten up while wearing it. But under the heading of "the show must go on," I submitted to this combination of discomfort and pain, did a brief monologue at the edge of the ice, jumped into the water, got a few laughs, and finished taping the routine.

Since I naturally didn't want my only pair of glasses to accidentally get knocked off and fall to the bottom of the frozen lake, I had taken them off. When I clambered out of the water and flopped down on the ice, two men helped me to my feet and directed me to a small van. In a few seconds I was inside the vehicle, on its floor—soaking wet and unfortunately still without my glasses—and bumping along an ice-rutted road to what I assumed was the lodge where I was supposed to get out of the painfully tight wet suit and back into my own clothes. To my surprise the van did not stop at the lodge but made a right turn and bounced off over deep, frozen ruts through a nearby stand of trees. Without my glasses I wasn't sure where we were going and for a few minutes didn't give the matter much thought, assuming that someone had taken my clothes to a more comfortable spot so that I could make the change there.

A moment later the van stopped. As I climbed out the side door I asked one of my kidnappers where we were. "Oh," he said, "this is Mrs. _____'s house. You're going to her party."

"The hell I am," I replied.

The faces of several guests floated past as I reluctantly splashed and sloshed into the house, still bent over like Igor, Dr. Frankenstein's helper, and was shown up a staircase to a second-story bedroom and bathroom. Neither of my abductors, it developed, had brought my glasses. In a moment they were gone. I struggled uncomfortably out of the wet suit and in a few minutes stood in the locked bathroom—completely naked, without glasses, without a stitch of clothing to put on, and of course without the slightest possibility of going downstairs, even if I had wanted to.

For quite a long time—perhaps twenty minutes—I heard no signs of life except the distant chatter of cocktail party conversation on the lower floor. Eventually an unidentified male voice called through the door, "How are you doing in there?"

"I'm sitting here naked," I answered, "because I have no clothes to put on. Nor do I have my eyeglasses."

"Oh," was the response, after which silence.

Another twenty minutes passed, and then one of the men from our show—God knows how he found out where I was—came upstairs carrying my clothes.

"How the hell did you get here?" he asked. "We've been looking all over for you."

"I got here," I explained, "because the idiot woman

refused to take no for an answer and had me literally kidnapped. Unfortunately for her purposes nobody brought my clothing, so I've been unable to mingle with her guests."

I then put on my clothes, was shortly thereafter reunited with my eyeglasses, walked downstairs, and without a word to the bystanders, all of whom looked guilty and embarrassed, walked straight out the front door, got into a car, and was driven back to continue taping the television show.

Some of the wacky characters who used to frequent the *Tonight* show also appeared on the Westinghouse series. There was Professor Voss, naked to the waist except for a strange necklace made of dried ears of corn, and our old New York friend Joe Interleggi, still picking up wooden tables with his teeth and whirling them around the stage (see Chapter 8). But a new oddball had been added to our midst.

An eccentric gentleman named Gypsy Boots bounded onstage like a madman every time he appeared. He spoke about three times louder and faster than was necessary and seemed to be bursting with excess energy.

There was invariably some rationale, however flimsy, for his visits. He wanted to convince me of the merits of drinking raw carrot juice, or of a diet consisting largely of mulberry seeds and crumbled linoleum, or whatever. Physically, he was a remarkable specimen. Gypsy was—is—about twenty years older than he looks. And he was a hippie before the word was ever invented in that he wore a beard, sandals, odd attire, ate a vegetarian diet, and chose not to conform to any number of society's social customs.

He would run onstage carrying a food blender, plug it in, jam it with carrots complete with the greens, whole apples, oranges, nuts, birdseed—froth it up into a foaming brew, drink deeply of it himself, and force me to do the same.

Gypsy also did crazy exercises, shouted slightly off-center pithy sayings, and in general turned the studio into a madhouse, to the accompaniment of numerous rimshots, cymbal crashes and chase music played by Don Trenner and his accomplices, who included the brilliant trombonist,

Frank Rosolino, guitar-player Herb Ellis and sometimes bassist Ray Brown.

I think Gypsy appeared only on our show—ours was probably the only one nutty enough to make him feel at home. Also, he was on with us so often that I guess the hosts of other talk shows or comedy programs assumed he was somehow my property, though I wouldn't have cared who else booked him.

Incidentally, from time to time Gypsy Boots can still be seen on television football games that originate in Los Angeles. The cameras like to pan the crowds to pick up shots of people with weird-looking hats, young women with bulging sweaters, or whatever. I occasionally see Gypsy's face at such moments.

Another character who appeared with us was the then-unknown Frank Zappa, the rock singer, although he never came on to perform music. One time I asked him what he was prepared to do. When he signaled for the curtains to open, an old automobile became visible. Then Zappa gestured to the orchestra to give him a little background music. At that point he and a couple of people he'd brought with him began attacking the car with sledgehammers. Within about five minutes they'd broken all the windows, crumpled the fenders, hood and doors, and reduced the car to a pile of junk.

Did the audience consider this entertainment? Your guess is as good as mine. Apparently they did. They laughed, applauded, jumped around to the rhythm of the music.... As they say—go figga.

As on my other shows, not all the bits were physically wild. Sometimes I would simply be given a shoeshine, a haircut, a shave, or a shampoo onstage. Twice a registered nurse from the Red Cross appeared and withdrew a pint of blood from my arm. Surprisingly, although I'm generally a shy person socially, I have no qualms about doing things in front of millions of people that other entertainers might feel too guarded or embarrassed to try.

In the instance of donating blood, as in a few others, I had more in mind than just getting laughs. Many people, I was aware, would've been willing to contribute blood to the Red Cross or other agencies but were simply afraid to do so. I reasoned that by putting the simple procedure on camera, making light of it, and obviously not suffering from the experience, I could use television to influence the conduct of a few of the millions who watched us each evening around the country.

Some routines that we'd come to do quite often started simply as a casual ad-lib. One, which I'd originated on *Tonight,* involved spontaneously making up comedy songs on the basis of whatever remark had just been ad-libbed. Because it's necessary to clear music performed on television through either the American Society of Composers, Authors and Publishers (ASCAP), or Broadcast Music Incorporated (BMI), secretaries would dutifully record the titles of the numbers, which were invariably inane-sounding. "It's an Icky, Icky Feeling," "Do We Have a Salami?" and "There's a Dragnet Out for Grandma" were a few of the actual titles, all of which must have puzzled many an official in the New York offices of ASCAP where they were processed.

A wonderfully useful routine emerged spontaneously on the show one evening when one of our cameramen brought in a special lens that could take extra-tight close-ups. Experimenting with it right on the air, we first placed a nickel on a music stand and spent several minutes engrossed by its appearance as it filled the whole screen. Somebody then found a dead insect backstage, and we marvelled at its magnified structural intricacies.

One night I got the idea of making a tour with the lens, around both sides of a ten dollar bill. We made the fascinating discovery that there are pedestrians strolling down a street on the backside of the bill; and that what looks like a late-1920s' automobile, with passengers, is also visible.

The lens proved invaluable, too, when we subsequently took close shots of an ant farm and a bee colony. The comic but educational routines with the lens would go on for a full fifteen or twenty minutes without the slightest possibility of boredom. On today's talk shows, producers get restless if a spot, even a fascinating conversation with a major guest, runs longer than six minutes.

One day shortly after I had started the Westinghouse series I ran into a friend, comedian Chuck McCann, while on a weekend trip to New York. McCann is known to modern audiences partly for his marvelous portrayals of Oliver Hardy in sketches with other actors performing as Stan Laurel. McCann invited me to come to his TV studio, saying, "My engineers have just discovered a trick here that I've been toying with the last few days." I walked into a control room where Chuck asked a technician to punch up a tape. The picture showed a tabletop covered with black velvet and littered with bread crumbs and crusts. McCann waved his hands above the assorted pieces of bread as if making magic gestures, and they suddenly began to assemble, to coalesce, so that in just a few seconds there was clearly one piece of bread instead of the scores of small fragments.

Now the gimmick of running motion picture film backwards had been known almost as long as motion picture cameras themselves. But the device was never terribly effective in silent-screen comedy because the audience could always tell that what they were seeing was achieved by means of reversing a film reel. Until the point of my meeting with McCann in 1963 it had always been considered impossible to reverse videotape effectively. But somehow Chuck and one of the engineers at his station had stumbled over a means of bringing this about. Obviously what Chuck had really done with the pieces of bread was rip them into smithereens. But the great plus in reversing videotape was that the viewer had absolutely no visual clues to explain the magical happenings on screen since a taped show looks no different than live.

Chuck showed me a few other little pieces of business of the same sort: "making" a head of lettuce, and a banana. "The reason I'm showing this to you," he said, "is that on my budget and with my limited facilities here there isn't much more I can do with this gimmick, but if you'll have the engineers on your show give my guys a call, we can explain how to do this trick."

I thanked Chuck profusely, instructed our engineers to phone his, and during the next year or two we did some of the wildest sketches using that technique never before seen on syndicated television. They were, oddly enough, difficult to write, mainly because they were tough to think of in the first place. In writing a backwards sketch you must obviously think backward, which is much more difficult than it might seem.

After toying with the reverse-mode tape during rehearsal one day, I suddenly thought of a great solution to the problem of keeping our viewers ignorant of the fact that during certain portions of our show they were seeing reversed tape. "I'll tell you what I'll do," I told our director, Steve Binder. "During this next little routine I will *walk backwards.* Later, when you run the tape it will look as if I'm walking forward, and that will make it impossible for people to realize what's going on here."

And indeed it did. For weeks after we began doing the sketches, many of which I performed with comedian Cliff Arquette as Charlie Weaver, viewers would write in or stop me on the street and say, "How did you do that trick the other night where you seemed to be painting a complete picture in just a few seconds?"

Now you know.

In 1967 I used the same gimmick on a series of comedy specials Jayne and I did for CBS, although in this case I played the same character in each sketch, a top-hatted magician we called *Ferno, The Great.*

Of the dozens of new and creative ideas that grew out of all the old shows, it strikes me now that the backwards-tape sketches represented the only idea of ours that was never "borrowed" by other comedy shows.

One of the biggest laughs I have ever heard on TV came one night when we were doing an all-Israeli show.

I had originally related entire shows to a specific ethnic culture when doing the *Tonight* show. Because it was so effective, we used the format again on Westinghouse. We did shows that were all-Japanese, all-Israeli, all-Italian, Mexican, Chinese, Irish, and Hawaiian. In each case we would serve the food of the land involved, feature its music, dancing, artifacts, and appropriate decor. At one point during the all-Israeli show, we concentrated for a few minutes on Israeli handiwork, showing lovely silk scarves, leatherwork, jewelry, and handcrafted items. The charming young lady who was our guide through the tour, so to speak, introduced me to a very old woman (in her nineties) who presided over a handsome display of silks, one of which she was embroidering. The young spokeswoman said, "I will have to answer all your questions about these things because the woman speaks no English."

For the next few minutes, any time I wanted to get information about the old soul's work I would say something like, "Could you ask her if she remembers the so-and-so." At one point, however, it occurred to me that I would like to purchase a particularly lovely head scarf to take home to Jayne. I said to the young guide, "Could you ask her, please, how much this item costs?"

"Five dollahs," the old woman said quickly, without even looking up.

I suppose that all over the world merchants recognize the English words *How much?*.

In our all-Japanese show, Jayne and I were served an authentic meal, plied with Japanese sake and other Oriental liquors, and instructed about Japanese culture generally. At one point, while chewing on a dish totally unrecognizable to me, I said, "This is very tasty. What is it?"

"That is ear," the man serving me said.

The director immediately cut to a tight close-up of my

face, which sent out the message we all transmit when we are dubious about the identity of something just eaten or swallowed. I choked out the words, "I'm eating an ear?"

The audience howled at my expression as the waiter responded, "Yes, ear."

"The ear of a *what?*" I asked suspiciously.

Jayne, having grown up in an Oriental culture, gently explained, "I think the gentleman means *eel.*"

Although it may sound odd, until writing this chapter I'd never fully grasped how much creativity and experimentation went into the production of the various talk shows which have occupied a total of twelve years of my television lifetime. The prime-time sketch comedy shows were equally funny, but except for the originality of the sketches themselves, the general form was more conventional. The very openness of the talk-show formula, by way of contrast, permitted us to do almost any damned thing we wanted, night-after-night, and since our production people shared my philosophy about the show, the degree of innovation now impresses even me as I look back.

Another aspect of the general zaniness of the series was my almost nightly use of double-talk words, phrases, and odd sayings. I don't recall how it all started, but I'd use a certain word or term and something about the audience's reaction would make me aware that it was worth repeating. Never was this calculated. As with the other comedians who have used double-talk, these things just seem to happen. It's odd, too, that in a given show where you might say 479 things only one of them catches the audience's fancy in a certain way.

An example of this from the Westinghouse series was once when I said, in complaining about something, "Of all the unmitigated gall—"

For some reason the audience laughed, I guess at the old-fashionedness of the phrase. So I added, "Or for that matter, of all the mitigated gall. And how does all that gall get mitigated in the first place?"

The Westinghouse series continued its craziness through the 1962, '63 and '64 seasons. When after three fun-filled years the program finally ended, I went back to network duty as host of the *I've Got a Secret* panel show for CBS. It's interesting that although *Secret* was seen in far more cities and by an audience larger by many millions than was the Westinghouse series simply because it was on an important network, the syndicated show is better remembered by critics today as a milestone of experimental comedy entertainment. David Letterman has said that while in college he watched it nightly.

The Westinghouse series was also notable for the opportunity it gave to scores of performers to make their television debut: The Supremes, The Carpenters, Lou Rawls, Bob Dylan, and Woody Allen are only a few of the then just-emerging entertainers who appeared with us. Singers Jennie Smith and Molly Bee also attracted a good many followers as a result of their frequent appearances on the program. The comedy feature called *Funny Fone Calls* that was first introduced on my 1951 CBS series also came to full flower on the Westinghouse show. Two record albums consisting of calls from the series are still on the market, with such indeed funny guests as Jerry Lewis, Mel Brooks, Louis Nye, Shelley Berman, Johnny Carson, Carl Reiner, and Bill Dana.

One of the more interesting theme shows I conceived during the run of the Westinghouse series was a 90-minute interview with controversial novelist Henry Miller, which we videotaped at his home.

I'd already met Miller socially but for the life of me cannot recall under what circumstances. He showed us copies of his various books printed in what must've been a dozen languages. He also was kind enough to present me with the gift of one of his watercolors which has ever since been displayed in our living room.

When an occasional Catholic visitor would express shock about my connection with Miller, I showed him on a nearby wall another original artwork, a Zen-like sketch that had been given to me by its creator, the near-saint Thomas Merton.

There were viewers of that particular series—like David Letterman—who saw practically every episode of it. But they can't possibly have seen the Miller interview because someone on the upper levels of Westinghouse management decided it shouldn't be aired.

I doubt that they'd seen the program before so summarily censoring it because Henry came off as the meek, mild-mannered fellow that he was, not at all the firebrand one might expect from having read his works. In terms of film-role typecasting, he would've been believable as a low-salaried bookkeeper or Christian clergyman in an obscure rural community.

Various scholars have written to me over the years, somehow having heard about the Henry-Miller-at-home show and asked at least for the courtesy of being able to view the tape. It's never been possible to accommodate them since to my knowledge the show was not only censored but physically destroyed. For whatever the point is worth, my discussion with Miller was quite tame. It was certainly in far better taste then the average Geraldo-Donahue-Oprah "Did Elvis Sleep With His Mother Before Or After He Returned From The Dead?" shows now so common.

In planning the last night of the Westinghouse series, I harked back—being one of the great back-harkers—to the idea that had occurred to me when the CBS series had gone off the air in 1953. Although the show had opened with typical theme music and thunderous applause, the cameras made a slow move from our stage to find me not entering in the usual way but already seated—in the middle of our totally deserted theater. We'd invited no studio audience. The script I wrote for the occasion, although it left room for ad-libbing, was largely a matter of thanking our millions of faithful viewers and reminiscing fondly about comedy high-spots of the preceding three years. One of these was a funny musical-comedy sketch that Jayne and I performed, with Gabe Dell as Dracula, in a series of horror-film classics we presented as if they'd been staged for Broadway by Rodgers and Hammerstein.

For my closing number on the show I performed a song I'd originally written for the score of *Sophie*, the Broadway musical based on the life of Sophie Tucker. The song had proved so depressing that it was removed from the show a few months before we opened in New York, but it seemed appropriate now. The lyric went as follows:

The final curtain
One day will fall for certain,
So when it does just bow very low
And close up the show
　　that day.

Did they applaud you?
It may have overawed you,
But keep in mind the curtain must fall
Once and for all
　　some day.

And though your heart is breaking
You'll just have to cry alone
'Cause mister, they've got troubles of their own.

The final curtain
One day will fall for certain,
And when it does, it's one of those things;
Just head for the wings
　　to stay.
The final curtain must fall
Some fine day.

Although that was the end of one talk-show series, I would, just a few years later, return to the form in another production that ran from 1968 through 1972.

Hosting talk shows is not an easy habit to break.

CHAPTER SEVENTEEN

Rounding Out The Sixties

From 1964 to 1967, as mentioned earlier, I hosted *I've Got a Secret,* the game show that had been on the air since 1952, replacing Garry Moore, the show's original host. With a 15-year network run, the series was probably the most successful panel show in the history of the medium. It placed in the Top Ten for four consecutive years during the late 1950s, and shows that I hosted were later syndicated and broadcast during the 1972-1973 television season. My wife Jayne had appeared as a regular panelist from 1952 through 1959, along with such other personalities as the genial quizmaster Bill Cullen, the acerbically witty Henry Morgan, and the charming actress Faye Emerson. Pretty ladies Betsy Palmer and Bess Myerson also made their mark as later celebrity panelists.

By the time I left *I've Got A Secret,* I was raring to get back into doing a sketch-comedy show, so that summer I contracted with CBS to do nine specials on which I featured Jayne. One of the sketches we did has since become recognized among comedy writers as a classic of sorts—a satire on a typical Jerry Lewis-type TV fund-raiser titled *The Prickley Heat Telethon.*

Between 1969 and 1972, Dick Cavett hosted a 90-minute ABC talk show from 11:30 to 1:00 each night, opposite *The Tonight Show.* He asked me to fill in for him for a week while he vacationed. I did so, and it has subsequently been a source of profound regret that I did not immediately arrange to acquire copies of the video tapes of those episodes, since each of them turned out to be as good a show as I am capable of doing.

When things go that well, of course, the factor of luck is always operative. For example, one of my oldest television comedy routines involves pointing a camera out at whatever street is adjacent to the studio and commenting spontaneously on what the camera reveals. Dick's producers wanted me to do the routine on his show, and we put it to good use every night. The camera was kept on all during the show; a small monitor just to the right of my desk showed me what was in view. Whenever things began to look particularly interesting, I would interrupt the flow of the on-stage action, ask for the outside camera to be punched up, and we were off and running.

One night I noticed that one of those New York Police Department tow-trucks had just stopped in front of the theater. As our studio audience was suddenly shown this real-life drama, a man's anguished voice floated out from the balcony saying, "Oh, no," as he recognized his car about to be taken away by the police. Given that stroke of good luck—mine, not the driver's—it didn't much matter what I said because the situation itself was hysterically funny. But we got no complaints about that particular routine.

What made everything hit the fan was the appearance, a couple of nights later, of comedian-writer-producer Bob Einstein. Fans of the old *Smothers Brothers Show* may recall Einstein as Officer Judy. He was also producer-performer on John Byner's *Bizarre* TV series, the star of his own *SuperDave Show,* and the brother of comedian Albert Brooks. That both brothers are witty and inventive practitioners of the comic arts is not unusual, I suppose, given that their father was a famous radio comic of the 1930s, Parkyakarkas, who was featured on *The Eddie Cantor Show.* Whenever Bob worked with me, he was never introduced as himself, since he has no act, but always appeared as a supposedly real-life personage.

Anyway, in this case, Einstein was introduced as Gil Drabowski, head of the Polish Anti-Defamation Society. The storyline of the ad-lib sketch Einstein and I then performed involved his pretending to be an irate spokesman for Polish-Americans who had come to lodge a public protest against Polish jokes. He threatened to sue various networks and programs and, to substantiate his case, read from a paper three or four commonly heard Polish jokes to which, he said, he took particular exception.

Few comedy routines I've ever heard have drawn bigger laughs than this one. The audience was at first embarrassed, since they believed that the man on stage was actually a Mr. Drabowski. But when he began to read Polish jokes—of the typically outrageous sort then heard daily all over the country—they lost all control because of the psychological dynamics of the situation itself. First of all, the jokes were funny, although they were certainly in poor taste. But the idea that an actual leader of an organization protesting jokes would read these same stories on the air made the situation—well, the point is clear enough.

At one moment Einstein (as Drabowski) said, "For example, Mr. Allen, here's an instance of a joke that we Poles find particularly offensive: What does a Polock use for underarm deodorant?"

The straight line itself convulsed the audience. In my response, I naturally did not use the word *Polock.* "Well, Mr. Drabowski," I said. "The only thing that occurs to me is the conventional answer: I give up. What *does* a Polish person use for underarm deodorant?"

"A can of Raid," Einstein replied.

Subsequently, telegrams of complaint began coming in from Polish-American organizations around the country, including one from Chester Grabowski, editor of the *Post Eagle,* a Polish-American newspaper. *The Dick Cavett Show* production office later advised me that several angry phone messages were received there as well, including death threats as well as threats of bodily harm. It must be reported that two letters with open, double-edged razor blades were received.

In a form-letter response, I made the following observations: Since the only person apt to be injured by such a weapon would be an innocent secretary, it is difficult to understand those who resort to such methods. (Ironically the secretary who opened these letters is herself of Polish descent.)

Also, when Jayne and I were driven from the theater after the program in the limousine commonly provided for that purpose, the driver of the car—a former policeman—was kind enough to point out that we were being followed.

When the car behind continued to follow us, we wrote down the license number. A few minutes later we were given the name and address of the owner of the car, by friends on the New York police force. Fortunately, nothing untoward happened.

The next afternoon, members of Mr. Cavett's production staff told me that Chester Grabowski (the *Post Eagle* editor who'd written) intended to come to the studio to demand satisfaction. I said, "Well, that's marvelous. When the gentleman gets here; please tell him that I'll be more than happy to have him appear as a guest on the program. That way he can express his views, and any Polish-American who might have been offended by the sketch will be satisfied that their sentiments have been made known."

The Cavett-ABC people agreed to deliver my invitation to Mr. Grabowski in the event that he showed up in the studio.

As viewers know, talk-show programs of this sort are interrupted every few minutes for commercials. In the studio, it's customary for the performers and production people to use these brief interludes to discuss the progress of the show and to deal with any problems that might have come up, in much the same way that a football team discusses strategy and tactics during a time-out period. Two or three times during the course of the program I asked, "Is Mr. Grabowski here yet?"

Eventually it was explained that he had indeed come to the theater but declined my invitation to come to the stage.

After the program that evening, Michael Zanella, the producer, came to me and said, "The Polish newspaper people decided not to accept your invitation to appear on the air but perhaps they'll feel somewhat better about the situation if you spend a few minutes with them in the Green Room [where guests are seated before going onstage] and talk to them."

"I'll be glad to," I said. I went to the Green Room, met Mr. Grabowski and two of his friends, and spent perhaps fifteen minutes in conversation with them. Since matters of taste and opinion are rarely arguable, I naturally took no exception to the emotional response of the three gentlemen to the routine that Einstein had done. When, however, Grabowski accusingly said, "We know who's behind all this," and made it very clear that he saw the entire Polish-joke phenomenon in America as an actual Jewish *plot*, I responded by saying that he was very much in error in regard to that aspect of the controversy. I also made it clear that I regretted that he had chosen not to appear on the program. Since my conversation with him was conducted on a gentlemanly basis, I found it impossible to understand his later imputations that I had invited him and his friends to appear on the program only to make light of them.

I've subsequently read Mr. Grabowski's account of the incident. He explains his reluctance to appear on the program by saying, in a *Post Eagle* column of August 23, 1971:

Well, we arrived, but we were not forewarned on the phone that we were going to be welcome on the show. Of course not, they wanted to catch us unprepared, and then try to make us look silly.... We did not bite, showing them that the Poles are not the meatheads that their sister-station [sic] depicts weekly on the *All in the Family* show.

Mr. Grabowski's comments called for the following response from me, in a letter that I sent to the *Post Eagle*:

It is not at all true that *they* wanted to catch the Polish spokesmen unprepared.

Since I doubt that Mr. Grabowski would claim the power of a mind-reader, it therefore follows that he could have had no way of knowing what my motivation was in inviting him and his friends to appear on the program. That motivation, in fact, was simply based on my understanding of the obvious: that it would have been both an act of fair play and also good theater to permit Grabowski and his colleagues to express their views.

Once the Polish spokesmen had taken a position of great seriousness in regard to the question they clearly considered highly controversial, it would have made no sense whatever to 'try to make [them] look silly.'

The quality of meatheadedness has apparently no correlation with the factor of race or nationality. Assuming that we could arrive at a definition of the term *meathead,* it would follow that all ethnic groups have their percentage of meatheads, which means there are a few Polish meatheads, just as there are Irish meatheads, Jewish meatheads, Italian meatheads, etc.

Elsewhere in his column, Mr. Grabowski says, 'The name used by Einstein was Grabowski.' Mr. Grabowski was apparently a victim of what psychologists call the Expectancy Illusion, in which one sees or hears what one expects or fears to see or hear. Neither Einstein nor I had ever heard of Mr. Chester Grabowski before this instance. In any event, Einstein was identified as *Gil Drabowski.*

I take no issue with Grabowski's suggestion that Poles 'must band together once and for all...in a fight against the media slander of our good image.' But I think all decent citizens—Polish or otherwise— will be alarmed by

Grabowski's statement that 'they only respect one method, that being *force*.' People are injured and killed by instruments of force....

Grabowski has repeatedly referred to Einstein as my straightman. The point is of minor importance, but the roles were, in fact, reversed. Mr. Einstein is a popular comedian; I served as *his* straightman in this particular instance.

One is naturally dismayed to see anti-Semitism blatantly revealed in Grabowski's newspaper accounts. I suggest that the gentlemen's Polish-American readers, and his spiritual advisers, give long and hard thought to his use of the phrase *the Jew Einstein*....

My letter suggested that the offending sketch—which was created by Einstein—would be better understood if considered in the context of a long and eminently successful series of routines he'd performed on my television shows during the previous several years. Each of them took the form of a put-on interview in which Einstein purported to be not an entertainer but a real-life individual with an interesting story. On one occasion, for example, he was introduced as an ex-convict who'd just served a great many years in prison and who, while incarcerated, had trained a small bird to do an incredible series of tricks. When at last the time came for the bird to go through its paces, it could not even be coaxed from the cage. The sketch finished with a television closeup of Einstein's heavily padded and gloved hand trying, without success, to grasp the bird so that it could be brought forth.

In another instance, Bob was The World's Strongest Man. He claimed to be able to take almost any sort of punishment; but when I landed an only-moderate punch on his midsection—at his request—he was nevertheless wounded and became rather surly.

Another time he was introduced as a professional football player who'd recently left the Detroit Lions. He described the meanness and savagery characteristic of line-play—the sort of thing, he said, that the public never becomes aware of.

The high-point of his account of a recent game came when he said that he'd seen a puff of smoke coming from the helmet of an opponent and realized that he had just been struck with a .22-caliber bullet!

On another occasion, Bob appeared on my show as Andy Bernard, the Coyote Man. He claimed to have been abandoned by his parents as an infant and raised in the wild, among friendly coyotes.

In another appearance he was a ping-pong champion.

During the same season that Einstein was doing this series of comedy sketches, he also appeared as Gil Drabowski, Polish-American Attorney. Oddly enough, although my program at that time was seen in many parts of the country, not a single letter of complaint was received. One possible explanation is that the number of viewers watching network television after 11:30 p.m. is greater than those watching daytime TV, although the original program was seen during the evening hours in some parts of the country. Or perhaps at the time of *The Dick Cavett Show* appearance, the Poles had started a fight-back campaign. As regards the four or five Polish jokes that formed the basis of Einstein's sketch, it's important, I think, that Einstein did not create any of them. They were—for better or worse—jokes in common circulation, part of the old American tradition of joke fads the origin of which will probably forever remain in obscurity.

I finished out the Sixties with my third talk-show experiment, produced by Filmways and Golden West, called simply *The Steve Allen Show*. Written by Bernie Kukoff, Jeff Harris, Elias Davis, David Pollock, and Mel Chase, it would run for five years—1968 through 1972—and during much of that time emanated from what is now called the TAV Theater on Vine Street, about half a block from Sunset Boulevard. Once again daily creativity and experimentation were the distinguishing characteristics of the series.

CHAPTER EIGHTEEN

Meeting of Minds

I spent most of 1970s doing syndicated series and comedy specials. In 1974, I helped write and served as performer on ABC's *American Academy of Humor TV Special,* a salute to humor and humorists. Then, for five seasons beginning in 1974, I hosted a hilarious annual ABC-TV spoof of the beauty extravaganzas that almost defy spoofing. Johnny Carson hailed *The Unofficial Miss Las Vegas Showgirl Beauty Queen Pageant,* produced by Jeff Harris and Bernie Kukoff, as "the funniest show of the year." This was kind of him since it was seen opposite his own *Tonight Show.*

In 1976, excerpts from our previous shows were syndicated into a series of twenty-three comedy specials so, although I was not at the time doing a regular series, I was still being seen on a consistent basis. The show, called *Laughback,* reunited many of the old gang in live-on-tape interviews and filmed highlights. Featured were, among others: Louis Nye, Jonathan Winters, Bill Dana, Don Knotts, Tom Poston, Foster Brooks, Gabe Dell, Jayne Meadows, Skitch Henderson, Tim Conway, Lenny Bruce, Abbott and Costello, Peter Ustinov, Andy Griffith, John Byner, Audrey Meadows, Pat Harrington, Jr., and Joe E. Brown.

The fruition of a long-held dream came in 1977 when PBS

aired the first show of the four-season, award-winning "ultimate talk show"—*Meeting of Minds*. The project actually had originated in 1959, as part of our weekly NBC Sunday night series. The initial segment was conceived as a discussion of crime and punishment with several prominent figures of the past: Freud, Hegel, Montaigne, Clarence Darrow, and Aristotle. Despite advance critical acclaim, the segment was canceled by NBC.

Not giving up the idea, I resurrected the format in 1971, on the Golden West syndicated series. And in 1977, the series, produced by Loring d'Usseau, at last found a home on the PBS network. Here, then, is the story of that dream, from the beginning.

I love to read. But this love, like others men may know, is in part a compulsion. I am powerless to resist the temptation to read. I perceive the magic, wondrous power of the printed word, and it disturbs me that many others do not share this simple insight. The great majority of people on our planet, which not so long ago we imagined was generally civilized, are still illiterate. These damnable polysyllabic words, such as *illiterate*, serve as mental filing devices but partly obscure the reality they were intended to convey. Think for a moment, really think, what it means to be unable to read. Of course we are all relatively illiterate in the sense that though there are hundreds of languages in the world, many educated people can read only one and perhaps an additional one or two stumblingly. But hundreds of millions, even in the twentieth century, can read nothing at all. This means that much of the best of human achievement, from all cultures, down through the long march of history, is largely closed to them. If they happen to live within walking distance of an ancient temple, a great cathedral, a sculpture by Michelangelo, a painting by da Vinci, if they are able to hear a performance of a symphony by Brahms or Beethoven, they are fortunate indeed, but few illiterates are so situated. And the degrading, dehumanizing social circumstances which may have contributed to their illiteracy make it extremely unlikely that they will avail themselves of even such opportunities as might present themselves. For the man who cannot read, Dostoevski and Bacon might as well have lived on another planet, Aristole and Aquinas might as well have never been born.

So far as can be scientifically determined, the important difference between man and the other thousands of animal species is that man thinks analytically and remembers. Reading, writing, printing, and publishing are extensions of this one fundamental difference. But if the ignorance that illiteracy invariably leads to is pathetic, tragic, what can one say of those who possess the gift of literacy but essentially waste it solely for purposes of diversion, practically never use it with an eye to enlightenment, moral betterment, or social responsibility? The child has at least an excuse for reading little more than comic strips, advertisements, or simple stories. But what of a college graduate who reads chiefly sensational tabloids, sports news, pornography, commercial advertisements, and the other forms of mindless fare produced in such enormous quantities by our culture because someone can turn a profit from it?

Well, all of this seems monumentally tragic to me; I therefore consider myself fortunate that I am seized by reading, as a result of which I am in a constant lifelong state of intellectual and/or creative excitement. I find no subject matter more stimulating than philosophy and history although I am willing, at rare intervals, to read a spy thriller or watch the visual equivalent on television.

To say that this endless reading is the *source* of many of my ideas would suggest that I simply find in books and articles ideas of others and take them as my own. No, my mind does not simply receive impressions. It talks back to the authors, even the wisest of them, a response I'm sure they would warmly welcome. It is not possible, after all, to accept passively everything even the greatest minds have proposed. One naturally has profound respect for Socrates, Plato, Pascal, Augustine, Descartes, Newton, Locke, Voltaire,

Paine, and other heroes in the pantheon of Western culture; but each made statements flatly contradicted by views of the others. So I see the literary and philosophical tradition of our culture not so much as a storehouse of facts and ideas but rather as an endless Great Debate at which one may be not only a privileged listener but even a modest participant. It was this last perception that led to the creation of *Meeting of Minds.*

After three years as host of NBC's original *Tonight* show in 1954, 1955, and 1956, I was assigned to produce a second program, a weekly prime-time comedy series, which the network carried for four years. On this program I from time-to-time referred briefly to books I thought deserved a wider audience.

By 1959 it had become clear that certain network and advertising people were made politically uneasy by the weekly recommendations of books, even though one Sunday I publicized one written by J. Edgar Hoover, simply because my publisher had asked me to. NBC would have preferred that I function in an intellectual vacuum, restricting myself to making audiences laugh rather than think. When I responded that it was precisely because I was able to do the former that I was in an advantageous position to accomplish the latter, the point seemed to carry little weight. The recommendation of books continued to be tolerated rather than approved. Then, in January of 1960, matters came to a head.

For some time an idea had been vaguely forming in the back of my mind of a method of imparting education without inducing boredom. In early 1959 I had made the following entry in a notebook:

> What I have in mind, however hazily, is probably a drama that would present characters embodying philosophical attitudes. Shaw and other dramatists have done something of the sort. There must be minds at hand capable of at least making this experiment.

About six months later I entered the following notation:

> If I had the time I would like to develop the vague idea that
> it might be worthwhile to create a television program of
> powerful intellectual content made attractive to the masses
> by virtue of being clothed in the garments of emotional
> conflict. Shakespeare, for example, makes us think at the
> same time he makes us feel. Perhaps present-day intellec-
> tuals should take a leaf from his book and try to develop a
> program that offers ideas in dramatic conflict. The busi-
> ness of debate is almost always exciting. Unfortunately our
> national conformist pressures probably make it impossible
> to broadcast any unpopular ideas, especially since sponsors
> frighten easily, understandably enough. But there must be
> some way to take constructive advantage, intellectually, of
> the emotional interests of the people.

There was some prophecy as well as inspiration in these
lines. By December the idea at last crystallized into *Meeting of
Minds,* a round-table discussion of weighty issues conducted
like any other panel debate except that the participants
would be actors portraying Thomas Aquinas, Abraham
Lincoln, Socrates, Meister Eckhart, Emerson, and others.

One night, while leafing through the Syntopicon of the
Great Books of the Western World Library, I found myself
examining the chapter on crime and punishment. I was
fascinated by the comparison among the ideas on this subject
of Freud, Aristole, Montaigne, Dostoevski, and Hegel. I
asked my friend journalist-critic Nat Hentoff to research this
chapter and assemble the various viewpoints into the form
of a dialogue. Within a couple of weeks we had cast such
distinguished actors as Everett Sloane, J. Carroll Naish, Ian
Wolfe, Lawrence Dobkin, and Phillip Coolidge in the above
roles, with Henry Hull playing Clarence Darrow. Our first
rehearsal was thrilling, although it revealed that the script
was overly long and needed additional dramatic values. I ran
it through my typewriter, brought the time down to about

nineteen minutes, and shortened the longer speeches by breaking them up with interruptions and angry interpolations by the participants.

Copies were sent to a number of friends. One, Norman Cousins of *Saturday Review,* reacted so favorably that he immediately planned a cover story on the subject and assigned Robert Lewis Shayon to write it.

Since by this time we had once again become aware of the familiar lack of enthusiasm on the part of some of those connected with our program, I had Norman's warm letter of response reproduced and sent to all interested parties.

At first reaction was improved, but in a few days requests began to come through that we cancel plans to broadcast the discussion. We were dumbfounded. If ever an idea had found its proper time, this was it. Television was being daily attacked by the nation's intellectuals, critics, and the public. There were good programs, a few with intellectual content, but for the most part they were relegated to the Sunday afternoon low-rated period. Here was a chance to bring something of rare value to an already guaranteed mass audience. When we heard that NBC wanted us to cut the spot, I felt as Edison might have if they had rejected the electric light while sitting in the darkness.

At first I could not take the network's objections seriously. None of the points its spokesmen made seemed valid. NBC's basic argument, that *Meeting of Minds* was not the kind of fare to present on a comedy-variety program, was easily parried. While it was true that something of this sort would seem peculiar if hosted by, say, Jerry Lewis or Red Skelton, it was not at all unusual in my own case. From my first days in television I had occasionally presented material of a serious nature. *Meeting of Minds* was not comedy, but variety is a more elastic word. A couple of years earlier, for example, Ed Sullivan had presented a pacifist film that dramatically delineated the horrors of atomic warfare. Public reaction was so favorable that a few weeks later he rebroadcast the feature. I do not recall anyone saying, "I was fascinated by the antiwar film Sullivan showed, but wasn't it a pity it was broadcast on a variety show?"

We soon became aware, by a shift in the network's arguments, that this suggested reason actually had nothing to do with the matter. It was simply what had been put to us at first in the hope that we would give in and that it would not be necessary for the network to reveal its true motivations. But within a few days we became aware that disapproval was tied to my connection with the National Committee for a Sane Nuclear Policy, as well as to having permitted the use of my name in an anti-death penalty campaign centered on the Caryl Chessman case. Although the debate was handled gingerly on the part of the network's representatives, it became clear at last that the old fear that the broadcast might antagonize potential customers was at the heart of the censorship. Our sponsor was an automobile company, Chrysler-Plymouth.

"I fail to see what is controversial about this script," I said. "Clarence Darrow does declare himself opposed to capital punishment but Hegel defends—"

"That's just it," a network man said. "Some people are going to think you prepared this script because of your feelings about Caryl Chessman." Chessman was the mass-murderer on death row that death penalty opponents made a *cause celebe.*

"But that's preposterous. Until this minute it had never occurred to me that there could be any connection. Nat Hentoff put the original draft together quoting from material he found in the writings of the thinkers involved. Anybody who sees this as a pro-Chessman plot is paranoid."

"Perhaps," the executive said, "but don't you see that you can't control other people's reactions? No matter how right you are, some people are going to misunderstand."

"I see no reason to deprive twenty million viewers of something wonderfully exciting and informative," I said, "just because of what a handful of crackpots might say."

At last, having reached an impasse, I pointed out that *Saturday Review* was coming out with a cover story on *Meeting of Minds* and that if we were to cancel the segment there would be a great hue and/or cry. I felt sure the cancellation would embarrass the network, the advertising agency, and the sponsor far more than they would be discomfited by the broadcast of the dialogue. In my opinion they would not be embarrassed by the broadcast at all, but would be proud to have had a part in it.

This argument had a telling effect and put an end to the discussion, for the time being. We went ahead with our plans. The men who had been sent out from New York to induce me to alter my position said a cordial good-bye and returned home. We assumed that nothing more would be said or done about the matter, but two days later we received word from the network's legal department that according to the terms of our contract we did not have the legal right to broadcast *Meeting of Minds*. There was nothing more we could do; I did not own the network. I sent Norman Cousins a letter of apology, substituted a comedy sketch, and advised the network that it could consider itself responsible for the salaries of the dismissed actors, which as I recall came to about $15,000.

As predicted, the cancellation received a great deal of attention, much more than the broadcast would have. The network, the agency, and the sponsor were subjected to bitter criticism.

Perhaps this kind of censorship will inevitably occur in television in the future because of the structure of the system, which makes all parties vulnerable in their bank accounts. The movie, radio, and TV blacklist came about, I suspect, not so much from any basic, informed revulsion for communism on the part of the television, radio, and advertising executives responsible but more from fear of a commercial boycott on the part of vigorously anti-Communist consumers.

The cancellation of *Meeting of Minds* brought in a flood of mail, including requests from individuals, schools, churches, and social groups for copies of the script. We sent them out and granted permission for various local productions around the country. I participated in one of these at a school auditorium in Los Angeles. It was tape-recorded and subsequently broadcast on the Pacifica Network FM radio stations in San Francisco, Los Angeles, and New York.

There the matter rested until 1964 at which time I was doing a nightly syndicated comedy-and-talk show for the Westinghouse Broadcasting people. They were pleased to learn of our plan to present *Meeting of Minds* in its original form. The telecast passed with nothing more earthshaking than a number of complimentary letters and reviews.

By 1971 I was doing another syndicated talk series, and this time decided to present *Meeting of Minds* in a more appropriate form, having realized that it was a mistake to limit the discussions to one subject. Even the greatest minds will tend to ramble and digress, though less so than the rest of us; this factor, I thought, would lend a more natural quality to the conversations. I wrote a totally new script bringing together President Theodore Roosevelt, St. Thomas Aquinas, Queen Cleopatra of ancient Egypt, and Thomas Paine of the American and French revolutions.

In rehearsals it developed that we had made an error in casting a certain actor to portray Paine. Under my direction his performance worsened, so he had to be dismissed. Unfortunately this left us without enough time to get another actor for the role. I therefore took it over myself and asked Peter Lawford if he would be kind enough to serve as host, a request to which he graciously consented.

The telecast was aired on a Friday. By Monday morning our office was flooded with about fifteen hundred letters from viewers who had seen the show on the Los Angeles station. I instructed our office staff to be prepared to hire additional personnel to take care of the avalanche of mail that would come in from the other cities around the country where the program was seen.

About two weeks later it occurred to us that we had seen no additional mail, which was certainly strange. When I attempted to discover the reasons my efforts at first were met with evasions and pretended ignorance. Eventually it emerged that the gentleman serving as distributor for the show had taken it upon himself to censor it from our entire network of syndicated stations, with the exception of our Los Angeles outlet. He reasoned, cleverly enough, that if we saw the show in Los Angeles we would have no way of knowing that it was not simultaneously being carried throughout the rest of the country. He would have gotten away with this, too, had it not been for the factor of the lack of congratulatory mail.

The disaster, however, turned out to have fortunate consequences. Since the program had been only a local show it was entered, by our executive producer Loring d'Usseau, in the local competition sponsored by the National Academy of TV Arts and Sciences. In due course it won three Emmy awards.

On the strength of this reassurance I personally financed the production of six additional one-hour programs and attempted to sell them to syndicators or networks. One by one various doors were opened and then unaccountably closed. Compliments were lavish but...no sale.

The only remaining hope seemed to be PBS, the "educational" network. Perhaps the most surprising turn of events of the whole long history of the *Meeting of Minds* project is that...well, it's not totally correct to say that the network turned the series down. Statistically very few people there ever became aware it had been submitted. But a couple of gentlemen in one of the eastern PBS cities decided, for reasons never made clear, that they weren't interested.

Having exhausted all evident possibilities I simply concentrated on other creative projects. *Meeting of Minds* would have been added to the list of thousands of other unsold TV "pilots" had it not been for an accident of fate. Shortly thereafter Loring d'Usseau, who had been executive producer when we did the 1971 telecast, happened to leave the Los Angeles NBC station and move to KCET, the local outlet for PBS, as program manager. Since Loring had received one of the three Los Angeles Emmys the program had won, it was obvious that he would not have to be sold on the project. I wrote him and he responded with immediate enthusiasm. Because the six scripts were already written we were, in a word, ready to go.

There was just one remaining problem: PBS has no money of its own but must seek funding for its programs. Fortunately a gentleman named William Clayton, an executive of E. F. Hutton and Co., saw one of our pilot tapes and became instantly enamored of the whole idea. Between Messrs. d'Usseau and Clayton they made it possible to proceed with the production of our first group of shows, six one-hour specials, the first of which was telecast nationally on January 10, 1977.

The program was, after a delay of some eighteen years, not only enormously successful but elicited a kind of mail none of us connected with its production had ever seen. What appealed to the thousands who wrote, I believe, was that they were actually given the opportunity to hear *ideas* on television, a medium which otherwise presents only people, things, and actions.

We certainly desperately need to become more familiar with such ideas. Modern man is going to have to examine the historical roots of modern practices if he is to even approach understanding them. *Meeting of Minds* encourages him to do so.

The distinctive feature of *Meeting of Minds* is that it does not consist of one-on-one interviews but rather of group discussions, stimulating conversations by important thinkers and/or doers of history. There have been other shows where Abraham Lincoln, say, was interviewed, as there have been programs in which Lincoln appeared in a dramatic context. But, except in the realm of literature, which provides much precedent, there has been nothing remotely resembling *Meeting of Minds*, in which Lincoln might be joined at the table by Julius Caesar, Henry VIII, and Aristotle. As host I spend the least possible amount of time interviewing our guests because the real excitement comes from their heated disagreements with each other.

It's important to note that the guests could never have met in reality, perhaps because they lived a thousand years or a thousand miles apart. Having George Washington speaking to Thomas Jefferson and James Madison wouldn't be all that surprising, but hearing him debate important questions with Augustine, Freud, and Lenin would be, at the very least, instructive.

As I have explained, it took some eighteen years to get *Meeting of Minds* on American network television on a regular basis. Some readers and critics viewed this optimistically, taking it to mean that you can't keep a good idea down, justice will eventually triumph, television will always make room for the worthwhile programs that industry spokesmen daily announce that they are searching for, etc.

Others, perhaps of a more pessimistic personal bent, concluded that if it took eighteen years to convince network executives of the value of something so obviously worthwhile then television was an even more desolate wasteland than former FCC Chairman Newton Minnow had supposed.

My own reaction has tended to oscillate between these extremes, although the oscillations have a rhythm in which I am often longer poised on the dark side of the spectrum.

I perceive myself as occupying a middle ground between scholars and the people. At the moment, however, the middle ground seems very thinly populated. It might be likened to a no-man's-land or barrier, which prevents, rather than facilitates, coummunication between the academy and the street, between gown and town. Through the personally fortuitous accident that I am chiefly employed in television I am in a position to share with a large number of individuals such information as I acquire in the process of my own education. There is frustration in this, of course, in that there seems some sort of vague, hard-to-define spirit—as insubstantial as Robert Frost's something-that-doesn't-like-a-wall—some force in television that doesn't particularly like what I'm doing unless it's comedy. For the most part the industry takes little notice.

Public reaction, on the other hand, has been so gratifying as to far exceed my expectations. I was quite prepared, in fact, to be strongly criticized, from almost every point of the philosophical compass, simply because the esteemed figures from history who appear on *Meeting of Minds* are not only complimented, and permitted to espouse their personal points of view, but they are also subjected—by others at the table—to criticism, some of it vehement. What would happen, I asked myself, when millions of Catholics heard Thomas Aquinas being taken to task publicly? What would humanists, atheists, agnostics, and freethinkers do when their hero Thomas Paine was attacked by Aquinas and Theodore Roosevelt, not to mention Queen Cleopatra of Egypt?

How would Lutherans respond to seeing the founder of their church pointedly criticized by Voltaire? How would feminists react at seeing Susan B. Anthony and Florence Nightingale subjected to penetrating questions?

Well, as it happened, the fears growing out of such considerations have proved to be groundless. Thousands of laudatory letters were received; fewer than a dozen took issue with us, and even then only with one aspect or another of the programs. Apparently the audience for *Meeting of Minds* perceived that we intended there to be no winners or losers in our dramatized debates, that every guest would be given full opportunity to defend himself or herself, and that the ultimate jury, in any event, was the one at home.

Our studio audiences, it is true, sometimes perferred one character to another. There was a certain amount of booing, for example, when Karl Marx made his first appearance, and there was a bit of derisive laughter at some of Martin

Luther's harsh comments about the German peasants of his time, about woman's place, etc. But by-and-large everyone seems to have recognized that my general purpose is nothing more than to awaken popular interest in the great debates of our cultural, intellectual, theological, and political history.

I am frequently asked if either all or most of the things our guests said were word-for-word quotations. That would be a perfectly reasonable ideal, but ideals are rarely realized. As regards some characters—Cleopatra and Attila the Hun for example—there is little or no record of what they said so all dialogue must be created for them. In the case of others—such as Aquinas—who left an enormous volume of written work, there is nevertheless not a great deal of direct quotation because one does not speak in the same form in which one writes. Most of what Aquinas wrote, if spoken, would simply not sound like natural conversation.

There were others—like Luther and Voltaire—who not only left behind a great body of written material but who were much quoted because their pithy manner of speech made them easily quotable. We were meticulously careful, needless to say, in attributing to our guests only those views they actually held.

By the second season, I was somewhat in the position of a football coach who's given the benefit of advice after a game but precious little assistance before. The primary reason for this was financial. Since the PBS network is noncommercial its programs have a bare-bones budget. We delivered each individual program of *Meeting of Minds* at a fraction of what the same show would cost if produced for ABC, NBC or CBS. For my own part that is a factor of no importance since the project was a labor of love, and I am fortunate enough to make my living by other means. But it did deny us what I'm sure would've been valuable academic reinforcement. Nonetheless, with the assistance of such cooperative people as Robert Philips of Oregon State University, Cutberto Hernandez-Torres, Professor Eugen Weber of UCLA, and my wife Jayne Meadows we hopefully produced programs—and later books and audiotapes—with demonstrable effectiveness as public education.

The Center for the Study of Democratic Institutions, the world-famous "think-tank" in Santa Barbara founded by the late Robert Maynard Hutchins, was kind enough, in 1978, to convene a panel of scholars for the purpose of making a critical analysis of *Meeting of Minds*. Portions of videotapes were viewed, scripts examined, formal papers delivered, and a discussion held, the proceedings—in somewhat truncated form—being eventually published in the January-February 1979 issue of the Center magazine.

I am also grateful to the staff at KCET-TV. Producer Loring d'Usseau, directors Bruce Franchini, Jeff Corey, and Diana Maddox, Art Director John Retsek, and Production Assistant Patricia Kunkel were all a part of making *Meeting of Minds* an award-winning presentation.

In the third year of production of *Meeting of Minds*, one pair of programs represented something of a departure from the series' usual formula. The shows in question were subtitled "Shakespeare on Love." I had been intending, for some time, to invite William Shakespeare to be a guest, but in considering who the other members of his group might be, it suddenly occurred to me that, rather than confront him with illustrious figures from history, it might be interesting to introduce him to some of his own creatures.

Shakespeare, like most great literary artists, painted on a very wide canvas. Three of his characters—Hamlet, Romeo, and Othello—had difficulties with that emotion which, though the sweetest, has always been a source of suffering and misunderstanding for human-kind, and what a damnably poignant reality that is. These famous three, I thought, would be wonderfully suitable choices. Certainly they had never before met their maker. It would be interesting to see what might happen if they were brought face to face.

In the original conception of *Meeting of Minds*, the version I had tried to introduce on NBC television in 1958, the idea had been to limit each discussion to one general subject. There is nothing wrong with that formula, so far as it goes.

There is certainly no doubt that stimulating discussions could be devised on democracy, war, pacifism, abortion, birth control, freedom, or any other significant idea. But it occurred to me, over the years during which I was occasionally attempting to make *Meeting of Minds* a television reality rather than merely a grand possibility, that we would learn relatively little about our famous guests themselves if we discussed only one broad subject with them.

There was also concern about the attention-span of even the more intelligent members of the American television audience. The decision gradually made itself, therefore, that while we would indeed have extended discussions on particularly important issues, we would, nevertheless, not limit our guest to a consideration of only one such issue. But now, as I began to develop the two programs featuring Shakespeare, I returned to the original formula and decided that it would be reasonable to deal with only the subject of love.

The title "Shakespeare on Love" flowed out at this point. And that was the name of the production that was eventually staged by the Shakespeare Society of America, at their theater in Los Angeles, that opened on May 26, 1975.

Although I served as host for the *Meeting of Minds* television series, I did not think it right to have a formal host or master-of-ceremonies for the theatrical production featuring Shakespeare. But there had to be someone who could provide more or less the same service, and yet be justified as part of the dramatic action. The solution: the Dark Lady of the Sonnets. Concerning this woman, very little indeed is known. For that matter, surprisingly little is known, with certainty, about Shakespeare himself, compared to what we know about, say, Martin Luther, Henry the VIII, or Abraham Lincoln.

It was obvious, once the theme of love had been selected, that we would have to deal with the famous sonnets. In reading them one day, it struck me that although Shakespeare and all his contemporaries had obviously spoken in the standard Elizabethan English common in his time, he was nevertheless perceived in such epic terms, because of his remarkable achievements, that it might be fun, and better art as well, to write a play, or at least the greater part of it, in Shakespearean-style iambic pentameter. While other writers might eventually have thought of this idea, only those who were themselves poets could have made it a reality, and, as it happens, I have written a good deal of verse since childhood, two volumes of which have been published.

Surrounding myself, then, during one three-day weekend, with collections of Shakespeare's plays and sonnets, I sat by the pool under a clear California blue sky and dictated the first draft of the play, needless to say quoting liberally from the three plays —*Hamlet, Romeo and Juliet,* and *Othello*—and the sonnets.

To enable the reader, before the curtain goes up so to speak, to judge how smoothly my own rhymed or rhythmic first lines harmonized with those of the master, I quote here a passage famous—among scholars at least—from *Othello,* concerning Jesus' advice that we love our enemies. The Moor says:

That this is wisdom of a pure astounding beauty
I'd be last to deny. But when we search
for instances, examples, writs of proof,
ah, there, 'twould seem, we enter realms so barren,
were we to march abroad till we had found
one single instance of a kiss bestowed
on hated brow, one moment of sweet love
for him who robs, or does us any harm,
we'd march, I fear, to our unholy graves.

In case the reader is trying to recall in which specific scene of the play these lines are found, I confess to having played a trick. The lines are not of Shakespeare's creation, but are my own, written in imitation of his style. Our gifted actors made the seams connecting original to imitation quite invisible.

Even many otherwise well-informed people have always assumed, because of the soaring emotion of the sonnets, that since they were written by a man, they must have been written to, for, and about a woman. As it happens, however, for the most part this was not the case. How I dealt with this discovery provided a certain amount of the play's tension and humor.

When, some years later, I was doing the *Meeting of Minds* series for PBS, it was necessary to revise the script somewhat so as to place myself into it, since I was the host of the ongoing series. But I contrived to get myself offstage as quickly as possible and let the original players speak for themselves. The brilliant cast which made my fantasy believable consisted of my wife, Jayne Meadows, as the Dark Lady of the Sonnets, Desdemona, and Juliet; William Marshall as Othello; Anthony Costello as Hamlet; Charles Lanyer as Romeo; Harris Yulin as Shakespeare; and, in smaller roles, Fred Sadoff as Iago and the ghost of Hamlet's father.

Another pair of shows during our third year featured St. Augustine of Hippo of the fourth century, the first major Catholic philosopher, a man of remarkable intellect whose views are still influential; the flagrantly immoral Empress Theodora of the Byzantine Empire; Thomas Jefferson; and, one of our few guests from the twentieth century, Lord Bertrand Russell, one of the leading scholars of modern times.

In doing research on Jefferson, I drew part of my information from Fawn Brodie's insightful biography of him. Since Brodie is an authority on matters historical, while I certainly am not, I relied on her word as regards reports that Jefferson had a mistress who happened to be black. (To me this would be no more scandalous than if he had a mistress of his own color, but that is a point, of course, on which others will form their own opinions.) After the telecast of the two shows featuring Jefferson and the others, I heard from a number of historians who expressed strong reservations about the reliability of Brodie's reports concerning the story of Sally Hemmings. It is unlikely, I suppose, that the full truth of the matter can ever be known, but I did want to set the record straight here that not all historians accept, as reliable, reports of a love relationship between Jefferson and Hemmings.

In that same season there was also a stimulating exchange involving Aristotle, Niccolo Machiavelli, Elizabeth Barrett Browning, and China's Sun Yat-Sen. I had, for some time, had a special interest in China and indeed not long after these programs would have the good fortune of being able to make three trips there, during one of which my son Bill and I were able to find his mother's birthplace. Jayne, as some readers may be aware, was born in China and spent the first seven years of her life there. She appeared on this pair of programs, too, as the delicate and romantic poetess Elizabeth Barrett Browning, and it was remarkable to see her move our studio audience to tears as she recited some of her famous poems.

The most difficult portions of the scripts to write—of all four seasons—were those involving the philosophers. The reason, of course, is that they dealt chiefly with ideas. It is easy enough to relate stories about actions, confrontations, wars, atrocities and scandals, but discussing abstract ideas was, as I say, somewhat difficult. Nevertheless, audiences reported no great difficuty in understanding what our visiting thinkers had to say.

Our fourth season proved to be as stimulating as the other three. In our nineteenth and twentieth programs of the *Meeting of Minds* series, we discussed chiefly the problem of overpopulation and the ongoing controversy concerning the merits of the free enterprise economy

I had earlier noted that "our series brought together individuals who could not have met in reality because they lived perhaps a thousand years or a thousand miles apart." To my surprise, in doing some background reading about birth-control advocate Margaret Sanger and India's Mahatma Gandhi, I discovered that they had, in fact, met on one occasion. Arranging a second meeting proved a strikingly effective means of bringing out certain particulars of the continuing dialogue about overpopulation since, though India is one of the countries that suffers dreadfully from it, Gandhi nevertheless thought there was something inherently evil about all human sexual activity unless it was engaged in for the sole purpose of having a child.

As for Adam Smith, he was a guest I'd wanted to bring to the program from the very first since he was the initial philosophical advocate for capitalism. I had, a few years earlier, communicated with a conservative author who I thought would be well equipped to take part in either the background research on Smith or the preparation of the script. To my surpsise, the gentleman chose not to take advantage of our invitation. I therefore had to do the great bulk of the work myself. I hoped, in so doing, that I would do complete justice to the free enterprise economy which, for whatever the point may be worth, I favor. I strongly feel, however, that capitalism must be called to moral account for whatever injustices it causes. Only in that way, it seems to me, can it be securely preserved as an economic institution.

As mentioned, we did not adhere to the original conception of discussing one general subject on the individual shows, with the exception of "Shakespeare on Love." The second exception came in our fourth season when I decided to devote two of our hours to a consideration of art. But that subject, of course, need not be narrowly focused, since art takes a variety of forms. Our three guests for these shows were Leonardo da Vinci, Niccolo Paganini, and William Blake, which meant that we touched on painting, music, and literature.

One unintentionally amusing result of the appearance of Paganini was that even many of my knowledgeable friends in the entertainment industry expressed puzzlement as to how we had so successfully dealt with the problem of having the great violinist actually appear to be playing his instrument, which he did frequently, to illustrate different points. In motion pictures, the theater, and television, it is always a difficult technical problem to make it seem that an actor, who may personally know nothing whatever about music, is actually playing a musical instrument. The usual technique is to have a gifted professional musician prerecord the music tracks and then later to film or videotape the actor, who synchronizes his or her physical movements with the sound track. (I had to do precisely this when I played the role of Benny Goodman in the motion picture account of the great clarinetist's life. It was necessary, in that instance, to take instruction on the instrument and to learn to play it somewhat, but this was chiefly so I would be able to hold the instrument in a professional manner and have my fingers on the right holes since, had I not done so, thousands of clarinetists around the world would have noticed the discrepancy.)

The same thing is true when singing is presented in motion pictures. Even if the actor's own voice is featured, he or she must still prerecord the sound tracks and then make his or her facial movements coincide with those associated with the original recorded performance. Even when you are lip-syncing to your own voice, it often requires a great many attempts before the job is done right. In fact, in many instances it is never done completely right, but those portions of separate tracks which are done correctly are edited together so as to construct an apparently faultless performance.

Well, the "secret" of the remarkable synchronization of Paganini's performance was explained by nothing more mysterious than the fact that the gentleman who played the role, Robert Rudié, happened to be a gifted concert violinist. He seemed to be playing because he actually was.

In the last pair of shows we dealt with "the Irish problem," by bringing together England's Oliver Cromwell, an important player in the drama of Ireland's subjugation, and that country's Daniel O'Connell. The debate provided yet another instance in which, though our figures were from history and the problems discussed of long standing, the dialogue nevertheless had a remarkably up-to-date quality.

The powerful Empress Catherine the Great, who ruled the Russian Empire, proved a particularly scintillating guest.

After four years of hectic but stimulating work we had completed twenty-four one-hour programs that, I have subsequently been glad to observe, have proved of great interest to educators in many parts of our country. A number of high schools and colleges, as well as individual teachers, have picked up the *Meeting of Minds* concept— always with my blessings, needless to say—and have found it an effective tool for getting students interested in the drama of history itself, many of its most important players, and their ideas. All of these ideas, to restate the obvious, have helped make our present world what it is, for better and for worse.

I am occasionally asked why, given the fact that few programs in the history of television have been so lavishly complimented as *Meeting of Minds*, the program was nevertheless not renewed by the PBS stations after its fourth season. Part of the reason is obvious: The stations could no longer afford to pay for the production costs of the series, relatively modest as they were. After all, every program produced for PBS faces the same difficulty and yet they all get on the air. They do indeed, but almost invariably with the help of generous underwriters (usually major American corporations).

With the exception of our first six programs, underwritten by a stock brokerage whose chief executive officer happened to personally fall in love with the concept, *Meeting of Minds*, despite its obvious virtues, was not endorsed by corporate America. I am reasonably certain that there is a great deal more to this peculiar state of affairs than has so far met the public eye. The explanation of this curious situation, I suspect, is that those who make such decisions on behalf of assorted foundations and large business firms were never entirely comfortable with a program in which all ideas were subjected to sometimes breathtaking scrutiny and criticism. The very same ideas were, of course, vigorously defended by their adherents but still, it would seem, there was an unacknowledged but palpable reluctance to be connected with a program that featured freewheeling discussions about important social, political, economic, philosphical, and religious questions that have yet to be resolved by the world jury.

If I am correct in this suspicion it is a great pity. The lack of financial support from corporations resulted in no personal handicap whatever; I performed my duties as host and writer of *Meeting of Minds* for the absolute minimum union-scale payments. When the series could no longer continue I proceeded on to more lucrative professional pursuits, but it is a shame that millions of students, and professional adults as well, were deprived of the enlightenment that this television series could easily have continued to bring about.

In any event, the twenty-four programs still exist on videotape. Eventually some video distributor will have the good sense to make all twenty-four programs available. For this happy end I have coined the advertising slogan "A university education in twenty-four hours."

The phrase sounds, at first, like a bizarre exaggeration, but it happens to have a great deal of justification. The programs are, after all, twenty-four in number and are individually one hour in length. Anyone who absorbed all of the ideas that were packed, with almost explosive pressure, into those discussions would be entitled to consider himself well-informed indeed.

There was certainly never any intention on my part that either our live broadcasts or video cassettes should replace reading. Indeed I have heard from many of our viewers that being introduced—in many cases for the first time in their lives—to major players in the drama of history has led to an immediate appetite for books by or about our esteemed visitors. That was music to my ears.

An interesting postscript supports this conclusion. In 1990 Prometheus Books released the scripts of all four seasons of the series in book form, and in the summer of 1991 Dove Books-on-Tape began distributing the shows on audiocassette.

Most of even the best fare ground out by the enormous mill of television is of only passing interest. Much I've done either has already been forgotten or will be not long after my death. But it seems probable that a thousand years from now people will still be watching the *Meeting of Minds* programs to their great profit. By that time they'll have no idea at all who the tall fellow with the horn-rimmed glasses is, but they will still, you may be assured, know who Aristotle, Socrates, Plato, Aquinas, and our other guests are.

CHAPTER NINETEEN

Television in the Eighties

On April 27, 1980, Jayne and I flew to the island of Jamaica where we spent a relaxing week as the houseguests of publisher Lyle Stuart and his wife Carole. Like all tourists, we swam, toured the local sites of interest, visited the nearby homes of Noel Coward and novelist Ian Fleming, and all-in-all had a delightful time.

On our third day at Stuart's estate perched high on a hill overlooking the blue sea, I received a telephone call from my secretary back in Los Angeles, who presented me with a sort of classic good-news/bad-news message. The good news was that NBC-TV programming chief Fred Silverman wanted to talk to me about an extremely urgent matter, this almost certainly meant that he was calling to offer me employment. The bad news was that he wanted me to get on a plane that very night and rush back to Los Angeles.

"Did you explain to Mr. Silverman that Jayne and I just got here?"

"Yes, I did," my secretary said, "but he was very insistent."

"Well," I said, "please call him back and tell him that I arrived here in a state of exhaustion, having been involved with a very heavy schedule recently. Tell him I'm naturally curious about his message and I'll be happy to talk to him, but they have this marvelous invention called the telephone, and unless the CIA or FBI are tapping our lines, no third party will know what we say to each other."

A couple of hours later my secretary called back. "Mr. Silverman, for some reason, doesn't want to discuss the matter on the phone," she said. "He wants to talk to you in person. He asks, if you can't fly out tonight, how soon can you return?"

The resolution of the problem was that Jayne and I would return to Los Angeles one day earlier than had been planned, and I would report to NBC the following morning for a brunch meeting.

The get-together took place in the network's executive dining room. Mr. Silverman sat at the head of the table, to my immediate right. My agent Irvin Arthur was across from me and another network executive, Perry Lafferty, was on my left. Silverman wasted little time on the sort of small talk—How-was-your-vacation?—that is apparently considered obligatory in all such instances.

He quickly came to the point. "I'll tell you what I have in mind," he said. "I don't know if you've heard, but Johnny is cutting down from ninety to sixty minutes, so he'll be on from 11:30 to 12:30 at night. Here's my suggestion: *Johnny Carson from 11:30 to 12:30; Steve Allen from 12:30 to 1:30!*"

There is something in almost all performers—something, in fact, against which their agents and managers often have to warn them—that tends to want to accept any offer of employment, even those that are not particularly advantageous to the performer. Fred was smiling at me broadly, waiting for an answer.

"Well," I said, "first of all I thank you very much for the proposal, and I agree with you that Johnny and I back-to-back would make for an unbeatable two hours."

"Right," Fred concurred. "The reason I was in such a rush to talk to you about this is that on Monday I'm meeting with the affiliates [the managers and owners of the network's various stations] and I know they'll give me a standing ovation when I announce this. Ordinarily I wouldn't be rushing you, but in this case we really do need an answer right away. You can see why."

He mentioned a weekly salary which, while it would satisfy the wildest dreams of the average person, was not exactly a dramatic figure, in the context of television network contracts.

"To tell you the truth, Fred, I'd like to cooperate with you and give you a quick yes or no right now, but I'm going to have to give the matter at least a little thought." This seemed to deflate him somewhat.

"Is there any particular question I can answer for you right now?" he asked. "Anything about the show itself?"

"Not really," I said. "As regards the show that would be no problem at all."

"Of course not," he agreed. "You invented this thing in the first place."

"But having done 13 years of talk-show duty I'm not sure I want to make a move back in that direction. I'm always available, as you know, to do prime-time comedy series or specials, but the middle of the night isn't exactly—"

"I understand," he said, "and I really don't want to rush you into an answer unless you're tremendously enthusiastic about it."

"We're all certainly enthusiastic about it here," Lafferty added.

The conversation continued on for a while but no new points were raised. Silverman said he would greatly appreciate it if I could get an answer back to him the following day because, he reminded me, he very much wanted to make that exciting announcement about the Carson/Allen combination; he knew it would electrify the affiliates, given that the network was going through general ratings doldrums at the time.

After we finished the meal and were walking out of the room Silverman approached my agent, Irvin Arthur.

"I have a good feeling about this thing," he said. "It'll work out great, for all of us. I'll just run it by Johnny now, but I'm sure there'll be no problem about that."

Had this scene been acted in a movie, the director would have called for a tight close-up of Irvin's face at that moment, perhaps even suggested a tense musical phrase to underscore the importance of what had just been said.

Seeing Irvin's quizzical expression, Fred reassured him, "Don't worry, I'm sure there'll be no problem."

The next day I called Irvin to tell him that I was inclined to accept the offer, but only subject to an agreement about financial terms, amount of vacation time permitted, etc.

"I'm sorry to have to tell you this," Arthur said, "but I just heard from NBC. Carson nixed the deal."

When news about what had happened leaked out, the network was, understandably, considerably embarrassed. I've always been personally fond of Fred Silverman and foresee no reason to change my mind. He was kind enough, not long thereafter, to assign me to do several comedy specials, all of which were warmly received. Another element of awkwardness was that Tom Snyder, who was at the time doing the *Tomorrow* show, following Carson's, which started at 1:00 a.m., was still on the air and naturally could not have been pleased to learn that the network had decided to replace him. At first there were flat denials, assertions that Johnny Carson had no authority to make such a decision, but eventually Brandon Tartikoff, who had taken over as President of NBC Entertainment, conceded that the matter had indeed been discussed with Carson but hastily added that "Johnny does not, *by contract,* have veto power."

With the exception of David Letterman, who took over the spot and who was willing to let Carson's production company control his program, all the rest of us involved came out of the experience with a bit of egg on our faces.

Throughout the 1980s, I kept busy doing a number of syndicated and network shows. First, in 1980-81 there was *The Steve Allen Comedy Hour,* six critically acclaimed NBC specials. In 1982 I did a number of prime-time comedy specials for NBC, and on several shows featured a newscast-satire called *Eyewitless News*. Because of the success of the sketches, I had planned to market the *Eyewitless News* formula as a series of separate programs for syndication, but an odd light was cast on the project in mid-May of 1987 when Johnny Carson did a newscast takeoff entitled—you guessed it—*Eyewitless News*.

In 1984 there was *Steve Allen's Comedy Room,* a series of six specials for the Disney cable channel in the talk show formula but involving only comedians as guests and only one subject for discussion: comedy itself. Also in 1984-85, I served as host on two series: ABC's *Life's Most Embarrassing Moments* and for cable, *Inside Your Schools.* The latter consisted of twelve monthly specials sponsored by the American Federation of Teachers and aired on TLC (The Learning Channel), cable's only adult learning network.

In 1985-86 *Steve Allen's Music Room* presented leading singers and musicians in the informal atmosphere of what seemed to be the Allen household, having fun around the piano. The series of six specials were presented on the Disney Channel.

Another syndicated series I hosted, in 1985-86, was *The Start of Something Big,* a weekly program about how now-common things began. We discussed the origin of the hot dog, the ice cream cone, the corset, the greeting card, etc.

Although I've been working in television comedy since 1948, I had not once in all those years encountered the slightest evidence of deviousness until I became involved with a short-lived CBS-TV series *Comedy Zone.*

To take the story from the beginning—

In January of 1984, a personable young fellow named John Manulis, an employee of the subdivision of the Nederlander real estate enterprise that concentrates on film and TV production, approached CBS with what the network thought was an intriguing idea. It was just one more attempt at a sketch-comedy show, but with the significant difference that the writers this time would not be TV comedy veterans, but Broadway and off-Broadway playwrights.

The network said, in effect, we like the idea; please show us some scripts.

So far so good.

Alas, the quality of most of the scripts, when they were finally turned in, had a sobering effect on the programmers.

It was not that they'd never seen work of such discouraging quality, but because of the reputations of the writers it had been expected that something either as good or perhaps significantly better than the TV sketch-comedy norm would be forthcoming. Except for a couple of sketches the material was not nearly so good as that of experienced television writers.

CBS's eminently reasonable solution: Bring in someone with an established TV comedy track record to convert the raw material into something broadcastable. It was also felt that the show should have a host, not only to introduce guests and sketches, but to give the viewer a sense of continuity from week to week.

The executive who welcomed the *Comedy Zone* project in the first place, Bob O'Connor, phoned me and said he'd appreciate it if I would consider signing aboard. At a subsequent breakfast meeting, held at O'Connor's request while I was in New York, it was clarified that the network wanted me to become not only the show's host but its head writer and comedy consultant or producer.

Although I was at the time doing a series of comedy specials for ABC, as well as two miniseries for the Disney Channel (*Music Room and Comedy Room*), I agreed to undertake the duties O'Connor had asked me to assume.

"I'm sure you'll be able to make an invaluable contribution," O'Connor said. He asked me to meet with Manulis and two of the theater writers who were working with him, Christopher Durang (author of the off-Broadway play *Sister Mary Ignatius*) and John Bishop. They had written some of the better material in the first draft, although there were elements in their sketches that were unlikely to get past the network's censors.

In any event, I immediately set to work, evaluated not only the first script but a tall stack of second-quality sketches and monologues other writers had contributed, and explained to young Manulis—in a series of memos—which of the sketches were good, which were faulty but salvageable, and which were hopeless.

In retrospect, it's easy to see that at this point I should have insisted on being named co-producer of the show so that my authority would have been equal to that of the then-inexperienced Mr. Manulis. Unfortunately, I assumed that this would not be necessary because of two factors: (a) The network had called me in *because* of my sketch comedy expertise, and (b) Manulis, partly because of his tender years, had theretofore created nothing whatever in the way of television comedy.

While some readers may assume that any successful comedian could serve in a production capacity on anyone else's show, this is by no means the case. Some comics have a good sense of what is right for them but are totally un-qualified to make creative and administrative decisions for others. Perhaps I should briefly mention here, therefore, that in addition to my own programs and hundreds of comedy concert appearances, I was once asked by Milton Berle to serve as his television producer, and also worked as head writer and host on the premiere telecast of NBC's *The Big Show*, undoubtedly the best variety series ever aired.

It gradually emerged, however, that the likeable Mr. Manulis considered his judgment about jokes and sketches as good as anybody's on earth. There was nothing personal in this. Even though his gifts would seem to be largely super-visory, John was reluctant to relinquish an ounce of creative authority.

As soon as I detected this, I sent him a letter, entirely cordial in tone, indicating that it was unlikely that I could continue to be affiliated with the program on such a basis, since I needed neither the money, the work, nor the headaches I could see looming.

Manulis, no doubt worried about what would happen if he went back to the network and said, "Steve Allen doesn't want to work with me on this project," said that he thought perhaps we could work out some satisfactory method of collaboration and urged me to stay on.

Had I known then what I later learned, I would have wished him well and stepped away.

I also realize now that I should have alerted the network at once about the emerging problems, but I thought that to do so might seem to be going behind Manulis' back. Unfortunately, there are professional situations where it's a mistake to try to Nice-Guy your way through and better to insist on a simple clearing of the air.

Another reason I didn't turn my back on the project was that I'd begun to write sketches and routines for the show, something I was competent to do because I'd written not only thirty years worth of successful comedy, but words and music for the Broadway musical *Sophie* and a play, *The Wake,* which had been produced in Los Angeles and various eastern cities, not to mention a couple of dozen books.

In any event, through hard work and additional effort on the part of several other writers, a second-draft script was presented to the network that looked somewhat better than what they'd so disliked weeks earlier.

The project began to look so promising to them, in fact, that they suddenly decided to do not just the one special that had been contemplated but five. I was asked, by CBS, to serve on the additional four shows, on the same terms.

During all of this, standard negotiations had been going on between my attorney, Seymour Bricker, and the Nederlander's attorney, a Mr. Feinberg. The fees that were negotiated for my services were merely par-for-the-course. Indeed, given the fact that I was performing three jobs, the payments were comparatively modest.

In any event, Manulis and his associate, a woman named

Gladys Rackmil, asked me to come to New York for a round of meetings with production personnel, where I spent two pleasant days exchanging ideas with other members of the team. I had for some time been urging Manulis-Rackmil to hire a comedy director. Generally, in television, the person known as *director* is like what, in the movies, is called a *cameraman,* in that he's in charge chiefly of taking the pictures, although he will supervise such details as scenery and lighting. But on comedy shows it's a good idea to have a separate comedy specialist—one accustomed to directing actors, not taking pictures. The Nederlander group finally perceived the wisdom of such advice and asked me to meet with a theater director named Gerry Gutierrez, who had done good work on a play written by Wendy Wasserstein, one of the *Comedy Zone* writers. I liked him and recommended that he be signed aboard immediately.

Now that the possibility of doing five shows rather than one had been presented, it occurred to me that I might want to serve as head writer only on the first because of the press of other work. I recommended, therefore, that if I made such a decision, the show should acquire another experienced television sketch comedy veteran to supervise—and if necessary, rewrite or edit—material submitted by the theater people. One of my former writers, Herb Sargent, now in his 60s, provides just such a service on *Saturday Night Live.*

The layman might suppose that if a writer is competent in one area, he or she could write almost anything. This is by no means the case. Most writers good at one form are inept at others. So some specialize in poetry, others in novels, others in essays, comic plays, short stories, advertising copy, and so on. That some of the program's contributors had achieved a degree of success in the theater—almost all off, not on, Broadway—by no means meant they could automatically be trusted to write TV sketches, particularly once five shows were commissioned, which meant that they would have to deliver the goods week-after-week.

It had, after all, taken them several months to produce the first draft of the first script, the one that had so disappointed CBS.

The fact that the Manulis-Rackmil group was inexperienced at sketch comedy now began to become significant as regards budget.

A couple of years earlier, I had produced six programs for NBC called *The Steve Allen Comedy Hour.* The critical reaction was unanimously complimentary, and the ratings were respectable. The shows had a budget of less than $450,000, and, at that figure, I made a sizable personal profit every week. But the Nederlanders were saying that they could not possibly do such a show for the same amount. Neither CBS nor I could make sense of their complaints, but since such details were none of my business, I didn't concern myself. Another complicating factor was that the talent agency, for doing nothing more than "representing the package," was to be paid $30,000 per show—a total of $150,000.

I *should* have been concerned about such details, as it turned out, because a way to make more money suddenly occurred to the Nederlanders. If I got hit by the proverbial truck and was no longer a part of the package, they reasoned, they could save a tidy sum each week and perhaps come up with an at least modest profit at the end of their brief production season. Thereupon they came back to the network and said, in effect, "We can't afford to pay Steve Allen what we have agreed to pay him."

"That's your problem," a network programmer responded. "We're offering you a certain figure. If you can't deliver the goods for that amount, just say so, and we'll put something else on the air."

CBS finally conceded a point by throwing another $50,000 per week into the pot, but when the Nederlander group continued to insist, "We still can't afford Steve Allen," one of the network people finally took the position that he didn't particularly care whether they did the show with or without your obedient servant, so long as it was delivered in time and was of acceptable quality.

Unfortunately Bob O'Connor, who had pleaded with me to save his already sinking ship, was away on a three-week vacation in Ireland at this crucial stage of the negotiations. By the time he learned that his superior, a canny specialist in demographic statistics named Harvey Shephard, had said that he personally didn't much care who the host of the show was, it was too late for O'Connor to explain that I was on deck only because he had asked me to be there. I had not sought the job.

Shephard knew nothing about the several months of work I had put in, nor was he then aware that O'Connor would not have had the project in good enough shape to present to him without my efforts.

The ball was therefore back in the Nederlander's court, where they were faced with a difficult problem: how to get me out of the picture and thereby save many thousands of dollars per week, when contractual terms had been agreed to, though not yet signed.

Perceiving that they could not simply fire me, they resorted to one of the oldest and least edifying ploys in economic practice. If you can't fire a worker or executive, you offer him an insultingly low salary, betting on the probability that he will turn it down.

The insulting offer was promptly made and, of course, rejected.

The Nederlander negotiator, nevertheless, said that they would at least live up to the part of the bargain that applied to the opening show.

No sooner had this point been agreed to than Manulis and Rackmil sent me a letter saying that my services would *not* be required in New York in mid-July, when the first show was to be taped, but from August third to the tenth instead. I mistakenly assumed this meant that the first show was to be taped two weeks later than scheduled.

Only later did I learn, after agreeing to the date change, that by August third the Nederlander group hoped to have two shows of the series already completed.

At this point, some of the general embarrassment began to leak out. Ms. Rackmil had, on my previous visit to New York, asked me to please call the editor of *TV Guide* so that advance publicity for the show could be arranged. I agreed to do this and had a pleasant chat with their current Bureau Chief Neil Hickey. At the time of the interview, of course, the Nederlanders were still assuring me that I would be the host of all five shows. That version of the story was therefore given not only to *TV Guide* but to other journalists who had begun to request information about the project.

The Manulis-Rackmil team by now, however, had other problems. The network, understandably, was demanding to see script materials for shows two through five, and had yet to be shown anything remotely broadcastable.

I had for some time been urging John to hire an experienced comedy producer. The network, also alarmed, now insisted on the same point, as a result of which veteran producer Joe Cates was taken on.

What Mr. Manulis will probably not know until he reads this is that one of his associates on the Nederlander team said to CBS at about this point, "Do you want us to ask Manulis to step down as producer?"

There was indeed sentiment for precisely this move at the network, but it was felt that since Manulis had indicated a willingness to hire Cates and Gutierrez, he would perhaps have the wisdom to take his hands off the wheel and permit the more experienced men to take over, while still retaining his title.

Another problem was that the theater writers, since only one of them had had television experience, were unaware of the standard procedure by which weekly sketch-comedy shows are created. Almost every first draft is weak but over the course of several days, and *always by a joint effort*, cuts and changes gradually strengthen the material. There's nothing unusual about this; it's the most sensible way to fly. But it's by no means the same as theatrical practice, according to which it's up to the playwright to rewrite his or her own work. There are times, of course, even in the theater, where the dramatist simply can't cut the mustard; at that point the production either collapses, or the writer swallows his pride and steps aside while a play-doctor is called in. A classic instance occurred when Clare Booth Luce was unable to solve certain problems in her script of *The Women*. Try as she might, she couldn't deliver. Finally the producers insisted that the experienced and talented humorist George S. Kaufman be called in. Kaufman saved the play, although Ms. Luce received the public credit.

Why CBS did not explain to the theater writers that, inasmuch as they were doing a *television* show and not a theatrical review, television rules would have to apply, I have no idea. But it was not done. I attempted to get that simple message, through Manulis, to the writers, but I have no idea whether he ever forwarded it to them.

In one of our meetings I said to the theatre writers, in perfectly cordial tones, "I have no personal interest in rewriting your material, but I very much hope that you will do one another the service of helping to rewrite one another's sketches since that's the way it's been done on television comedy shows for the past thirty-five years."

Something that Ms. Rackmil will not know until she reads this is that an individual closely connected with her team (who does not wish to be identified) next sent a message, designed to reach my ears, that he felt very unhappy about the way I'd been dealt with. "I think the whole affair has been very poorly handled. I wish I could do something about it, but my hands are tied because of my position."

Through all this, there were differing points of view among the CBS programming people. One camp argued, "It's an outrage the way the man is being treated." The other felt, "We have nothing against him personally, but hey, if somebody has to be thrown overboard, well, that's show business."

Fortunately one hideous embarrassment was avoided at the last possible minute, but only because I took charge of the situation. Both CBS and the Nederlander group had asked me to help in publicizing the show, for the obvious reason that for the first several months I was the only member of the cast that had been set. The network and the Nederlanders, in fact, asked me to fly to Phoenix to address a gathering of television critics on the subject of *Comedy Zone*. I agreed to cooperate and even canceled a lucrative Midwest concert booking to do it. When a couple of days before I was supposed to fly to Arizona I began to hear rumors about my position with the show, I called Harvey Shephard, said the tickets had already been ordered for my flight, and asked him to tell me directly if it really made sense for me to publicize the show if there was some question about my continued connection with it. "There is a problem," Shephard admitted. "And it hasn't been resolved yet. You're probably right in thinking you ought not to go to Phoenix."

I shudder to think what would've happened if I hadn't called Shephard.

Parenthetically, I kept trying to arrange to have other experienced comedy performers booked, but none of these suggestions met with much enthusiasm from the Manulis-Rackmil group. To be specific, I had run into the gifted comedy actor Dabney Coleman while waiting to board a morning jet to New York and had told him that he would be marvelous for one of the new show's sketches. He became interested but when I brought up his name the following morning at a production meeting, Manulis actually said, "I'd rather not give out the big plums in the script to guest stars. I'd rather save them for members of the regular company." Since the regular players had not as yet been mentioned, much less auditioned and hired, and would all be TV unknowns in any event, I was dumbfounded.

"John," I said, "naturally we will want to accommodate whoever your regular players turn out to be. But please trust me, when you can book a top comedy actor like Dabney Coleman, you shouldn't waste one second speculating about the matter."

Because of Manulis' continuing reluctance, however, Mr. Coleman was not booked until weeks later, and then only as a result of the *network's* insisting that stars be hired, and fast.

To say that things did not go well the week of the taping of the first show would represent a dramatic new achievement in understatement. Mr. Gutierrez, understandably accustomed to the relatively leisurely pace of theatrical direction, in which one has months to get a production ready, was frustrated at the combined ineptitude and recalcitrance of some of those who were supposed to be taking his direction.

One afternoon my friend Joe Cates, theretofore mild-mannered and cooperative, blew up and read the riot act to everyone in the studio, in the process delivering himself of a few pungent sentiments about a particular routine—a comedy song about cocaine, if you can believe it.

CBS's top officer at the time, Tom Leahy, having heard rumors that things were not going well, dropped by the studio to see what was going on. He was so disappointed that consideration began to be given to airing at least some of the shows of the series in late-night rather than prime-time, which is to say, throwing them away. As one network executive later put it, "It had become clear to us that the production group—and chiefly the writers—were literally incapable of coming up with five good shows."

But the network—alas for its interests—was already contractually committed to provide funding for five programs, a decision they had made months earlier largely because I had been the supervisor of comedy on the show. CBS then initiated negotiations, hoping to reduce their commitment down to three programs. Had they been able to simply dictate the decision, it would've been to cut back to the original one-show arrangement.

Again there was the problem of the contract. Nederlander could insist on the deal for five, running the risk of alienating an entire commercial network, a choice to avoid if possible.

As the shakiness of the first show became painfully apparent, the decision was finally made to follow advice that I'd offered weeks earlier. "It's only the first show that will be reviewed," I had said. "At the moment, the script for it is still, after months of effort, far from strong enough. Presumably the writers are now contributing sketches for shows two through five. If anything particularly strong shows up, you ought to add it at once to show one, since if you open with good reviews and respectable ratings the general impression of success and quality will be created even if the following four shows are much weaker."

This advice, after some initial resistance, was finally followed, although it had the "oh, swell" effect of weakening the script for show two, the one on which I was now to appear.

For several weeks, incidentally, my secretary had been asking to see the first drafts of sketches that I would be involved with as performer. *Literally nothing was forthcoming.* Finally the word came through, "We haven't really decided what Mr. Allen will be doing on the show. In fact, we had hoped that he would write his own material, or come up with his own ideas."

This, mind you, from a production company which for months had boasted to me of the brilliance of its writing staff.

Which raises an interesting question: Were the vaunted off-Broadway writers just not-so-hot after all? No, not really. All of them are talented, albeit in varying degrees. Unfortunately, *Comedy Zone* was not written for the theater but for television. And the esteemed theater folk were not nearly so good at writing hysterically funny comedy sketches as experienced writers for television.

The problem, of course, concerned a great deal more than

the simple factor of funniness, since some of the sketches that did not work for *Comedy Zone* were quite funny. The problem was that the writers didn't seem to understand that the national audience that watches television is very different from the audience that goes to the New York theater.

Another factor was that in its earlier phase of high hopes, CBS wanted to put the show on right after *60 Minutes,* at eight o'clock Sunday night. But some sketches that might have worked well enough on, say, *Saturday Night Live,* would have shocked the Sunday night prime-time audience.

By mid-July the producers had had another jolt. Some of the stars who'd booked for the first two shows simply refused to do the sketches submitted to them. I was not at all surprised by the news. Indeed, one of the performers, a professional comedian, put the matter very plainly about a sketch that had been given to him. "It isn't funny," he said.

Film actress Dyan Cannon, after being set for the first show, had finally refused to come in from Mexico, for reasons that remain unclear. Dabney Coleman became un-nerved and argumentative due to his lack of confidence in the material he was given. Mariette Hartley was almost reduced to tears by rehearsal tensions.

Comedian Robert Klein, who did a sketch on the first show without entirely understanding it, wryly suggested that the series should be called *The Subtle Zone.* Another dis-gruntled guest performer suggested *The Weird Zone.*

Monday afternoon, July 23rd, in New York, I was asked to report to a four o'clock rehearsal to go through a sketch called *Mr. Wonderful.* I arrived early and remained at the rehearsal facility for two full hours, during which time not only was the sketch not rehearsed, it was never even mentioned.

I enjoyed the afternoon, nevertheless, largely because it gave me the opportunity to socialize with guest performers Steve Landesberg (who I had urged be booked), actress/director Penny Marshall, and Marty Nadler, a clever young jokewriter who had, a few minutes earlier, turned in his notice because it had become apparent to him that he would have no more luck improving the theater writers' sketches than I had had.

Incredible as it sounds, after several months of preparation the show was actually scrambling for guests on a last-minute basis. Landesberg at first evinced little interest, but finally agreed to work on the second show, which was music to my ears since he was precisely the kind of naturally funny performer I had been prodding the producers to book. Back in April I'd written a routine for Sid Caesar, a satirical exaggeration of one of those hidden-camera television commercials in which some pain-numbed sufferer describes his headache in unnecessarily rich detail. Sid turned out not to be available, but Manulis, who was in trouble finding strong enough material for the second show, remembered the routine and asked what I thought of having Landesberg do it. I loved the idea. Within ten minutes we had copies of the script in hand, and Landesberg and I went off to an adjacent room and ran through the routine, which played very well.

Parenthetically, although Manulis was careful to give the New York writers on-screen, *during*-the-show, printed credit for their various sketches, he neglected to do so for me as regards this sketch.

The wise and talented director Penny Marshall, booked to work on the show I was hosting, said, "There seem to be two factions on this show. One group wants to make it just good old-fashioned funny, and the other group says, 'No, it should be some sort of theatrical experience.'"

"If the second group prevails," I told her, "then they shouldn't call the series *Comedy Zone.*"

Penny sincerely wanted to find a way to get out of her commitment but realized she was stuck. Nevertheless, her agent phoned her at one point and asked her, "Do you want me to get you out of this thing?"

It is not unprecedented in television, of course, that a given sketch should be considered over the heads of the audience, too hip for the Midwest, or something of the sort.

But in such instances, the comedy players, at least, should understand perfectly what they are doing. So far as I've been able to determine, *Comedy Zone* was the first—and probably only—series in the history of television in which, as regards certain sketches, not even the actors were clear as to what they were involved with, or what messages they were supposed to convey.

Although part of the essential rationale for the avant-garde sketches was that they were breaking absolutely new comic ground, this turned out not always to be the case. In one instance, a musical version of a soap opera was proposed, with the action taking place in "General Hospital." A clever idea, but certainly not original, since I'd done precisely the same sort of sketch on the *Tonight* show back in 1955, under the title *Give My Regards to Bellevue.*

One of the writers, who does have talent, was apparently unaware that his sketch had already been done, quite precisely, by Miller and Lyles, a Black comedy team of the 1920s and '30s. The gimmick of their exchange was that the straightman would start to ask a question, and the comedian, Flournoy Miller, would provide an answer before the question was finished. They performed the sketch at the Daley 63rd Street theater in New York in 1921, in a revue by Noble Sissle and Eubie Blake called *Shuffle Along.*

Guest-booking continued to be troublesome. When the possibility of booking my wife Jayne as a guest was proposed, I was told by Manulis that Penny Marshall found herself insecure about having other major female guests on the show, particularly one who was attractive. "It's been very difficult for us to book her at all," one of the executives explained. "We're a little nervous about risking losing her by booking another major woman."

There was no evidence of this in Penny's attitude. She was obviously seriously disappointed with the material she'd been given but good-egged her way through the week. In any event, when a firm offer for Jayne's services was finally made, my wife responded with an immediate and firm no-thank-you.

By Tuesday, things were in such a state of disorganization that even the makeup, hair, and wardrobe people were complaining. "It's gotten so bad," one worker told me, "that we can't even get an accurate production schedule out of these people. The schedules they give us don't bear any resemblance to what actually happens."

On Wednesday, a good deal of new debris hit the network fan. A problem had come up in that the CBS Standards and Practices department—the network's censors—had objected to the punchline of an amusing sketchlet written by the talented Jules Feiffer in which a desperate wife (played by Penny Marshall) accuses her husband of never taking her seriously and just coming up with stupid jokes no matter how often she appeals to him for substantial, meaningful response. At the end of the monologue, Penny stands on a chair, a rope around her neck and announces that she's going to kill herself, at which her husband looks up and says, "Amy, is that your nose, or are you eating a banana?"—a deliberately old insult-joke. The network felt that the serious national problem of suicide ought not to be dealt with in so playful a fashion.

(Earlier that week, by coincidence, comedian Buddy Hackett and a number of other Hollywood entertainers had organized a benefit to raise funds for a suicide prevention center.)

As a writer myself, I didn't feel that the sketch was socially harmful, but there was, as I say, contention about it. The network executive who delivered the bad news to the production group suffered the fate of the bearers of unwelcome messages down through the centuries—he was subjected to a tirade of personal abuse lasting for a good many minutes. Had this been the only explosion of its sort, the executive, who was familiar with the volatility of some of television's creative and/or production people, would have attributed it to temperament and continued to pursue the argument on its own merits. Unfortunately, the outburst came at a time when the network had lost all confidence in the project and wanted very much to walk away from it.

Accordingly, the programmer told the producer that he personally was withdrawing from the project but would communicate the producer's views to the network. When he did so a few minutes later, one of his counterparts in the Los Angeles network headquarters called and said, "You were absolutely right to decide to get the hell out of there. You don't have to take that kind of crap. And you're right to tell them they can now do the shows any way they want but that we reserve the right, after delivery of the tapes, to decide whether we want to put any of them on the air."

When a few minutes later one of the Nederlander executives was apprised of this bad, if inevitable, news, the response was, "Oh, please, don't abandon the project. Maybe what we'll have to do is get rid of Gerry Gutierrez, if he's the one chiefly responsible for insisting that the scripts remain unchanged." He wasn't.

The discussion merged into a consideration of the prospect of even dismissing the highly competent Mr. Cates, too, and replacing him, that very afternoon, with Bill Perksy, one of my former writers who'd become a successful comedy director and producer.

As of taping day, Friday, the general inefficiency not only continued but worsened. I had been called the night before and told to be ready for a car pick-up at 9 a.m. sharp, in order to arrive at the studio by 9:30. Even this was cutting things dangerously close, since the first sketch, in which I would work with the talented Broadway actor Joe Montegna, was to be videotaped at 10:30! Not at all to my surprise, there was no car waiting when I reported to the front entrance of the Ritz-Carlton at precisely nine o'clock.

The possibility of taking a cab naturally presented itself, but a phone call to the *Comedy Zone* production offices brought the assurance the "the car should be there any minute." A torrential rain, in any event, had made taxis scarce and several other men were already huddled under the marquee waiting for the few available.

At five minutes to ten, the doorman was finally able to get me a cab. Arriving fifty-five minutes late for TV work is, in itself, not a particularly big deal except that in this instance it meant that the entire day's production schedule would be domino-theoried out of whack.

After another comedian and I did a long warm-up, to get the theater audience practiced at laughing, the taping went surprisingly well and an ad-libbed routine I'd taped on the street in the city's garment district was particularly well-received. But by this time, the Nederlander group had decided to fire Gutierrez, God knows why. I returned to Los Angeles on July 29.

As of July 31 there were more dramatic developments. A media rumor circulated in New York that Gutierrez's firing had been done, reluctantly, by the Nederlanders only because CBS insisted on it. Since this was precisely the opposite of the truth, Bob O'Connor was incensed when the report reached his ears. He called the Nederlander executive actually responsible for the firing and delivered a few blistering comments on the subject of blame-shifting.

That same day producer Cates said to the network's Los Angeles programmers, "The second show is so much better than the previous week's program that you would be smart to ask Steve Allen to step back into the picture and host the rest of the series for you."

Fat chance.

To me, Cates said, "All your memos about the show—about the sketches, everything—were absolutely right. They should have listened to you."

By now, network program chief Shephard had decided there was no way *Comedy Zone* was going to be given the plum Sunday-night spot following *60 Minutes*. The programming department's reasoning was that the time-slot was too precious to risk dropping in a program that had been in such rocky shape even before the first show had been taped. When Shephard finally did see the first production, his reaction was glum. He therefore decided to follow Cates's advice and use the second program—the one I hosted—as the premiere show and put it into a reasonably good time spot, at eight o'clock on Friday night, August 17th.

When I finally saw an edited tape of the show, I was moderately appalled. Some of the sketches were incredibly weak and had the air of cute, promising skits one might see in a college production. The only one produced by the New York group that was strong and funny was a sketch about political paranoia by Jules Feiffer.

Although I'd painstakingly and repeatedly explained to Manulis that, in the 1980s, television sketches could not be as long as sketches of the '50s and '60s, even some that had funny moments went on too long. A Russian translation sketch—much like routines from my own show done some twenty years earlier—was at least two minutes overlong. A one-joke sketch about writing horror movies, titled *Ghost Writers* was originally about twenty pages in length. A CBS programmer insisted on cuts, with the result that six pages were deleted. Joe Cates helped a bit more by simply starting the tape about two-and-a-half minutes into the sketch, eliminating the beginning altogether. It was still too long, despite a strong performance by the funny Bob Dishy.

Another mistake made by the Nederlanders concerned the casting of the regular players. The conscious philosophical decision of the theater-oriented organization was actually made to "hire actors, not comedians."

I love actors. I *am* an actor. But if those were the rules, the name of the show should have been changed to *Acting Zone*. I do not mean to suggest that actors cannot be funny, nor that comedians cannot act. Robin Williams, Dan Aykroyd, Bill Murray, Tom Hanks and some other young comedians act very well indeed. But sketch-comedy shows succeed in part due to the natural *funniness* of the performers on them.

Consider *Saturday Night Live.* The players featured on my comedy shows—Don Knotts, Louis Nye, Tom Poston, Tim Conway, the Smothers Brothers, Bill "Jose Jimenez" Dana, Dayton Allen, Gabe Dell, Pat Harrington. These men were funny just standing there. They made written material seem stronger than it sometimes was. But when you use straight actors you do not have that advantage. There must have been over three hundred clever comedians working in New York who could have been considered for *Comedy Zone.* Unfortunately they were ruled out on the bizarre grounds that they were funny.

To sum up --

There was perhaps no conscious villain in this whole unhappy drama. The theater writers didn't think anyone else should have authority to change so much as a comma of their scripts. That would have been okay, except that some of those scripts were just terrible. Almost all the great television comedy sketches of the past forty years, as I have said, had been written not by individuals but by *teams,* or, even more often, by groups. So by insisting on their theatrical prerogative the writers accomplished nothing more than to ensure the failure of what could have been a stimulating experiment.

What is clear is that, to my knowledge, no other comedy series in the history of television has experienced such a high percentage of rejected material. Traditionally, a small percentage of what's prepared, even by professional writers is, for various reasons, deemed unsuitable. In the case of *Comedy Zone,* far more material was rejected than was found acceptable.

Can anything be learned from this peculiar experience? I hope so. The original mistake was that of the network's programming people. Had they been aware of theatrical tradition, according to which the writers' rights are carefully respected, they would have explained to the Nederlander group at the start that inasmuch as the writers had now come into television, TV rules of the game would have to apply. At that point, the writers could have agreed, or gone their separate ways.

A pity. TV needs sketch comedy in prime-time. *Saturday Night Live,* though marvelous, airs awfully late at night.

In 1988 I returned to radio with *The Steve Allen Radio Show,* a wild daily three-hour comedy-fest which ran initially on New York City's WNEW and, after a few months, expanded to the NBC radio network. The show featured announcer/sidekick Mark Simone, with almost daily visits by *Saturday Night Live* writer Herb Sargent, comedian Bob "Super Dave" Einstein, and dozens of other popular comics and wits, including Jay Leno, Larry Gelbart, Mel Brooks, Richard Belzer, Jackie Mason, Milton Berle, Mort Sahl, Bill Maher, Martin Short, Richard Lewis, Roseanne Barr and Elaine Boosler.

That same year I also hosted a series of thirteen syndicated televisions specials, called *Host-to-Host,* which featured interviews with other interviewers: Phil Donahue, Merv Griffin, Dick Cavett, Joan Rivers, Ted Koppel, Hugh Downs, Geraldo Rivera, David Frost, Larry King, Robert Klein, Charles Kuralt, Regis Philbin, and Morley Safer.

The actor/singer Richard Kiley and I, as mentioned earlier, were school-boy friends. Occasionally, so long ago, we would talk about how old we felt, as distinguished from our actual ages. I think we were fifteen when the question first came up, and I remember saying, "Oddly enough I don't feel fifteen."

"How old do you feel?" Dick asked.

"Thirteen."

The pattern, such as it is, has persisted to the present day. Though I was thirty-one when I started hosting the *Tonight* show I somehow felt, at the time, about twenty-five. As of the present year, 1992, I am seventy years old but feel ten years younger. What had in my twenties seemed chiefly an indicator of immaturity appears far more advantageous as I approach the end of my life. If the observation will in any way encourage those who fear the approach of their later years, then, I am pleased to share the news that as regards my assorted professional activities I am much more proficient at them now than I was in times past. As for jazz piano playing, for example, I play much better than I did twenty years ago. The exercise of such wit as I can boast is much faster and more incisive than it was in earlier decades, and all the books and songs I write, too, come at a faster pace and with greater facility. There can be, therefore, no thought of retirement. Those performers who have sold chiefly their physical beauty are eventually so cruelly treated by time that their faces and bodies are no longer marketable, but this has no connection with the art of comedy. At the moment of this writing Bob Hope, Milton Berle and 97-year-old George Burns, all much older than myself—are still performing regularly.

This book, obviously enough, has been an account of only my professional adventures in broadcasting, and not a revelation of my experiences as pianist, composer, author, public citizen, lover, husband or father. More intimate aspects of my existence, in any event, have been well covered in two of my early novels, *Not All Of Your Laughter, Not All Of Your Tears,* and *The Wake,* as well as such autobiographical works as *Mark It And Strike It* and *Beloved Son: A Story Of The Jesus Cults,* and a number of books of poems and short stories.

I consider myself most fortunate to have spent half a century in the theatrical profession. Perhaps the fact that I was born into it, my mother and father having done comedy in vaudeville, accounts for my always having felt at home in theaters, night clubs, and radio, TV and film studios. Although I have been treated kindly by both my professional peers and the human race generally there is more than enough room—indeed a requirement—for humility in all of this. Though I have been blessed, by what I assume are accidents of genetic nature, with a number of marketable talents, I have always had the somewhat wry understanding that a large part of my fame rested not on those abilities but rather simply because I was one of television's products—famous for being famous, as the saying goes. The American people, I perceived early, have surprisingly little interest in talent—many seem incapable of perceiving it—but have a morbid fascination with success. What else could possibly explain the fact that some extremely talented people have never achieved the acclaim they would have enjoyed in a more rational world, while at the same time some individuals with little or no discernable talent whatever have become superstars. It doesn't make sense, of course, but then the same point could be made about the physical universe itself, and that subdivision of it called life. The seeker who looks for fairness in the grand scheme will always be doomed to disappointment for the simple reason that what he looks for has never existed. Indeed the only possibility of ultimate justice, however remote, lies in the afterlife. It is certainly no attribute of human existence as we know it. But if there is no innate fairness to life there is still a great deal of beauty, and always the possibility, and occasional realization, of love.

As for television itself, it continues to be chiefly junk-food for the mind, with all too rare exceptions. God bless those exceptions—Ted Koppel's *Nightline*, Charles Kuralt's and Charles Osgood's Sunday morning hour of beauty, *60 Minutes*, psychoanalyst David Viscott; fine dramatic series like *Law And Order, Brooklyn Bridge* and *I'll Fly Away;* or situation comedies like *Cheers* and *Northern Exposure*. Thank God, too, for the brilliant series that have been available on public television during recent decades. There are other programs that are well done, needless to say. Burt Reynolds' *Evening Shade, Dear John, Golden Girls, The Cosby Show* and a few others. *Saturday Night Live*, though often offensive to the majority of television viewers is, particularly in recent years, exceptionally funny. It is absurd to assume that such happy deviations from the norm constitute evidence that television might someday improve to some statistically significant degree. It cannot happen. The reason is that the environmental context in which television exists—American society—is itself deteriorating in ways too depressing to count. To speak in defense of simple manners, in today's America, is to be considered old-fashioned. To recommend civility and rational discourse is to be considered irrelevant. The art of comedy can be used as a perfectly functional dipstick to measure the degree of our social and ethical collapse.

In the 1950s we simply laughed at Jackie Gleason, Milton Berle, Ernie Kovacs, Bob Hope, Red Skelton, Jack Carter, Jack E. Leonard, Jan Murray, Red Buttons, Morey Amsterdam, Martha Raye, Lucille Ball, George Burns and Gracie Allen, Jack Benny, Edgar Bergen, Victor Borge, Sid Caesar and Imogene Coca. We could watch them in the company of small children with no discomfort.

As of 1990 the majority of Americans were offended, to one degree or another, by much of what passed for suitable family entertainment on television and radio. The producers of one 1990 sitcom, apparently incapable of creating actual wit of the sort weekly provided by *Cheers* or *Murphy Brown,* decided to go with the flow, despite the fact that the current flow is carrying us all along right into the sewer. They made an innocent five-year-old say, "It sucks." The very sort of language parents forbid their children to use is now being encouraged not only by anything-goes cable entrepreneurs but also by the once high-minded networks. We may therefore paraphrase the ancient moral admonition about money now to read: Love of Ratings is the root of all evil.

We're not just talking about television here. Much of modern entertainment in general already involves vulgarians addressing barbarians. But the underlying questions are vastly more important. Why are ratings important? Because they translate into dollars. The bankers, corporate executives and country-clubbers who own network stock, plus the advertisers, far from resisting the present aesthetic and moral collapse, as their class would have in times past, are actually abetting the ugliness.

Marketplace factors are largely responsible for having thoroughly debased popular music, a billion-dollar industry, since the tastes of poorly educated teenagers with discretionary income dominate the field. Most of today's "punk" and "heavy-metal" lovers have yet even to hear the music of Gershwin, Porter and Rodgers. Forget Beethoven.

The best humor, when it's not simply purely playful, says something witty and wise about the issues it confronts. Among the horrifying problems of our civilization at present is the collapse of the American family, which has assumed such proportions that many now react to the word *family* as if it were just another noun like *skateboard* or *television*. Humans can do without skateboards or TV but they literally cannot long survive as a rational, emotionally healthy species without a secure family structure.

The reason, to belabor the obvious, is that the family is the soil in which each year's new crop of humans grows. It is mostly the failed family, therefore, which has produced our present millions of prison inmates, rapists, drug addicts, burglars, muggers, sexual psychopaths, nonprofessional whores of both sexes and all-around general goofolas.

Very well, then—agreed; that is the problem. The solution of today's comedy specialists, with few exceptions, is to make vulgar light of what is, in reality, tragically heavy. As for those trying to treat as deep a wound as our society has ever suffered, instead of encouraging them, today's comics deride them. It is sadly clear that even those who acknowledge the right rules of social conduct will often fail to live up to their own honestly professed codes. Tragically, what the dominant voices of our culture—with their access to center-stage of popular music, radio, TV, films and the comedy concert circuit—are saying today is "screw virtue."

If you think our society is sick now—stand by.

This relates, of course, to the debate about censorship and the question as to whether the large segment of American society that perceives the moral dangers in totally unrestricted artistic expression has any say at all concerning the use of public funds by the National Endowment for the Arts. The question is a perfectly fair one: Though artists have the creative right to produce work that may express racial, sexual or religious hatred, does the state have the correlative obligation to endorse such expression with already inadequate taxpayers' money?

The matter is by no means justly resolved by reflexive condemnations of censorship, which in any event already exists, in law, or are slander and libel perfectly acceptable?

Even the maligned networks do censor their programs. When the Prince of Filth, Andrew Dice Clay, appeared recently on that bastion of free speech *Saturday Night Live,* several of his more revolting remarks were, quite properly, censored.

High time.

See you on TV.

INDEX